# CHRISTOLOGY

# CHRISTOLOGY
## Origins, Developments, Debates

*Gerald O'Collins, SJ*

BAYLOR UNIVERSITY PRESS

*Cover Design* by Hannah Feldmeier
*Cover Image*: The Risen Lord, 2001, Color on Paper (gouache). Courtesy of the artist, He Qi © 2013 / www.heqiart.com.

Library of Congress Cataloging-in-Publication Data

O'Collins, Gerald.
  Christology : origins, developments, debates / Gerald O'Collins, SJ.
  216 pages cm
  Includes bibliographical references and index.
  ISBN 978-1-4813-0256-2 (hardback : alk. paper)
1. Jesus Christ—Person and offices. 2. Jesus Christ—History of doctrines. I. Title.
  BT203.O255 2015
  232—dc23
                                        2015014114

# Contents

Preface                                                            vii

## PART ONE

1  Christology—The Last Fifty Years                                 3
2  Revisiting the Person of Jesus                                  17
3  Revisiting the Work of Jesus                                    31

## PART TWO

4  Paul as a Witness to the Risen Jesus                            49
5  Peter as Witness to Easter                                      65

## PART THREE

6  The Priesthood of Christ and Followers of Other Faiths          89
7  Jacques Dupuis and Religious Pluralism                         109
8  Jacques Dupuis and Karl Rahner                                 131


Notes                                                             143
A Bibliography of Gerald O'Collins, SJ (2000–2013)                173
Works Cited                                                       189
Credits                                                           201
Index of Names                                                    202

# Preface

Carey Newman proved a strongly active participant at the four "summits" that I cochaired in New York: on the resurrection (1996), the Trinity (1998), the incarnation (2000), and the redemption (2003). Oxford University Press published the proceedings of all four symposia, which brought together an ecumenical and interdisciplinary team of scholars from the United States, the United Kingdom, and elsewhere.

Since those golden days in New York, Carey has become the editor of Baylor University Press, and I finished thirty-two years of teaching at the Gregorian University (Rome) and returned to live in Australia (from 2009). Carey noticed that I was continuing to publish articles in the area of Christology (Who is Christ in himself?), which also necessarily involves work in soteriology (What has Christ done for us?). He invited me to gather together and publish eight recent articles. I hope that they can advance reflection on and spark insights into the heart of Christian faith: the person and "work" of Jesus Christ.

This book appears on the occasion of the fifty-year celebration of the Second Vatican Council (1962–1965). Called by Pope John XXIII of blessed memory, the Council gave a great impetus toward the unity of Christians. In its own small way, may *Christology: Origins, Developments, Debates* help believers everywhere toward appreciating and following the One at the heart of the ecumenical movement, our Savior, Jesus Christ.

Three general chapters (about Christology and soteriology) will be followed by two essays in the area of resurrection studies ("Paul as a Witness to the Risen Jesus" and "Peter as Witness to Easter") and an essay on the eternal priesthood of Christ. As its title indicates, "The Priesthood of Christ and Followers of Other Faiths" extends our focus to include also "the theology of religions." In this area, which could be more happily titled "the Christology of religions," the writings of Jacques Dupuis (1923–2004) continue to be enriching and influential. Hence I add two further chapters: "Jacques Dupuis and Religious Pluralism" and "Jacques Dupuis and Karl Rahner."

This book ends with a bibliography of my publications since 2000. My earlier bibliography is to be found in Daniel Kendall and Stephen T. Davis, eds., *The Convergence of Theology* (Mahwah, N.J.: Paulist, 2001), 370–98. Since many of the articles and books that I have published from 2000 concern issues in Christology, I add a complete bibliography for those years.

I wish to thank very warmly Andy Nguyen, SJ, for his generous and indispensable help in preparing this book. It is dedicated, with gratitude and affection, to all my Baptist friends in Australia, the United States, and elsewhere.

—*Gerald O'Collins, SJ*
Australian Catholic University (Melbourne)

# PART ONE

# I

# Christology—The Last Fifty Years

Where was Christology, as developed not only by Roman Catholics but also by other Christians, heading when the Second Vatican Council closed on December 8, 1965? Any adequate stocktaking should take note of what was ending and what had already begun and would affect the future direction of Christology.

## ENDINGS AND BEGINNINGS

The very influential Paul Tillich had died on October 22, 1965, but with the three volumes of his enduringly significant work, *Systematic Theology* (1951–1964), already published. Tillich's Christology, like the rest of his theology, was shaped by a "method of correlation," which presented the revealed truth of Christ as answering questions raised by the cultural situation. At its best this method is reflected in the "human questions and divine replies" approach of Vatican II's Declaration on the Relation of the Church to Non-Christian Religions (*Nostra aetate* 1) and more fully in the Pastoral Constitution on the Church in the Modern World (*Gaudium et spes* 3, 4, 10, and 21). At its worst, by allowing the cultural situation to dominate, the method could produce a triumph of (supposed) relevance over (real and life-giving) orthodox faith in Christ.

Sickness prevented Karl Barth (1886–1968) from attending Vatican II as an observer, and he was to die with his major work, *Church Dogmatics* (1932–), still unfinished. For Barth, human reason and philosophy cannot attain knowledge of God, which comes only through the gracious revelation given in Jesus Christ. Barth based his high Christology and, indeed, all of his theology on the Word of God communicated in the Bible.[1]

Barth's famous contemporary Rudolf Bultmann (1882–1976) had engaged with him in notable debates: for instance, over the historical status and nature of Christ's resurrection. In general, Bultmann argued for an almost complete break between history and Christian faith, leaving only the bare fact of Christ crucified as necessary for faith. Present in the proclaimed word, Christ calls hearers to decide and accept in faith the radical demands of the Gospel.

Before Barth and Bultmann died, their influence had already begun to wane. Bultmann, as we have just seen, maintained that, beyond the sheer fact of Christ's existence and death on a cross, historical conclusions cannot and should not affect, let alone support, faith in him. This was to isolate faith from history and rely on our direct experience of Jesus here and now. Many theologians and exegetes—in particular, Roman Catholic, Evangelical, and Orthodox scholars—had never accepted Bultmann's veto, which his fellow Lutheran Ernst Käsemann and others among his former students challenged in the 1950s.

The year before Vatican II came to a close, two landmark books appeared in German, written by a pair of younger theologians, the Lutheran Wolfhart Pannenberg (d. 2014) and the Reformed Jürgen Moltmann (b. 1926). In *Jesus: God and Man* (German orig., 1964), Pannenberg, who had studied with Barth, outgrew him by appealing to critical rationality in defending the historicity of the resurrection and in taking over from the speculative idealism of G. W. F. Hegel such themes as the horizon of universal history and the notion of truth being found in the whole (that is to say, in the totality of history). The three volumes of Pannenberg's *Systematic Theology* (German orig., 1988–1993) presented in fuller form the doctrines of God, creation, Christology, and so forth. But his 1964 work had permanently made its mark by arguing against Barth and Bultmann for a Christology "from below"—in the sense that critically established knowledge of the historical Jesus belongs essentially both to faith in him (as divine and human) and to systematic Christology. While historical conclusions can and should support faith, Pannenberg argued that faith has no privileged access to history and historical facts.

In *Theology of Hope* (German orig., 1964), Moltmann moved beyond his earlier dependence on Barth. Inspired by Käsemann's exposition of Paul's apocalyptic eschatology—by Gerhard von Rad's theology of the Hebrew Scriptures, and by Ernst Bloch's philosophy of hope—Moltmann rehabilitated future-oriented expectations and expounded the resurrection of Christ as the promise of God that should underpin—so he argued against Bultmann's otherworldly individualism—a common commitment to transform human society in the light of the universal future of God's kingdom. Moltmann's work helped prepare the way for black Christology, liberation Christology, and feminist Christology. He was to take his own Christology further in such later works as *The Crucified God* (German orig., 1972) and *The Way of Jesus Christ* (German orig., 1989), the former highlighting the cross as God's loving solidarity with those who suffer, and the latter presenting a messianic Christology. *The Crucified God* proposed that, in the passion and death of Christ, the whole story of human suffering became the suffering of the triune God.

If we are to understand and interpret Vatican II and its aftermath, we need to recall *ressourcement* theology, which developed from the late nineteenth century and expressed itself in the biblical movement, the liturgical renewal, the ecumenical movement, the patristic renewal, and the revival of Thomism. This theology aimed at retrieving ancient, life-giving sources for reflection that had been ignored over the centuries. Some of the leaders in *ressourcement* theology (e.g., Yves Congar, Jean Daniélou, Henri de Lubac, and Karl Rahner) became *periti*, or expert consultants, at the Council and worked closely with the bishops in producing the conciliar texts.[2]

In the years before the Council opened, Rahner (1904–1984) developed fresh thinking in Christology through lecturing and writing on such topics as (a) Christ's human knowledge and self-consciousness, (b) his resurrection, (c) the enduring importance (as "not an end but a beginning," or, more exactly, as "an end *and* a beginning") of the Council of Chalcedon's teaching on Christ's one person and two natures, (d) Christ's redeeming work and the followers of non-Christian religions, (e) the significance of evolutionary views for Christology,[3] and (f) Christ as *the* symbol of God. The early volumes of Rahner's *Theological Investigations* (German orig., 1954–1984) gather together articles that record developments in Rahner's christological thought. His mature christological synthesis would come in the monumental *Foundations of Christian Faith* (German orig., 1976).

Rahner's work embodied at least five significant changes in modern Christology: (a) the shift from a static to an existentialist and evolutionary interpretation of human existence; (b) the shift from focusing principally, or even exclusively, on the ontological question (who and what is Jesus in himself) and only secondarily (at best) reckoning with what he has done for us; (c) the shift from (at best) considering Christ's resurrection from a merely apologetical point of view to exploring its dogmatic or doctrinal significance; (d) the shift from ignoring those who do not share Christian faith to reflecting on how the saving grace of Christ reaches and affects them;[4] and (e) a shift to new philosophical thinking and language.

Apropos of (e), where the preconciliar, Roman Catholic manualist Christology (and theology, in general) borrowed its concepts from a barren and artificially clear neo-scholasticism, Rahner took up the transcendental Thomism of Joseph Maréchal and, even more, the existentialist philosophy of Martin Heidegger, with whom he had studied. Rahner signaled a shift in Christology to a philosophical pluralism, in which different theologians would draw on analytic philosophy,[5] various forms of existentialism and idealism, feminist philosophies, classical Indian philosophy, other Asian philosophies, some Marxist conceptuality, phenomenology, postmodern thought, updated forms of classical Aristotelianism, and so forth.

Rahner himself argued that human beings and their questioning reveal a drive that leads them beyond themselves towards the Absolute. This led him to develop a Christology of human self-transcendence. He interpreted the incarnation not only as the divine self-communication in the person of the Son but also as the limit case of what is possible for humanity in its dynamic openness to the Absolute. This is not to reduce Christology to anthropology, as has been sometimes alleged. Rahner never wavered in holding the incarnation to be the free self-communication of God.

Unlike Rahner, Hans Urs von Balthasar (1905–1988) played no part in the proceedings of the Second Vatican Council, but, like Rahner, he was already developing, even before the Council opened in 1962, theological and christological themes that were to bear fruit for decades to come.[6] As regards particular questions, von Balthasar interpreted Christ's "descent into hell" as utter alienation from God, and (like Rahner) broke with a long tradition by accepting that, during his earthly life, Christ exercised faith. Von Balthasar's central contribution came in the seven volumes of *The Glory of the Lord* (German orig., 1961–1969), for which *Love Alone* (German orig., 1963) served as an introduction. Here he presented the priority of beauty, understanding the glory of the beautiful God to be the central reality of biblical revelation and to enjoy a certain precedence over truth and goodness. It is through beauty, which inspires our love, that we come to know and accept what is true and good. Von Balthasar gave Christology a thoroughgoing Trinitarian focus, as did some others (e.g., Moltmann), albeit from a different theological perspective.

Early in his career, von Balthasar had won his ecumenical spurs by a fine work on the theology of Barth (German orig., 1951). But his enduring contribution to Christology came not through developing a Barthian-style Christology of the Word but through championing a more spiritual and worshipping approach. This followed, or at least resembled, some notable Orthodox theologians and writers (e.g., Fyodor Dostoevsky) by putting the beautiful Christ at the center.[7]

## THE SEVENTIES AND EIGHTIES

If asked to name *the* outstanding contribution to Christology from the 1970s, many would pick *Jesus the Christ* (German orig., 1974) by Walter Kasper (b. 1933).[8] This work brilliantly synthesized biblical, traditional, and philosophical material. Like Pannenberg, it gave adequate attention to the resurrection of Christ and relevant material from his public ministry—unlike manualist Christology that could be one-sidedly and nonhistorically engrossed with the incarnation as such. Kasper's Christology exemplified (a) a shift in Christology (and theology, in general) from an uncritical to a critical reading of the Scriptures and, in particular, of the New Testament and the Gospels. When handling his biblical sources, Kasper, like most Catholic theologians in the post-Vatican II situation, drew on both Protestant scholars like Käsemann and Catholic authors like Rudolf Schnackenburg. Not only at the scriptural level but also in general, Christology had become thoroughly ecumenical. (b) Where many manualists, when citing the fathers of the church, lifted proof texts from a widely used and frequently reprinted anthology—Marie Joseph Rouët de Journel, *Enchiridion patristicum*[9]—Kasper quoted and referenced directly Athanasius, Augustine, Irenaeus, Maximus the Confessor, Tertullian, and other ancient authors. The patristic renewal enriched this Christology. (c) Finally, strands of German idealism, coming from J. G. Fichte and F. W. Schelling as well as from Hegel, helped shape the conceptuality and arguments of Kasper. He aimed to illustrate how a particular history has universal relevance: Jesus *is* the Christ. In carrying through his project, Kasper exemplified what Bernard Lonergan called the shift from classical to historical consciousness.

A certain political consciousness helped trigger a largely Latin American movement, which was inspired by the Exodus, prophetic calls for justice, and Jesus' proclamation of the kingdom. Liberation theology struck deep roots wherever unjust structures, economic dependence, and political domination oppressed great masses of poor people. Its better exponents included Juan Luis Segundo (1925–1996), Jon Sobrino (b. 1938), and, above all, Gustavo Gutiérrez (b. 1928), whose *A Theology of Liberation* (Spanish orig., 1972) signaled the start of the movement.

From *Christology at the Crossroads* (Spanish orig., 1976) and *Jesus in Latin America* (Spanish orig., 1982) down to a book dedicated to eight murdered friends, *Jesus the Liberator* (Spanish orig., 1991), and beyond, Sobrino has proved in Christology the leading voice of liberation theology. Viewing from the standpoint of the victims who Christ is and what he does, Sobrino calls for a transformation of society and a life of service based on the ideals of justice, peace, and human solidarity. Such liberation Christology embodies a spirituality of active discipleship.

One feature of the seventies and eighties was the increasing help that Christology received from biblical scholars: for instance, from Raymond Brown (1928–1998), James Dunn (b. 1939), Martin Hengel (1926–2009), Geza Vermes (1924–2013), and others. Let us see some of the details.

Author of *Jesus: God and Man* (1967) and coeditor of the widely read *Jerome Biblical Commentary* (1968; rev. ed., 1990), Brown contributed much to theological development through these works and through such books as *The Virginal Conception and Bodily Resurrection of Jesus* (1973), *The Birth of the Messiah* (1977; rev. ed., 1993), and *Exegesis and Church Doctrine* (1985). He would continue to offer biblical help to Christology through the two volumes of *The Death of the Messiah* (1994) and *An Introduction to New Testament Christology* (1994). Brown was also one of the leading exegetes who "blew the whistle" on the somewhat ill-conceived use of scriptural material in Edward Schillebeeckx' work in Christology, *Jesus* (Dutch orig., 1974).

Dunn's thesis director, C. D. F. Moule, had provided well-based guidance with *The Origin of Christology* (1977), as he did with an earlier work that he edited, *The Significance of the Message of the Resurrection for Faith in Jesus Christ* (1968). Dunn himself produced a landmark book with *Christology in the Making* (1980; new ed., 1989); it has been extensively used by teachers and students of Christology.

A leading German exegete, Hengel published works that enjoyed much currency in theology: *The Son of God: The Origin of Christology* (German orig., 1975) and *The Atonement: The Origin of the Doctrine in the New Testament* (German orig., 1980). The former book explained how the first Christians identified Jesus "in himself," while the latter clarified how they came to understand Jesus "for us" or what he did to atone for human sin.

A 1973 work by the Jewish scholar Vermes, *Jesus the Jew: A Historian's Reading*, encouraged Christian theologians and biblical scholars to take seriously the Jewishness of Jesus and the Jewish matrix in which his story and the origins of Christianity unfolded.[10] In the light of what happened academically (wider concern with Jesus the Jew) and what had happened historically (the unspeakable horror of the Holocaust), it was astonishing to find the Jesus Seminar (founded in 1985 by Robert Funk and John Dominic Crossan) renewing a long discredited picture of Jesus as a kind of itinerant sage and Greek-style Cynic philosopher.[11] Highlighting their odd kind of wisdom interpretation of Jesus, the members of the Jesus Seminar ran counter to what Käsemann and other biblical scholars had reestablished: the deeply Jewish, apocalyptic thrust of Jesus' proclamation of the divine kingdom. The Jesus Seminar, like some liberal writers of the past, highlighted Jesus' ethical teaching at the expense of his dramatic eschatological message about the reign of God breaking into our world. It was no wonder that many leaders in New Testament scholarship—such as Dale Allison, Raymond Brown, Richard Hays, Luke Timothy Johnson, John Meier, and N. T. Wright—objected to much in the methods and skeptical "findings" of the Jesus Seminar. These critics once again encouraged specialists in Christology to recognize that the Gospels are substantially reliable in putting us in touch with the historical Jesus, as well as warning them not to neglect his future-oriented proclamation of the kingdom.

## FROM THE NINETIES TO DATE

*Biblical Scholarship*

From the nineties down to 2013, biblical scholars have continued to provide Christology with notable help: for instance, in arguing effectively against those who continue to propose that Jesus was simply an outstanding teacher of ethics, a final prophet, or a wandering wonder-worker. According to this view, Paul or others wrongly credited Jesus with a divine identity and created a Christ of faith, who misrepresents the true Jesus of history. They perverted the faith *of* Jesus into faith *in* Jesus as divine Lord and Son of God. They wanted to strip away the later dogmatic overlay and return to the very noble but merely human Jesus of Nazareth.

Contemporary biblical scholarship, however, highlights passages where Paul, the earliest Christian writer, quoted even earlier traditions that involved a high Christology and the worship of Jesus: for instance, the hymn found in Philippians 2:6-11. The apostle also cited a prayer in Aramaic that Greek-speaking Christians living elsewhere shared with the first Christians in the Holy Land: "Marana tha [Our Lord, come]" (1 Cor 16:21). Like Paul but before Paul, the first Christians believed in Jesus as divine Lord (and Son of God) and worshipped him accordingly. This belief and practice did not first emerge later through a gradual process but was there from the beginning, as Larry Hurtado's *Lord Jesus Christ: Devotion to Jesus in Earliest Christianity* (2003) documents meticulously.

The year 2003 proved an annus mirabilis for biblical publications like Hurtado's that provide notable assistance to those working in Christology. Wright's magisterial *The Resurrection of the Son of God* presented Jesus' resurrection as something startlingly new within the context of Jewish expectations about the fate of the dead.[12] In the same year, Dunn published *Jesus Remembered*, an account of what critical biblical scholarship maintains that we can responsibly say about the history of Jesus.

From 1991 Meier has published four volumes in his monumental *A Marginal Jew: Rethinking the Historical Jesus*, with a further, fifth, volume still to come. These volumes supply experts in Christology with abundant material as they examine and seek to draw conclusions from the preaching and activity of Jesus.

*Six Trajectories*

In plotting the story of Christology in the last two decades, let me pick out six trajectories, which at times overlap: (a) feminist Christology; (b) wisdom Christology; (c) various Christologies developed in African and Asian contexts; (d) the growing impact of Christologies produced by Eastern Christians; (e) a rich harvest of studies of the redemption that inaugurated the twenty-first century; and (f) the challenge of both holding one divine plan to save human beings through Jesus Christ and recognizing various religious traditions as ways of salvation.

Feminist Christologies coming, for instance, from Rosemary Radford Ruether (b. 1936) and Elizabeth Schüssler Fiorenza (b. 1938) have taken a crusading form in rightly protesting against a dominant male chauvinism. But a feminist label seems less than appropriate for other women scholars, such as Eleonore Stump (b. 1947). Her philosophical studies have enjoyed an indirect impact in Christology. But sometimes she has dealt directly with theological questions, as in the essay "Aquinas' Metaphysics of the Incarnation."[13] Sarah Coakley (b. 1951) provided another brilliant essay in the same volume: "What Does Chalcedon Solve and What Does It Not? Some Reflections on the Status and Meaning of the Chalcedonian Definition."[14]

Caroline Walker Bynum (b. 1941) has made a lasting mark through her studies of medieval spirituality and ideas of redemption. Against the background of a conventional opposition between Anselm and Abelard (that she challenges), she introduces Angela of Foligno, Catherine of Genoa, Julian of Norwich, and other mystics, and enriches our grasp of the redemption theory that underpinned medieval piety.[15]

In 1995 Fiorenza published *Jesus: Miriam's Child, Sophia's Prophet: Critical Issues in Feminist Christology*, a book partly inspired by the theme of wisdom. But one cannot claim that a well-rounded Christology in the key of Wisdom (Sophia) has yet been produced. With Fiorenza and others, like Celia Deane-Drummond, Denis Edwards, and Elizabeth Johnson, I share a sense of the possibilities offered by such a Christology and have done some interim work in its cause.[16]

A search for justice and the common good has shaped not only the liberation thinkers of Latin America but also the leaders in African Christology (e.g., Jean-Marc Ela and John Mbiti) and the contributors to Asian Christology (e.g., Arockiam Alangaram and

Peter Phan).[17] Both in Africa and Asia, initiatives in Christology have grown exponentially and have also been notably spurred by the desire to enculturate faith in Jesus. The contributors aspire to a Christology that is fully African or Asian and completely Christian—that is to say, they look for a living Christ for Africans and Asians. In both Africa and Asia, however, they are challenged not only by the vastness of the continent but also by the diversity of languages, cultures, peoples, and histories.

Eastern Christianity—represented by such theologians as Sergius Bulgakov, Paul Evdokimov, John Meyendorff, Dumitru Staniloae, Kallistos Ware, and John Zizioulas—encourages doing Christology in the key of beauty and the context of worship. This style of Christology, drawing on the early councils and leading Greek fathers of the church, works out of the setting of the Church at public worship. It bears witness to the divine beauty of Christ, revealed and actively present in the liturgy.

Some of those Eastern theologians just mentioned are long dead: Bulgakov, for example, died in 1944. But their influence in both East and West continues and in some cases grows. An English translation of Bulgakov's *The Lamb of God* was elegantly published in 2008.[18]

As the twentieth century drew to a close and the new century opened, numerous important studies on redemption and related themes have come from such scholars as Ian Bradley, Robert J. Daly, Colin Gunton, Alan Hultgren, John McIntyre, Bernard Sesboüé, Richard Swinburne, Frances Young, and others. Some of these recent works—for instance, by Paul Fiddes— were outstanding.[19]

These authors have helped to heal the long-standing and unfortunate divide between Christ "in himself" and Christ "for us." One may distinguish Christology from soteriology, but we lose much by separating them.

In the preface to the second edition of *Christology* (2009), I remarked that in recent years Christology has received its richest input from a broad range of biblical scholars and from writers who have wrestled with the question of Christ's saving work being mediated through the Holy Spirit to the whole of humanity. While making this claim, I also drew attention to some systematic studies in Christology (e.g., by Oliver Crisp and Robert Jenson), and some valuable studies in patristics (e.g., by Lewis Ayres, Sarah Coakley, Brian Daley, Andrew

Louth, and Richard Price) and in medieval studies (e.g., by Caroline Walker Bynum, Richard Cross, and Marilyn McCord Adams). I also recognized how such philosophers as Ingolf Dalferth, Stephen Davis, C. Stephen Evans, Brian Leftow, Alvin Plantinga, Eleonore Stump, Peter van Inwagen, and Richard Swinburne have proved lively debating partners with those in systematic Christology. Nevertheless, I attributed greater significance to (i) publications in the biblical area, which have continued to supply indispensable resources to theologians, and to (ii) the debates over the grace of Christ being mediated to those who do not belong to visible Christianity. I have already made a case for (i). Let me now attend to (ii), but limiting myself to one outstanding figure in that field, Jacques Dupuis (1923–2004).

Thirty-six years in India—where he taught Christology and other branches of theology, published a great deal, and emerged as *the* theological adviser to the Catholic Bishops' Conference of India (CBCI)—prepared Dupuis to write the book for which he will be mainly remembered, *Toward a Christian Theology of Religious Pluralism* (1997).[20] Written in English, as well as appearing in French, Italian, Portuguese, and Spanish, this work combined not only enormous scholarship but also the fruits of Dupuis' experience. At the age of eighty, he spoke of his time in India: "My exposure to the Indian reality has been the greatest grace I have received from God so far as my vocation as a theologian and a professor is concerned."

Dupuis' case for inclusive pluralism (understood in his terms) triggered a vast debate about the role of Christ's humanity for the salvation of human beings. Over a hundred reviews in major journals, along with numerous articles in journals and chapters in books, evaluated his views. *Toward a Christian Theology of Religious Pluralism* also brought Dupuis dozens of invitations to deliver lectures across Europe and in Asia and North America.[21] His book addressed major questions that remain highly relevant: How can we profess faith in Jesus Christ as the one Savior of humankind and at the same time recognize the Holy Spirit at work in religions and cultures everywhere? What, from a Christian perspective, is the role of the world's religions as visible paths to salvation?

A subsequent, more popular, work, *Christianity and the Religions* (2001),[22] clarified some of Dupuis' positions and introduced the expression "inclusive pluralism," which he used to sum up his theology of religions. The Festschrift that Daniel Kendall and I edited for Dupuis' eightieth birthday (December 2003), *In Many and Diverse Ways*,[23] contains much information and comment on his life and theology, as well as a complete bibliography of his publications up to 2003 and a full bibliography of reactions to *Toward a Christian Theology of Religious Pluralism*.

After the death of Dupuis, I wrote *Salvation for All*, a book that (i) assembles and assesses the biblical testimony about the salvation of God's other peoples, and then (ii) presents some systematic conclusions about the role of Jesus for the salvation of the world.[24] The book, I would argue, provides further underpinning for the inclusive pluralism of Dupuis. Its language about the universal presence of Christ (as divine Wisdom) and of the Holy Spirit differs from his, and the book moves ahead by appealing to Hebrews to profile the saving faith of "outsiders."

After Dupuis died on December 28, 2004, his views have continued to be cited, approved, and criticized. Most of those who now write on Dupuis concentrate on his *Toward a Christian Theology of Religious Pluralism*; only a few also take into account his subsequent *Christianity and the Religions*, in which he clarified his inclusive pluralism, qualified his language about the complementarity (between Christianity and other religions) by calling it "asymmetrical complementarity," introduced some teaching from the Third Council of Constantinople (680–681) (to support his position about the actions of Christ's divine nature and human nature being distinct but inseparable), and made other changes. In a chapter below ("Jacques Dupuis and Religious Pluralism"), I present and evaluate some of the discussion that has appeared in English from 2005 to date (including William R. Burrows, *Jacques Dupuis Faces the Inquisition*).[25] The essay also draws attention to the debate about Dupuis' views that continues in Italian and other languages.

Apropos of the last fifty years of Christology, I am painfully aware of how much more could be discussed: for instance, the kenotic self-limitation and self-abasement of the incarnation; the endemic misunderstanding of something dear to Melito of Sardis, Augustine of Hippo, and Martin Luther, the interchange of properties; the application to the redemption of ideas from René Girard; and the imagining of Christ through the visual arts, literature, music, and film.

Let me end by drawing attention to four works that can fill out what has been happening in Christology over the last fifty years: Gerald O'Collins' *What Are They Saying about Jesus?*, Giovanni Iammarrone's edited volume *La Cristologia contemporanea*, Edward T. Oakes' *Infinity Dwindled to Infancy*, and Francesca A. Murphy's forthcoming edited volume, *The Oxford Handbook of Christology.*[26]

# 2

# Revisiting the Person of Jesus

In *The Way of Jesus Christ*, Jürgen Moltmann pointed to one of the major "constraints" for those who undertake such a theological project: "No contemporary Christology is ever completely new. Every Christology is part of a grateful and critical dialogue with the christologies of [our] predecessors and contemporaries."[1] When writing *Christology: A Biblical, Historical, and Systematic Study of Jesus*,[2] I also attended to what had gone before and to the christological input coming from leading biblical scholars, historians, and theologians of modern times. I planned to write my own Christology, but in a "grateful and critical dialogue" with others.

In the years after the first edition of *Christology* appeared in 1995 and then the second edition in 2009, numerous reviewers have presented and evaluated the book. It seems worthwhile taking up dialogue with them and reacting to their questions, insights, and corrections. Without such a response, any conversation would remain incomplete. The reviews are gathered together in alphabetical order in the notes at the end of this chapter, and full publication details are given. My discussion that follows provides the name of the reviewers and relevant page numbers for quotations. The reviews raised at least four general issues: the question of an expertise that creates expectations; the degree of engagement with modernity; the contribution of liberation Christology; and the use of the latest proposals from biblical scholars.

## EXPERTISE CREATING EXPECTATIONS

Inevitably, the particular expertise and reading of reviewers color and even shape their evaluations. To make this point, one might single out three reviewers of *Christology*: James Dunn, John Parr, and Lewis Ayres.

Dunn opened his review with a flatteringly positive judgment: "There are few who have the necessary breadth of knowledge and reading to attempt an integrated study in what have become the separate disciplines of biblical, historical and systematic theology. Fewer still make the attempt. And very few succeed. This is one of the very few." As a leading New Testament scholar, Dunn appreciated that "fully half the discussion" was "on the biblical material as such," judged that throughout "excellent use" was made of that material, and praised the "unusual" familiarity with "biblical scholarship" (Dunn, 133).

. Other scriptural scholars—such as George Montague, Carey Newman, and Pheme Perkins—also came up with similarly positive reviews, but not all the experts proved equally happy. Parr, for example, found three problems with the section on the history of Jesus. First, it should have "contextualized Jesus' ministry" in "contemporary Judaism's struggles to come to terms with the impact of Roman rule and Greek culture on Palestine" (Parr, 304). Parr rightly called attention to the significance of the social and religious context in which Jesus proclaimed the kingdom of God, but this context was not primarily Palestine as such but rather Galilee, which has been studied brilliantly by Sean Freyne, Mark Chancey, and others. The quest for Jesus should not be separated from the quest for the historical Galilee. Moreover, *pace* the Jesus Seminar (and seemingly Parr himself), the historical Galilee of the early first century was solidly Jewish and not struggling with, let alone shaped by, the impact of Hellenistic culture. Something of the "impact of Roman rule" could have featured, albeit briefly, in my presentation of Jesus' ministry, but, more importantly, I could have included something about the different Jewish groups (and the "struggles" between them) that John Meier has examined, above all, in volume three of his magnum opus.[3]

Second, Parr objected to what he called my "imposing dogmatic categories on the Gospels. So, Jesus' authority becomes a matter of his 'divine status' rather than his insistence that he, and not his rivals, speaks and acts for God at time of crisis for Israel" (Parr, 304–5). But should we dismiss a relatively "ordinary" term, "divine status," as a "dogmatic category"—that is to say, a fundamental philosophical concept of a doctrinal nature (such as "hypostasis," "physis," or "prosōpon," which emerged in later christological controversy)? Since Jesus insisted that he spoke and acted for God in ways that set him apart from others, this inevitably raises a question (that should, of course, be answered with due sensitivity to what the Gospels allow us to conclude): Who did Jesus think he was? Can we reach any conclusion about his sense of his own identity and, hence, of his status?

Third, Parr argued against "his [Jesus'] father-son language" suggesting "an ontological relationship rather than a particular quality of spiritual experience." I share Parr's concern with "the varying textures of human and Christian experience" (Parr, 305)[4] but fail to see why one should propose here a "rather than." What might we conclude—once again, using the Gospels with appropriate sensitivity—about the particular quality of Jesus' spiritual experience? Could it lead us to suggest that, beneath and behind this experience and the language in which he expressed it, there existed, in reality or in being (that is to say, "ontologically"), a father-son relationship?

It was out of his top-class expertise as a patristic scholar that Ayres reviewed the second edition of *Christology*.[5] He appreciated my desire to engage with the biblical sources and make christological reflection more directly scriptural. But he regretted that I did not draw more on patristic and medieval authors when "examining some key questions in modern debates about Christ." He judged that I made "extensive use only of modern biblical scholarship," and wished that I had introduced more, for instance, from the works of St. Augustine of Hippo and St. Thomas Aquinas (Ayres, 28). Let me make four points in response.

(1) The importance of the patristic and medieval authors is beyond question. Yet they belong to the history of *reception*, and not to the *origins* of Christianity constituted by the history of Jesus and his apostles, which for all time the uniquely inspired Scriptures recorded and normatively interpreted. To be sure, it is at their peril that theologians ignore large sections in the history of reception, and it is a disaster when they ignore the whole history of reception. But the history of reception remains just that, and should never be privileged over against the history of origins.

(2) It was not only Ayres but also Parr (Parr, 304) who wanted a longer discussion of christological developments—from the fathers of the Church, through the medieval period to modern times. But, as was stated clearly in the preface to the first edition, I set myself to write my own Christology and *not* a complete history of Christology. In any case, selectivity was necessary, if the book was not to grow beyond the proportions desired by the publishers. If Ayres reads a book that I coauthored, *Jesus Our Priest*,[6] he may be happier about the extent to which it could incorporate the Christian tradition. Given a relative neglect of the Letter to the Hebrews and the theme of Christ's priesthood, it was possible to present and evaluate how official teachers and theologians over two thousand years had received and understood that priesthood and our sharing in it. Even so, to do full justice to the whole Christian tradition and its reception of Christ's priesthood would have called for much more attention to liturgical texts and practice (than we allowed ourselves) and to Christian art and architecture (which we had to neglect).

(3) When I took up such a "key question in modern debates" as the relationship between the divine and the human mind of Christ, Ayres wanted me to remember "answers extensively developed" by ancient and medieval authors and referred specifically to Augustine's Letter 137.[7] That letter certainly explores the incarnation with "sophistication," but it never addresses the question of the "two minds" of Christ and how they might relate. Unlike the issue of his "two wills," this is a modern question and not a "perennial" question; it has not been posed and answered "over and over again in different modes through Catholic tradition" (Ayres, 28).

(4) I wholeheartedly agree with Ayres that, together with the results coming from modern biblical study, "tradition" is a major resource for "reading Scripture" and is, in fact, "a commentary on Scripture," alongside the results coming from modern biblical study (Ayres, 28). But I would add that philosophy is also a major resource. In developing, for instance, a Christology of *presence* or reflecting on redemption as a work of *love* (as I did), theologians need to draw on philosophical resources to achieve some degree of clarity and coherence in the positions they develop. Despite the study of Platonic, Stoic, Aristotelian, and other schools of philosophical thought that his work in patristics has required, Ayres never mentions philosophy and the role it has played in christological thinking since the second century.

Christian theology in general and Christology in particular have proved the greatest employment agency for philosophy the Western world has ever seen.

## ENGAGEMENT WITH MODERNITY

Unlike Ayres, Denis Carroll considered my "dialogue with the tradition" to be "superb," but, like George Newlands (Newlands, 783–84), he judged my "engagement with modernity" to be "less so." He explained that "the linguistic, conceptual and political questions raised from the 1960s onwards are addressed but fit uneasily to [into?] the author's scheme." As specific examples, (a) he cited the scant attention I paid to the possibilities of Christology in an evolutionary perspective, and (b) he queried my observation that "talk about his social critique and counter-cultural behaviour can submerge the religious dimension of Jesus' activity" (Carroll, 318).

As regards (a), *Christology* (1995) did introduce the evolutionary perspective of Pierre Teilhard de Chardin, and *Christology* (2009) enlarged this slightly. Beyond question, it is high time that someone, preferably a theologian with a strong scientific background, retrieved the best insights of Teilhard and produced a full-scale evolutionary Christology, one that allows theories of evolution to illuminate the person and work of Jesus, but not a Christology that cuts Jesus down to size and forces him into a preconceived evolutionary framework. The sometimes uncritical enthusiasm for Teilhard's writing that marked the 1960s has waned; we now need his "second coming," which would exploit what he has to offer for Christian thought and action in the third millennium. In my own *Jesus Our Redeemer*, I showed my own appreciation for what he contributes to thinking about the redemption.[8] But both in *Christology* (1995) and in *Christology* (2009), the primary aim, as stated, was to expound my own views, not to tell in detail the story of the best christological developments, either ancient or modern, evolutionary or otherwise.

As regards (b), I was contrasting the best work coming from research into the sociohistorical context of Jesus' ministry with the worst products in this field. To exemplify the latter, I cited Burton Mack, whose one-sided stress on social critique and countercultural behavior submerged the religious dimension in the activity of Jesus and his first followers.[9] Other names could be added, like that of

Robert Funk.[10] Anthony Saldarini, who reviewed *Christology* (1995) along with Funk's *Honest to Jesus*, complained that Funk "has capitulated to the post-Enlightenment culture into which he seeks to bring Jesus" (Saldarini, 12). One gets a measure of how far this capitulation can go when Funk endorses "responsible, protected recreational sex between consenting adults."[11] One does not need to be a raging fundamentalist to shake one's head over Jesus being enlisted in support of recreational sex.

Nevertheless, rejecting such one-sided and sometimes bizarre pictures of Jesus in his social and political setting should not take us to the other extreme and join the latter-day followers of Rudolf Schnackenburg. In his classic *God's Rule and Kingdom*, he wrote, "The salvation proclaimed and promised by Jesus in this reign and Kingdom of God is *purely* religious in character."[12] Did Jesus take no stand on social and political issues? Here "political" is not to be reduced to national, still less nationalistic, issues. It refers to all matters of public and civic concern. Without going as far as Schnackenburg, John Meier assures his readers: "Jesus was not interested in and did not issue pronouncements about concrete social and political reforms, either for the world in general or for Israel in particular. He was not proclaiming the reform of the world; he was proclaiming the end of the world."[13] In a 1998 essay that was largely a debate with Meier, I argued that Jesus "broke open and changed the contemporary social structures by the ways he spoke and behaved," and I went on to spell out certain aspects of "his liberating work for integral human progress."[14] Some of that material should have been incorporated in *Christology* (2009).

Leaving aside the two specific issues raised by Carroll, I believe that he (as well as Newlands and Charles Wilson[15]) are correct in calling for more engagement with modernity. To be sure, both editions of *Christology* address some of the issues,[16] but they should have contained, or at least evoked, more about the cultural, political, economic, and other changes (both positive and negative) that characterize *modernity*. When we reflect today on the person and work of Jesus, we do so in a world that has seen an urbanization that has brought a widespread flight from villages to life in enormous urban centers, an unprecedented rise in the world's population, a globalization that has radically changed the functioning of national and international economy, a revolution in communications, an exponential growth in religious and cultural pluralism (that questions the Church's mission to proclaim the gospel), ecological decay, climate change, nuclear proliferation, a greater respect for personal dignity that seeks to end a widespread denial of basic human rights, savage civil wars, and the rest. Robert Imbelli rightly wanted "more explicit consideration of the 'pathological' elements of human experience" (Imbelli, 27). Right at the time when I was committed to writing *Christology* (1995), I coauthored an article on what Imbelli named "the wilful refusal of love," or what I would call "wilful hatred."[17] Some of that material might have entered *Christology*. The best and the worst of modernity should not be neglected.

Remembering David Brown, a theological colleague whose scholarly writing persistently draws in valuable and challenging examples from modern art, literature, and music, I find Carroll's gentle reproach even more convincing.[18] Peter Bernardi may have appreciated my "references to artistic works" (Bernardi, 353). Yet the painters and writers I invoke—for example, in *Christology* (2009) and elsewhere—are repeatedly classical figures. It is only rarely that I cite such artists as Francis Bacon, Marc Chagall, or Andy Warhol, or such authors as Chinua Achebe, Shusaku Endo, Gabriel García Márquez, Seamus Heaney, James Joyce, Eugene O'Neill, Iris Murdoch, Salman Rushdie, Dylan Thomas, Mario Vargas Llosa, or Virginia Woolf.[19] Here too Christology should play itself out in counterpoint with modernity. Nevertheless, I may deserve a little credit for changing the image on the cover of *Christology*. Where the first edition displayed a classic mosaic of Christ from the Basilica of Saints Cosmas and Damian (Rome), the second edition used a wonderful modern portrayal of Christ calming the storm, created by a contemporary Chinese artist, Dr. He Qi.

Apropos of modernity, Saldarini, showing himself somewhat more satisfied than Carroll, wrote, "O'Collins . . . gathers up modern themes, concerns and insights into a classic synthesis tuned to modern ears. The topics may be familiar and unexciting (resurrection, Son of God, Trinity, councils, divinity and humanity, virginal conception, redeemer, etc.), but the explanations are clear and attuned as much as possible to modern thought and sensibility." But, Saldarini added, he does not grapple with "questions and doubts that have confused and tormented the modern soul," and "serenely assumes" in his readers "a sympathetic acceptance of God, Christ, and the Christian tradition." This means that "the task of [his] theological inquiry into Jesus remains seriously incomplete" (Saldarini, 12, 14). Here something comes into view that I never set myself to do in either edition of *Christology.* The subtitle was and has remained "A Biblical, Historical, and Systematic Study of Jesus," and does not at the end qualify the study as *also* being "apologetical." In his long and probing review of *Christology* (2009), James McGrath defended me over this issue: "O'Collins is writing as a Christian theologian, and historic Christian doctrine provides his theological framework. His aim is to formulate a coherent Christian view of Jesus, not to persuade skeptics to adopt it" (McGrath, 487).

Nevertheless, Saldarini rightly pressed home the need to tackle modern questions and doubts, so as to present to troubled human beings the case for accepting Jesus as a credible answer to their search. Egan also looked for more help for the "marginal people" and those who want to know how the Christian understanding of Jesus "actually affects" their lives. In other books I undertook those apologetical (Saldarini) and pastoral (Egan) tasks, notably in *Jesus: A Portrait.*[20] But, even there, was I largely preaching to the converted?

## LIBERATION CHRISTOLOGY

A third general issue raised by several reviews concerned liberation theology. Parr noted my "lack of engagement with Christologies of liberation" (Parr, 305), while Robert Moloney missed any "account of the contribution of liberation theology" (Moloney, 134). They both saw that in *Christology* (1995) Jon Sobrino featured only twice (pp. 240, 251); the second edition gave him more entries in the concluding bibliography. Once again I might plead in my defense that I was not providing accounts of various modern schools of Christology but writing my own Christology. If I should have written at length on liberation Christology, I should also have done so in the case of Hans Urs von Balthasar, Karl Barth, Bernard Lonergan, Jürgen Moltmann, Wolfhart Pannenberg, and others. But, for better or worse, I set myself to do my own work and thinking, and not to provide an adequate survey of contemporary contributions to Christology. Yet there is a little more to be said.

The courageous witness of Sobrino, Gustavo Gutiérrez, and some other exponents of liberation theology (like Ignacio Ellacuría) has always won my deep admiration. As regards liberation theology in general, I have persistently championed its place among the major "styles" of theology that the Christian Church needs.[21] As regards Sobrino in particular, I defended him against accusations made by the Congregation for the Doctrine of the Faith.[22] Nevertheless, I must admit that—apart from (a) his aim to shape Christology on behalf of the victimized nonpersons in our world and (b) his insistence that implementing justice, peace, and human solidarity will enable us to grasp more fully the meaning of Christ's resurrection from the dead[23]—I have not found themes to appropriate in my own christological thinking. I may be badly mistaken, but too much of what I read seemed derivative, and I looked in vain for a full-scale development of what the suffering victims of this world themselves make of Christ's person and work.[24]

## USE OF RECENT PROPOSALS

Among other issues raised in his review of *Christology* (2009), James McGrath put the question, should systematic theologians follow, wherever possible, the consensus view when they draw on biblical scholarship? Is it "best to seek to be as up-to-date as possible, even drawing on recent publications that seek to challenge the consensus view, or to remain with the consensus"? He pointed out the "danger" of any choice: "To the extent that a particular view comes to be judged unpersuasive, this will affect the volumes that drew on and built on it. This happens with consensus views as well, of course, but usually only in the longer term." McGrath had in mind the use I made of Richard Bauckham's "most recent work on eyewitness testimony of the Gospels. Bauckham's arguments are certainly generating discussion, but the extent to which they will be found persuasive and considered of lasting value remains to be seen" (McGrath, 486–87).

Some years ago Dan Kendall and I raised the same issue and argued that "where available, the consensus of centrist exegetes" should "guide systematic theology."[25] We went on to explain, "It is obviously ill-advised to take over into theology adventurous, even maverick, theses advanced by individual biblical scholars or a small

group with its own particularist agenda. One might dub this practice
rushing to apply in theology the latest thesis from the banks of the
Seine or the Neckar. To some extent, Edward Schillebeeckx did just
that in his 1974 Christology."[26] Was I doing the same by using Bauckham's work? In my defense I plead that, since in biblical studies no
general consensus exists on the origins of the Gospels, I had to choose
one approach. I took over Bauckham's proposals about eyewitness testimony, using as well the widely accepted scheme of three stages in the
transmission of witness to Jesus' words and deeds: the initial stage in
his earthly life when his disciples and others spoke about him; second,
the handing on by word of mouth or in writing of witness to him after
his death and resurrection; and, third, the authorial work of the four
evangelists later in the first century.[27] Rather than planning to be "as
up-to-date as possible" about Gospel origins, I happened to receive for
review Bauckham's major study and, somewhat to my surprise, found
it convincing, or at least the most plausible version I had come across
about the origins of the four Gospels.[28]

Thus far I have responded to four general questions reviewers have
raised for discussion. Let me turn now to four more specific topics: my
introduction of "presence" as an organizing principle for Christology;
the importance of the theme of Christ's relationship to followers of
other religions; the virginal conception; and the role of the historical
Jesus for systematic Christology.

## THE SIGNIFICANCE OF PRESENCE

Imbelli singled out my "path-breaking exploration" of the theme of
presence as a systematic category and argued that "the Lord's continuing presence" made *Christology* (1995) "particularly relevant for the
Church's liturgical life" (Imbelli, 26). Ann Nickson (Nickson, 143),
Pheme Perkins (Perkins, 26–27), William Portier (Portier, 154), and,
even more insistently, James Heft wanted "further development" of
ideas about presence" (Heft, 548)—not least because that would help
deploying the resurrection as "the interpretative key" for the whole of
Christology. Certainly more remained for me to do, "if the possibilities of Jesus' presence among us are to be realized" (549).

In *Christology* (2009), I added two further themes about presence
to my 1995 list of seven.[29] Then, in an article on the liturgical presences of Christ, these aspects of presence grew to ten.[30] In *Salvation*

*for All*, I dedicated a chapter to the universal presence of Christ and the Holy Spirit.[31] But all of that is hardly enough. Currently I am directing a doctoral dissertation on the Christology of presence, hoping that dialogue with a brilliant student may take me further along the track in thinking about Christ and his presence.[32] Part of the difficulty that I have experienced toward developing fuller ideas about "presence" has come from the lack of interaction on the part of other theologians, not to mention philosophers. "Interesting" has been the standard response, but real challenges and additions to what I have written have not been forthcoming.

Ayres declared what I wrote about "Christ's presence to the world in different modes" to be "a powerful meditation." He suggested that this theme could be taken forward by exploring "the extent to which theologians from the tradition" have written about "the divine presence" in its "mystery" (Ayres, 28). But I wished to explore the presence of Christ, not precisely the divine presence as such. Here I found little to draw from the tradition.[33]

Several reviewers queried the "feminine" dimension that I listed in my account of presence. Carroll wrote, "I found O'Collins's listing of male/female characteristics and his application thereof to Christ's presence somewhat unconvincing" (Carroll, 318). Faced with the biblical presentation of Christ as Lady Wisdom, the homely image of the mother hen that Jesus applied to himself (Luke 13:34), and some traditional teaching about "Jesus our mother," I believed that the feminine should be introduced and that this involved drawing some distinction between the feminine and masculine. Picking up the reflections of the late Walter Ong, I attempted this task, conscious that the whole area was "controversial and deeply conditioned by one's own culture."[34] But Klyne Snodgrass may well be right: "Presence is no more feminine than masculine, and Jesus' reception of children or his insistence on losing life in order to find it do not betray feminine traits. They betray caring, human traits" (Snodgrass, 257).

## Christ and the Religious Others

Heft wanted my chapter on Christ as "The Universal Redeemer" to be "extended, given both the importance of the issue of Christ's relationship to other religions and the amount of scholarship recently dedicated to that topic" (Heft, 547–48). Heft himself has contributed notably in that area, not least by the book he recently edited and for which he wrote an insightful introduction.[35]

Heft's suggestion led me to enlarge for the second edition the chapter on Christ's redemptive impact on all humanity.[36] Even more than Leslie Houlden, who wanted to hear more on "other faiths" (Houlden, 15), Heft prompted me into writing two books in the area of what we might call "the Christology of the Religions."[37]

## THE VIRGINAL CONCEPTION

When reviewing the first edition of *Christology*, Montague expressed a wish to see more space given to the virginal conception (Montague, 169). The second edition has doubled the treatment of this theme,[38] engaging with difficulties against the virginal conception and expounding further its significance in the whole story of salvation. I was glad to discover that Ayres found this "particularly helpful."

In both editions, borrowing a distinction from some philosophers, I distinguished between *essential* and merely *common* human properties and wrote: "Clearly, enjoying a biological father as well as a mother is a common property. But can we establish that it is also an absolutely essential property."[39] Queries coming from Dunn (Dunn, 133) and Parr (Parr, 305) suggested that I should have explained further this distinction. Medieval theology compared the story of Adam's origin (as pictured in the book of Genesis) with the standard origin of human beings, without introducing the terminological distinction between "truly essential" and "merely common" human properties. It understood the first Adam to be created without originating from either a human father or mother, while Christ, the New Adam, was conceived and born from a human mother but not from a human father. Unquestionably, when retrieving today such a comparison between the two Adams, we need to recognize the mythical status of the Genesis story and views about human origin coming from evolutionary science. Nevertheless, the medieval comparison can encourage a modern, philosophical question: Does the standard origin of a living organism rule out all possibilities of any other origin? Or is there, for example, a possibility that God might make an exception for very good reasons?

## THE HISTORICAL JESUS' IMPACT ON SYSTEMATIC CHRISTOLOGY

McGrath, apropos of the specific issue of preexistence, raises a major question for those who elaborate a systematic Christology. Let me explain. He asks, "If, as O'Collins acknowledges, Jesus [in his human mind] did not think of himself as pre-existent, then it is unclear why one ought nevertheless to insist on this doctrine's importance in a systematic theology for our time" (McGrath, 486). Here McGrath risks privileging one-sidedly the public ministry of Jesus and what he said (or, at least, implied) about himself, almost as if the divine revelation through *and of* Jesus was completed with his life and death and there was no room for a postresurrection development taking place, albeit partly on the basis of Jesus' own self-interpretation.

Any (normally tacit) presumption that nothing is revealed in the post-Easter situation obviously plays down the role of the risen Jesus and his Holy Spirit in illuminating the apostolic generation about the meaning and implications of what they had experienced of the earthly Jesus (see, e.g., John 14:26, 15:26, 16:13-14). The preexistence Christology of Paul and John authoritatively went beyond the self-interpretation of Jesus through their experiencing his resurrection (that is to say, the risen One) and his Holy Spirit. That post-Easter experience was, to use McGrath's language, "data adequate enough to persuade" (McGrath, 486) apostolic leaders of the truth and importance of Christ's eternal preexistence.

## CONCLUDING CONSIDERATIONS

This chapter has sampled some of the major questions raised by over thirty reviews that evaluated the first and second editions of *Christology*. Space precludes doggedly taking up every point, including justified criticisms. McGrath, for instance, rightly queried my citing Pannenberg to "settle" the issue of whether or not Paul "could have envisaged resurrection without an empty tomb" (McGrath, 487). Yes, rather than merely citing an eminent theologian, I should also have drawn on N. T. Wright's magisterial study of the resurrection to establish that, for Paul, a resurrection without an empty tomb would have been unimaginable.

John McIntyre is the most notable figure missing in my conversation. In the second edition of *The Shape of Christology*, he spent a chapter in close debate with me over the philosophical exploration of the Council of Chalcedon.[40] He showed where we converge and diverge in the reasons we offer for the lasting validity of the Chalcedonian Definition and the role it continues to play in reflecting on the person of Christ. To take up the debate with McIntyre would require a small booklet, and, sadly, it would be a posthumous debate, as John died in 2005.[41]

# 3

# Revisiting the Work of Jesus

In 2003 I cochaired in New York a symposium on the redemption that was interdisciplinary, ecumenical, and international. A
year later Oxford University Press published the proceedings, *The
Redemption*.[1] A number of those who took part in the symposium
and contributed to the subsequent book felt that their discussions and
the chapters they wrote had provided the prolegomena for a systematic study of redemption. They wanted one or more of the symposiasts
to compose such a work. That desire prompted me to prepare and
publish *Jesus Our Redeemer: A Christian Approach to Salvation*.[2] I
might well have done so anyway, since my 1995 *Christology* treating
Jesus "in himself" needed to be complemented by a book treating
Jesus "for us."[3]

In following up the 2004 joint work and my own work of 2007, I
published in 2008 *Salvation for All* and in 2010 coauthored *Jesus Our
Priest*.[4] This chapter will revisit *The Redemption*, *Jesus Our Redeemer*,
and *Salvation for All*, leaving *Jesus Our Priest* aside for later study.[5]
The three books now being revisited were widely reviewed, and that
allows for reflections on soteriology that take the form of a dialogue
with the reviewers. In the course of this chapter, I will discuss reviews
of these three books and will refer to them with in-text citations.

## The Redemption

After the preface and my introductory chapter, "The Redemption:
Some Crucial Issues," the thirteen chapters of *The Redemption* took
up biblical questions (Christopher Seitz, Gordon Fee, N. T. Wright,

31

Jean-Noël Aletti, and Peter Ochs); themes from the patristic (Brian Daley) and medieval (Caroline Walker Bynum) periods; foundational and systematic issues (Eleonore Stump, Stephen Davis, and C. Stephen Evans); and the redemption as a theme in literature (Robert Kiely), art and music (David Brown), and preaching (Marguerite Shuster).[6]

Several reviewers registered their favorite articles. As well as entering into debate with the "intriguing" essay by Evans, Boersma called Bynum's chapter (which, among other things, challenged the conventional opposition between an Abelardian and an Anselmian theory of atonement) "a most welcome antidote to some of the commonplaces that we find too often in theologies of atonement" (Boersma, 111–12). Murphy wrote of Bynum's "brilliant analysis of the late medieval obsession with blood" and found my introductory chapter "very helpful" (Murphy, 445, 447). Loughlin judged Bynum's chapter "exhilarating," Brown's contribution (on the Lamb of God, the descent into hell, and the prodigal son in European painting and music) "masterful," and my introduction "exemplary," and added that "there is something of interest in every essay" (Loughlin, 214). Moloney concurred: "It is an excellent collection. There is not one superficial essay in the entire book" (Moloney, 373). Geldhof highlighted as "an excellent study" Daley's account of major themes in the soteriology of the church fathers and concluded that "all the articles" not only "reflect sound scholarship but they also present intriguing ideas and interesting suggestions in such a way that they certainly foster further reflection and discussion" (Geldhof, 264, 266).

While observing that "as a collection it [*The Redemption*] is bound to be uneven and perhaps technically frustrating in parts," Wales considered the book "an interdisciplinary and ecumenical feast. It will remain an indispensable tool for those who want to go deeper in their grasp of the mystery" of redemption (Wales, 1).

Ticciati, however, stated that only "a few essays stand out as worth reading" but named the chapters by Daley and Bynum as "offering good, clear introductions to their respective fields which are both innovative and provocative as historical accounts and raise challenging questions for constructive theology today." She dismissed Davis' essay (which contrasts the systems of karma and grace) as dissolving into "a completely meaningless exercise." She judged "the overall conception of the book" as "extremely problematic" and not "a genuinely interdisciplinary exercise" (Ticciati, 368, 369).

To dismiss a seventeen-page chapter by a well-published analytic philosopher with strong theological interests as "a completely meaningless exercise" means perhaps no more than saying in a loud voice, "I do not find his essay interesting and helpful." Ticciati shares, however, a concern of Boersma about what constitutes a "genuinely interdisciplinary exercise" in theology. She wants "collaborative work" that is both "constructive and exploratory" (Ticciati, 369). (Incidentally, it might be more logical to describe such work as first "exploratory" and then "constructive.") She questions whether *The Redemption* represents the most fruitful approach to interdisciplinarity: "What we have . . . is more like a series of windows into a variety of specialist fields: none of the essays engage in conversations across disciplines, and few raise genuinely cross-disciplinary questions, thereby opening up the space for such conversations" (366).[7] For his part, Boersma recognizes that "every now and then, the authors make cross-references to each other's papers. Mostly they argue their own case without reference to the other participants' work. The result is a lack of cohesion" (Boersma, 109).

But is there room for collaborative symposia that result in works that are not tightly cohesive? Or does *only* a collaboration that, from start to finish, dedicates itself totally to cross-disciplinary questions and conversations between several fields count as interdisciplinary? Can we tolerate "soft" interdisciplinary meetings that bring together specialists in a variety of fields and that encourage interaction between them at the meetings themselves and in subsequent publications? I raise these questions out of the experience of cochairing five interdisciplinary meetings that all resulted in joint works published by leading publishers.[8] In my commitment to bringing scholars together, running the meetings, and then publishing some results of these symposia, I declined to set the bar too high. Rightly or wrongly, it seemed thoroughly worthwhile persuading leading scholars in various disciplines to attend (not always easy!), open windows, let others know what they were doing in the specialist field, and wrestle, to the degree that they were capable and willing to do so, with the challenge of understanding and interpreting "the others" and of producing collaborative results. I remain convinced that such "soft" interdisciplinary collaboration can be thoroughly fruitful for the participants themselves and for subsequent readers of the published results. Ticciati's desire for what she calls "genuinely interdisciplinary endeavours" (Ticciati, 369) is admirable. But how *easily* could that desire be translated into reality in the context of an international, interdenominational meeting of leading scholars (and not merely malleable beginners) from different disciplines?

Reviewers of *The Redemption* also noted lacunae. Thus Boersma rightly observed that "there is no sustained treatment of the relationship between Christian liturgy and the doctrine of redemption" (Boersma, 110). Loughlin, while applauding Kiely's treatment of "the theme of self-redemption in much North American writing," regretted that he "ignored the musical stage and the cinema screen" (Loughlin, 214). Murphy wanted further exploration of "the coming together of soteriology and political theology," "the contemporary search for non-violent atonement," and the possibility of constructing a feminist theology of the cross "without returning to damaging forms of self-denial and sacrifice." She added, "To regret what was not included or developed is in no way to diminish one's appreciation of the exciting and rewarding survey of contemporary thinking on redemption and the hope that it may be a foundation for a fuller and more comprehensive systematic study" (Murphy, 447). In fact, I used *The Redemption* as a foundation for my own fuller systematic study, *Jesus Our Redeemer.*

## JESUS OUR REDEEMER

Most reviews of *Jesus Our Redeemer* were gratifyingly supportive and may have let me off too lightly.[9] Cornwell called the chapter on the resurrection "truly illuminating" (Cornwell, 31) and had only positive things to say about the rest of the book. Crosbie, Ezigbo, Imbelli, and Mostert likewise had nothing but praise for the volume. Imbelli flatteringly remarked, "[O'Collins] continues to improve with age, like a fine Shiraz in his native Australia." But let me leave the compliments behind and discuss three issues that came up: the redemption of the nonevangelized; penal substitutionary theories; and the redemption of unbelievers.

### The Nonevangelized

First, Shults highly recommended the book as "a significant and creative contribution to contemporary soteriology." Apropos of the chapter on "the salvation of non-Christians," he remarked, "O'Collins leaves open the possibility that those who are not in the church may still be drawn into fellowship with the transforming love of God" (Shults, 205).The question of salvation for the nonevangelized, which would lead me to write *Salvation for All*, has lost nothing of its urgency but continues to be debated vigorously.

A veteran leader in evangelization, Ralph Martin, has recently argued that "the conditions under which people can be saved who have never heard the gospel are very often, in fact, not fulfilled."[10] This is tantamount to saying that the majority of people *cannot be saved* and hence presumably finish up damned for all eternity in hell. The heart of Martin's book is the claim that the Second Vatican Council's Dogmatic Constitution on the Church, *Lumen gentium* in "the Council's main teaching," to be found in the last three sentences of article 16, maintains that "very often the possibility of people being saved without hearing the gospel is not realized."[11]

The three sentences (in fact, only two in the original Latin) do not make this claim; rather, they draw on Paul to stress that satanic forces and other difficulties very often threaten the salvation of the nonevangelized. One has to torture the Vatican II passage in question to make it mean, "Very often the possibility of people being saved without hearing the gospel is not realized." Dire threats to salvation are not equivalent to the absence of the very conditions for the possibility of salvation.

Moreover, in proposing his chilling thesis, Martin ignores much of Vatican II's teaching on the salvation of human beings, whether they have been evangelized or not. The Constitution on the Sacred Liturgy, *Sacrosanctum concilium*, which was the first document promulgated by Vatican II and which fails to appear in Martin's book, contains much that concerns human salvation.[12] Article 83, for instance, reads: "Jesus Christ, the High Priest of the New and Eternal Covenant, when he assumed a human nature, introduced into this land of exile, the hymn that in heaven is sung throughout all the ages. He unites *the whole community of human kind* with himself and associates it with him in singing the divine canticle of praise" (emphasis added). Such a union of all people with the incarnate Christ, a vision that reaches back to some fathers of the church, fulfills a very basic condition under which people can be saved. Martin likewise fails to consider what Vatican II's Decree on the Church's Missionary Activity, *Ad gentes* taught about "the seeds of the Word" sown by God and "hidden" everywhere, and, in particular, in "religious traditions." This was to point to the "secretly present" Christ, the "author" of the elements of "truth and grace" found "among the nations" (arts. 9, 11, 15, 18).

In discussing the Pastoral Constitution on the Church in the Modern World, *Gaudium et spes* Martin interprets in a minimalizing fashion article 22 and its statement that, through the Holy Spirit, all human beings can be united with the crucified and risen Christ. What is worse, Martin passes over in silence further relevant teaching about the Holy Spirit found in *Gaudium et spes*. The Spirit gives all human beings "the light and strength" needed "to respond to their supreme calling" (art. 10); through the Holy Spirit, the risen Christ is a work in the hearts of human beings everywhere (art. 38).

The theme of the Holy Spirit's universal activity was taken up by Pope John Paul II, not least in his 1990 encyclical *Redemptoris missio*. Martin pays some attention to that encyclical but completely ignores what the pope wrote about "the Spirit's presence and activity affecting not only individuals but also society and history, peoples, *cultures and religions*" (art. 28; emphasis added). Vatican II and then John Paul II indicated how not only Christ himself but also the Holy Spirit have created very basic conditions under which human beings, whoever they are, can be saved.

Martin's passion to encourage the Church at large to become again much more missionary minded is justified and admirable.[13] But a seriously misleading interpretation of the Second Vatican Council should not be offered as a way toward underpinning such a fresh commitment to evangelization. The question of the prospects of salvation for "the others" will recur with a vengeance when we come to discuss reviews of *Salvation for All*. In the meantime, however, let me register my gratitude that in his review of *Jesus Our Redeemer* this question had already been raised by Shults.

## Penal Substitution Theories

Second, along with praise for "a challenging and stimulating volume" (McGowan, 304), McGowan complained of "a straw man" being erected by my "insisting that penal substitutionary theories require us to believe that an angry God is propitiated by the death of his Son into becoming a loving God. I do not know of any advocates of penal substitution who take such a position" (303).

Cornwell, Imbelli, Mostert, and Shults also remarked on what I wrote in criticism of penal substitutionary theories. Cornwell, for instance, observed, "O'Collins performs a welcome demolition job on penal substitutionary theories of the atonement, those which, in the words of a famous preacher, affirm that 'the lightning of the wrath of God struck Christ on the Cross instead of us' " (Cornwell, 31). Mostert called my chapter on such theories "one of the best" and quotes approvingly my conclusion: "There is perhaps a sense in which Christ, participating in the human predicament, came under divine judgement, but 'not in order to propitiate and appease an angry God' " (Mostert, 245; citing *Jesus Our Redeemer*, 159).[14] Shults reported that "O'Collins rebuts attempts to support penal *substitution* with these texts [Ps 22; Isa 53; Rom 8:3-4; 2 Cor 5:21; Gal 3:13], and concludes with a critique of the notion that God's anger is placated by Jesus' suffering" (Shults, 205).

Unlike McGowan, these four reviewers (Cornwell, Imbelli, Mostert, Shults) never suggested that I was erecting a straw man when dealing with theories of penal substitution. I did indicate where such a view was to be found in the works of Protestant Reformers and Roman Catholic preachers and where it lingers on in the views of some modern authors.[15] McGowan may well be partly right. The notion that God's anger was appeased by Jesus' suffering on the cross is *less commonly* held nowadays, but it has not disappeared. Take, for instance, the entry "Propitiation" in *The Testament Christian Dictionary*: propitiation means "appeasing divine anger by sacrifice that atones" for sins or offenses against God, and satisfying "the needs of divine justice."[16]

Before leaving the theory of penal substitution, in my *Jesus Our Redeemer* I argued that, despite his strong stress on the divine love being the heart of redemption, St. Thomas Aquinas unwittingly helped open the door for those who were to develop theories of the atonement as penal substitution.[17] Rik van Nieuwenhove, not in a review but in a book chapter, "strongly disagreed" with me for suggesting that Thomas prepared the way for views of penal substitution. He argued that Thomas' soteriology was neither penal nor substitutionary.[18] But his argument has now been convincingly answered by Brandon Peterson. In a recent article, he has shown in detail how, in a certain sense, Thomas' brand of satisfaction theory did unwittingly prepare the way for penal substitution theories.[19]

## The Salvation of Unbelievers

Thirdly and finally, a comment by Stephen Bullivant should be retrieved. Attending closely to the teaching of *Lumen gentium* he asks, "How, within the parameters of Catholic theology, is it possible for an atheist to be saved?"[20] In the course of developing his own answer, he correctly remarks that, when writing about "the salvation of non-Christians," many authors think of the "members of the world religions." They hardly mention either "the existence of millions of non-religious unbelievers" or "that these too are unambiguously included" in the assurances of *Lumen gentium* 16.[21] Taking an example from my *Jesus Our Redeemer*, he notes that the "excellent chapter on 'The Salvation of Non-Christians' directly addresses only the salvation of religious people." Bullivant adds that "this approach is also reflected" in my *Salvation for All*. Bullivant correctly judges that "the common elision of 'non-Christian' with 'non-Christian religious' is unfortunate. Atheists are thus the forgotten subjects of *Lumen Gentium* 16."[22]

In *The Second Vatican Council on Other Religions*, I paid some attention to the "upright" atheists (and agnostics).[23] But, given the scope of that book, I regularly limited myself to the followers of other religions.

Yet Bullivant's comment makes me regret failing to attend to "upright" atheists in my earlier *Salvation for All*. In his review of this latter book, D'Costa also raised the same issue. Given that I made much of Hebrews 11:6, to which D'Costa refers as "the formal requirement of faith in God," what about the "nontheists," by whom D'Costa presumably means atheists and agnostics (D'Costa, 397)? Let me now move to *Salvation for All* and dialogue with its reviewers.

## SALVATION FOR ALL

Thus far I have located twelve reviews of *Salvation for All*, with one reviewer discussing the book in two journals.[24] I am grateful to find the book judged a "useful and thoughtful book" (Bradshaw, 762); a "discerning reading of biblical testimony regarding God's universal salvific will" (Burrell, 26); a "gentle and generous reading of the Bible" (Clooney, 128); "the most comprehensive treatment to date of biblical resources which demonstrate God's universal work of salvation" (Cornille, 130); "an important contribution in lifting up muted biblical voices" (Fritschel, 430); a work containing "much that is good and generous and accurate and theologically acute" (Griffiths, 137); and "a treasure-trove of theological insights" (Phan, 125).

Like Cornille and Fritschel, in his first review (in *American Theological Inquiry*) Siniscalchi agreed that by "discussing the entire biblical witness to God's love for persons who lived outside the nation of Israel under the Old Covenant and the Church after the Messianic age," my book filled "a great need" (Siniscalchi, 187). Bradshaw concurred: "Probably correctly, he [O'Collins] thinks that there has not been a Christian study of biblical material relating to the question of the unevangelized. . . . His book certainly fills the gap in its learned and accessible discussions of the relevant texts in the Old and New Testaments" (Bradshaw, 761). While noting antecedents to my theological conclusions in the thought of F. D. Maurice and Karl Barth, he agreed that my work was the first comprehensive treatment of the *biblical* witness to the universal benevolence of God who calls all to salvation (762).

The reviewers raised many serious questions that together could give rise to a companion volume. Let me limit myself to some issues that concern (1) methodology and terminology, (2) biblical material, and (3) theological challenges.

But first I feel the need to set the record straight about my attention to the theology of religions. Siniscalchi opened the first of his two (very positive) reviews of *Salvation for All* by remarking that I had never before "dedicated my energies to the theology of religions" (Siniscalchi, in *American Theological Inquiry*, 187; in *Downside Review*, 74). Phan made a similar observation (Phan, 121). In fact, for years I had been writing book chapters and articles about Christ and those of other faiths. *Salvation for All* was my first complete book in that area, but it was in 1981 that I started publishing on the theology of religions.[25]

## Methodology and Terminology

First, D'Costa queried the legitimacy of looking only at the "positive" texts in Scripture: that is to say, those passages witnessing to the divine benevolence toward all human beings. "A synthetic vision," he wrote, "is only attained through a complete survey and balance of the positive and negative together" (D'Costa, 397).[26] But I never promised to produce such a "synthetic vision" and provide the full story. My aim was limited to exploring the full biblical witness to the universal benevolence of God—something that simply had not been done before and that seemed worth doing for the sake of furthering theological reflection on "the others" and interfaith dialogue.[27] In any case, to set out completely the troublingly negative or apparently negative judgments of God on the religious "others" would require a second book, as Clooney recognized (Clooney, 127–28).

Apropos of terminology, Ipgrave thought it "surprising" that I used "universalism" to describe the divine benevolence toward everyone. "Universalism," as he rightly observed, "normally refers to the teaching that all will be saved, rather than that salvation is offered to all" (Ipgrave, 449). By adopting this term, I made it possible for Mark Scott to imagine that I endorsed the kind of "universalism" frequently attributed to Origen.[28] But I never proposed reflecting on this question: How many will accept the offer of salvation and be finally saved? I should have used an adjective and written rather of God's "universal benevolence"; that would have avoided any misunderstanding.

Also apropos of terminology, Griffiths took me to task for writing of various "religious traditions" and so, "unreflectingly" and wrongly, presupposing that Christianity and Judaism may also be called "religions." He warned against employing the language of "religion" and proposed dividing "the world" into three categories: "Jewish, Christian, and pagan, where the last term means simply neither Jewish nor Christian."[29] He invited me to "think with the Church" in this matter (Griffiths, 134). Presumably that includes thinking with Vatican II. But the Council never used the word "pagan" (*paganus*), even if occasionally vernacular translations from the original Latin carelessly introduced that term when rendering the conciliar language of "nations" (*gentes*) and "peoples" (*populi*). Furthermore, the Council employed the term "religion" (*religio*) seventy-one times, speaking of "different religions" and "other religions" (e.g., *Nostra aetate* 1 and 2), and—an expression that seemed abhorrent to Griffiths—of "the Christian religion" (*Lumen gentium* 11, 26, 35, and 50; *Ad gentes* 16; and *Gaudium et spes* 19). Vatican II obviously had no inhibitions about adopting the terminology of "religion(s)" and "the Christian religion."

Unquestionably, "religion" can be and at times has been a misused term. But this did not deter other reviewers of *Salvation for All* from writing repeatedly of "the theology of religion(s)," "theologians of religion," "other religions," "religions other than Christianity," "the religious others," "religious traditions," "interreligious encounters," and "interreligious dialogue" (see, e.g., Clooney, Cornille, and Phan, *passim*). Thus Griffiths was at odds with the terminology employed not only by the Second Vatican Council but also by other reviewers of *Salvation for All*. In particular, he dismissed as "late-modern jargon" (Griffiths, 135) the term "interreligious dialogue," a term taken up and not dismissed by the modern papacy, as we shall see.

The proposal of dividing "the world" into the three categories of "Jewish, Christian, and pagan" obviously enjoys "brevity" and "clarity." But I doubt whether colleagues in theology will find "many advantages" in the proposal (Griffiths, 134). Whatever about its origins, "pagan" now carries too many unpleasant connotations (e.g., of pagans being "irreligious," "unenlightened," and even "perverse"). Hindus, Buddhists, and followers of other world religions would not be happy about being lumped together under the category of "pagans." But Griffiths announced that he wished to use "pagan," and assigned it the meaning of "simply neither-Jewish-nor-Christian" (134). He went on to write twenty times of "pagan(s)." But should (or can) one "simply" assign a personal meaning to "pagan" and ignore common usage, in which the word has too many unpleasant connotations and an ugly history? In any case, like many others, I feel uncomfortable about adopting such negative labels as "non-Jewish" and "non-Christian," even if Vatican II incorporated that language in the title of its 1965 "Declaration on the Relation of the Church to Non-Christian Religions." That landmark document was preceded by the creation in 1964 of the Secretariat for Non-Christians, happily renamed under Pope John Paul II as the Pontifical Council for Inter-Religious Dialogue. Did Griffiths want Pope Benedict XVI and does he now want Pope Francis to change once again the name of this office and call it The Pontifical Council for Dialogue with Pagans? Significantly, "pagan" is not a term used by the other reviewers of *Salvation for All*.

Before leaving questions of terminology, apropos of the issue of Israel learning from its neighbors, I wrote, "In the story of Israel and its contacts with the nations, one would need to torture the data before proposing the existence or even the concept of inter-religious dialogue."[30] Having declared that such a concept was not applicable, I found it a little strange when Griffiths described this passage as "one of the most jarring juxtapositions" in my book "between late-modern jargon and scriptural rhetoric" (Griffiths, 135). More accurately, Phan recognized me as simply saying, "It would be anachronistic to speak of an interreligious dialogue between Israel and the nations" (Phan, 122).

### Biblical Questions

As regards biblical matters, I found nothing but joy in the way Clooney developed his review in terms of the figure of Melchizedek. The scriptural witness to that Canaanite priest-king and his place in Christian liturgical developments more than justify the conclusion that "we know Christ better by taking Melchizedek to heart" (Clooney, 128). How differently Melchizedek has been treated in a recent work by Garry Wills![31] Some or even much of the thrust of that book could be summed up as telling us, "We know Christ better by demolishing Melchizedek."

With an eye to my discussion of the Jewish material, D'Costa alleges that "when non-Israelites are positively treated it is *always* in the context of their acknowledgment of Israel's God" (D'Costa, 397; emphasis added). Sometimes this is true: for instance, in the case of Namaan the Syrian.[32] But it is certainly not true in the case of the Ninevites: "A shift to belief in and worship of YHWH as such, along with the adoption of the Mosaic law and practice, was not the issue. God was content to let the Ninevites remain what they were religiously, provided they underwent a moral conversion from 'their violence and evil ways.' "[33]

Cornille rightly notes that the Scriptures do not contain much detailed witness to the revelatory and salvific work of God in other religions (Cornille, 132–33). God may be understood, for example, to speak through "outsiders" (e.g., Balaam). But the book of Numbers has nothing to say about Balaam's religion playing or not playing a "constitutive role" in his prophetic speech. When Cornille inquires about "the value and truth of the religions of the outsiders" (133), we need to move beyond any hints found in the Scriptures[34] to the teaching of Vatican II: "The Catholic Church rejects nothing of what is true and holy in these [non-Christian] religions" (*Nostra aetate* 2). So obviously there are things that are "true and holy" in these religions as such and not merely in the faith and practice of individual believers.

Cornille reports helpfully the distinction between the "message" and "mission" of Jesus, recognizes the universal scope in the message of Jesus, but remarks that "he [O'Collins] follows most New Testament scholars in admitting that Jesus probably did not understand his mission to extend beyond the Jews" (Cornille, 130). Yet I spent pages indicating how the activity of Jesus extended beyond Jews to others: for example, to those in the predominantly Gentile area of the Decapolis.[35] To be sure, it is easier to establish the universality of Jesus' *message*. But he responded to the needs of the others, whoever they were, and signaled that the final gathering of the Gentiles had already begun in and through his *mission*.

Cornille is right to say that I did not consider whether Jesus' own sense of mission might have developed. She asks, after being directed originally only to the "lost sheep of the house of Israel," did his sense of mission come to include the Gentiles (Cornille, 131)? The Gospels provide a few hints in support of this development. But, since it is difficult to establish the chronological sequence between events in the ministry of Jesus, I was content to present readers with a more central and clearly founded conclusion; whatever the sequence or developments there might have been in his intentions, Jesus reached beyond Israel during his earthly ministry. He did not see his message *and mission* as exclusively directed to "the lost sheep of Israel," but reached out also to the Gentiles.

Finally, before leaving the biblical area, let me comment on a remark by D'Costa about the Letter to the Hebrews. He maintained that in Hebrews the "context of those who have faith in the true God . . . is carefully related to the history of the covenant with Israel" (D'Costa, 397). An examination of the text will not vindicate this claim. When listing "a cloud of witnesses" to faith (11:1–12:2), Hebrews introduces twenty-five times "faith" but never refers to a "covenant with Israel," not even when summarizing the history of Moses (11:23-29). Elsewhere, Hebrews speaks merely seven times of "faith" and then only once seems to point to the history of the covenant with Israel (6:12). All in all, Hebrews shows a wider use of "faith," and this significantly supports identifying the "faith in the true God" available for "outsiders."

## Theological Challenges

Finally, let me respond to some of the theological challenges developed by those who reviewed *Salvation for All*, and start with a comment from Cornille. She wrote, "Even though distancing himself from the expression 'anonymous Christian,' the position [of O'Collins] is in fact closely in line with that of Karl Rahner" (Cornille, 132). It may be worth recalling here that Rahner, after speaking of "anonymous Christians" and "anonymous Christianity," did not use such terminology in the masterpiece of his mature years, *Foundations of Christian Faith*.[36] Apart from being offensive to the followers of other religions (who can react by speaking of Christians as "anonymous Hindus" or "anonymous Buddhists"), talk of "anonymous Christians" and "anonymous Christianity" distracts from the heart of the matter: the grace that comes from and leads to Christ himself. Apropos of my being "closely in line" with Rahner's views on "the others," those who read *Salvation for All* will find very little.[37] My explicit discussion of Rahner's views came in a later book.[38]

Phan, after accurately summarizing the content and intentions of *Salvation for All*, probed superbly the theological implications of my biblical findings. His questions suggested writing a short book in reply. Let me take up briefly four issues he raised: first, the possibility of God being covenanted (albeit not equally) with people other than Israel and members of the Church (Phan, 123). I think that the universal scope of the covenant with Noah,[39] as well as the witness coming from various Old Testament books such as Amos, Jonah, and Isaiah,[40] should encourage us to acknowledge some kind of covenantal relationship between God and communities of believers other than Israel and the Church. What Amos and further biblical witnesses say or imply about God's relationship with various peoples illustrates the outworking of the universal covenant with Noah and justifies talking of "God's other peoples."

Second, Phan brought up the issue of prophetic and priestly "outsiders" mediating the blessings of God to others, including Christians (Phan, 123–24). Using the figure of Melchizedek, Clooney in his review documented how such mediations have taken place and continue to take place.

Third, Phan noted how I drew on Hebrews and on Vatican II to acknowledge that "outsiders" can have true faith and not merely human (religious) beliefs elaborated through a merely human search for God. He contrasted this position with the Congregation for the Doctrine of the Faith's document *Dominus Iesus* of the year 2000: there the CDF distinguished between the "faith" of Christians as a graced response to revelation and the "belief" of non-Christians as the result of a human search for God (Phan, 124). Phan was correct in recognizing an incompatibility between the two positions.[41]

Fourth and finally, Phan raised the question of the relationship between Jesus and the "saints," "prophets," and "founders" of other religions. His remarks (Phan, 124–25) and some from Griffiths persuade me to modify my position. While continuing to endorse what I wrote, following a lead from St. Augustine about those "outsiders" who are truly saints and genuine prophets,[42] I admit the need to develop arguments to show how important founders who lived centuries *before* the coming of Christ were affected by him in ways that might justify calling them his "delegates and agents." Phan rightly noted how this opens up the question of the causality involved. Here one should also bear in mind what Paul (1 Cor 10:4) and various early fathers of the church wrote about Christ's activity during the Old Testament history.

At least some of what (earlier or later) religious founders taught and did could partly disqualify them from being recognized as being (or being persistently) such delegates or agents of Christ. Some of what they did and taught could lead people away from any "mysterious existence" in Christ. To some extent, they may have been "agents of absence, advocates of lack, entrepreneurs of evil" (Griffiths, 136). Even tentative judgments here depend on well-conducted empirical investigations and call for another book, which would take us well beyond the scope of *Salvation for All*. Some religious "outsiders," as well as some Christian leaders, have at times commended and undertaken things that have taken them and others away from Christ.

To conclude, my sincere thanks to those who reviewed *Salvation for All* and the other two volumes. Our agreements and disagreements should have at least one happy result: understanding and interpreting the redemptive work of Jesus Christ remains a very complicated and challenging task. Putting us in the presence of the very central mystery of redemption, our debates illustrate some of the major issues that arise for those who reflect on that mystery.[43]

# PART TWO

# 4

# Paul as a Witness to the Risen Jesus

In a recent correspondence with an American scholar, the question emerged about the preferable way to translate *ōphthē*, which occurs four times in 1 Corinthians 15:5-8. Contemporary translations into English (in particular, the NIV, NJB, NRSV, REB, and RSV) render this first aorist passive indicative of *horaō* as "he appeared." My correspondent suggested an alternative, a divine passive: "Jesus was shown by God to Cephas" (1 Cor 15:5), and then to the others. He recalled not only that in the early Christian tradition God is the agent of the resurrection (e.g., 1 Thess 1:10; Rom 10:9) but also that Galatians 1:15-16 ("he revealed his Son to me" or "in me") presents God (and not Christ himself) as the agent of this revelation or appearance to Paul. He might have added that a divine passive occurs very close to the fourfold use of *ōphthē* under discussion: "He [Christ] was raised [*egēgertai*]" or, if you like, "was woken from sleep" [from the sleep of death] (1 Cor 15:4). In this verse a scholarly consensus recognizes a divine passive and understands this resurrection or waking from sleep to have been effected "by God." It might be argued that finding a divine passive in verse 4 could encourage us to detect such a divine passive also in verse 5 (*ōphthē*).

This correspondence prompted me into revisiting the question of translating *ōphthē* as well as thinking further about the language used by the New Testament witnesses to report the Easter encounters. Are contemporary translations correct in translating "he appeared," or should we render the fourfold usage of *ōphthē* in the passage "he was made manifest" or "he was shown" (and in both cases one is to

49

understand "by God")? Let me first examine some wider data and possible translations.

## ELIMINATING ONE POSSIBILITY

A few earlier translations—notably, the Authorized Version (AV) or King James Version (KJV), the New Testament in Modern English by John Bertram Phillips (1958; rev. 1970),[1] and the first edition of the New American Bible (NAB, 1970, but not its revised version of 1986)—rendered *ōphthē* followed by the dative in 1 Corinthians 15:5-8 as "he was seen by." The AV translated the verb as "he was seen of." First Corinthians has earlier used the active (perfect) form of the same verb (*horaō*) when Paul asks: "Am I not an apostle? Have I not seen [*heōraka*] Jesus our Lord?" (1 Cor 9:1). If we have the active form in 1 Corinthians 9:1 ("I have seen Jesus"), does the meaning of the passive form correspond in 1 Corinthians 15:5-8 (Christ "was seen by Cephas" and others, including Paul)?

However, if we think of accepting the translation "he was seen by," we should expect the verb to be followed by *hypo* and a noun or pronoun in the genitive. That is the case, albeit with the aorist passive indicative of another verb (*theaomai*), in Mark 16:11: "He was seen [*etheathē*] by her [Mary Magdalene]." But, instead of *hypo* and the genitive occurring in 1 Corinthians 15, we have *ōphthē* followed by the dative ("he appeared to Cephas" and so forth), just as we have in similar New Testament passages, universally it seems, translated today "appeared": for instance, "there appeared to him [Zechariah] an angel of the Lord" (Luke 1:11); "there appeared to them Elijah with Moses" (Mark 9:4); "there appeared to them divided tongues, as it were of fire" (Acts 2:3).[2]

For any translation of 1 Corinthians 15:5-8 and Luke 24:34, it is clearly relevant that there are numerous examples of a Hebraism preserved in the Septuagint (LXX), which, when (generally) translating the Hebrew *wayyērā* (niphal imperfect), uses *ōphthē*. Joseph Fitzmyer calls this a case of a "semitized Greek verb."[3] The first such occurrence in the LXX comes with a theophany found in Genesis 12:7: "The Lord appeared to Abraham and said, . . ."[4] It was this usage of *ōphthē* for theophanies that was applied to the encounters with the risen Christ.[5] Here, as Fitzmyer explains, the aorist passive "took on an intransitive meaning, 'appeared.' "[6] In an earlier generation, Joachim Jeremias recognized this same usage as being originally Hebrew and Aramaic, and translated *ōphthē* in 1 Corinthians 15 as "Christ appeared."[7] Even earlier Joseph Thayer had proposed "showed himself" (or "appeared") as the appropriate rendering of the verb as used in 1 Corinthians 15.[8]

The origin of the kerygmatic fragment that Paul quotes in 1 Corinthians 15:3-5 might affect the translating of *ōphthē*. (a) Did the fragment render in Greek a Semitic original coming from an Aramaic-speaking community (perhaps Jerusalem)? (b) Or was it drawn from a Greek original, borrowed from a Jewish-Gentile, Greek-speaking church (perhaps Antioch)? Jeremias argues for (a), but Fitzmyer points out that the evidence is far from conclusive.[9]

However, the disagreement between Jeremias and Fitzmyer over the origin of the fragment does not seem to affect the translation: "he let himself be seen," or "he appeared." Neither of them proposes a divine passive: "he was shown," or "he was made manifest [by God]." Fitzmyer speaks of the passive taking on "an intransitive meaning." Raymond Collins renders *ōphthē* as "he appeared," translating it "in an intransitive sense."[10] Anthony Thiselton, who translates the verb as "he appeared" or "he became visible," points out that "he appeared" occurs with a dative ("to Cephas") and in a "reflexive sense."[11] Wolfgang Schrage, who also prefers to translate the verb as "he appeared" or "he let himself be seen," writes of a "deponent or middle form."[12] But the labels ("intransitive," "reflexive," "deponent," or "middle") seem a secondary matter. Collins, Fitzmyer, Jeremias, Schrage, and Thiselton all endorse the common translation: Christ "appeared," "became visible," or "let himself be seen." Like all current English translations, none of them propose "he was seen by." Despite its passive voice, *ōphthē* does not have for them a passive meaning.

We have cited current English translations of and commentaries on 1 Corinthians. What do the authors of New Testament grammars and dictionaries say? Daniel B. Wallace observes that when "*ōphthē* is used in the New Testament with a simple dative, the subject of the verb consciously *initiates* the visible manifestation. In no instance can it be said that the person(s) in the dative case initiate(s) the act. In other words, volition rests wholly with the subject, while the dative noun is merely recipient."[13] In other words, the verb, while passive in form, is intransitive in meaning: the subject "appeared to" whoever is mentioned in the dative. The older Blass-Debrunner *Grammar of the New Testament* also recognized what it called a "passive with intransitive meaning" in *ōphthē* as used in 1 Corinthians 15:5-8, specifying this further as an "intransitive-deponent meaning."[14]

Rather than speaking, like Wallace, of *ōphthē* in its four occurrences in 1 Corinthians 15 as being "intransitive" in meaning or, like Blass-Debrunner, of an "intransitive-deponent" meaning, the Bauer-Danker *Greek-English Lexicon of the New Testament* categorizes them as passive but in "the active sense: became visible, appear." It cites various examples not only of the risen Christ "appearing" (as in 1 Cor 15) but also of "appearances" of angels (e.g., Luke 1:11; 22:43) and of Moses and Elijah at the transfiguration (Mark 9:4).[15] Bauer-Danker has its own label ("the active sense"), but it lines up with the commentaries and grammars we have examined by understanding *ōphthē* in 1 Corinthians 15 to mean "Christ appeared," "became visible," "showed himself," or "let himself be seen."

## "HE WAS MADE MANIFEST BY GOD"

Unlike Collins, Fitzmyer, and Thiselton, in his commentary on 1 Corinthians Schrage examines some earlier suggestions coming from Karl Heinrich Rengstorf, Gerhard Friedrich, and Josef Pfammatter, and considers the possibility of a divine passive and hence of interpreting *ōphthē* as being a paraphrase (*Umschreibung*) for the divine action: "God has let Christ become visible [*Gott hat Christus sichtbar werden lassen*]." Schrage points to the parallel with a passive form in 1 Corinthians 15:4 that we recalled above (*egēgertai*). Since Christ has been raised or woken from the sleep of death by God, he has also been made visible or manifest by God. Secondly, Schrage thinks that one might also appeal to a parallel in Acts 10:40: "God raised him [Jesus] from the dead and allowed him to appear [*edōken auton emphanē genesthai*]."[16] Thirdly, Schrage recalls that for Paul, as for the earliest Christians, God is the agent of the resurrection (see, e.g., Rom 10:9), and adds, "It goes without saying that, for Paul, ultimately it is God himself who brings about the appearance of Christ." Fourthly, after stating that the gospel he preaches came "through a revelation of Jesus Christ" (Gal 1:12), Paul makes it clear that Christ is the object rather than the subject of this revelation by declaring, "God was pleased to reveal his Son to [or in] me" (Gal 1:15-16). In the apostle's own comment on his Damascus road encounter, it is the initiative of God that is to the fore.[17]

Nevertheless, Schrage emphasizes that the subject of the formula—*ōphthē Kēpha* (1 Cor 15:5), a formula found also in 1 Corinthians 15:6, 7, and 8—is Christ, just as in the LXX God "is repeatedly named as the subject of a theophany signified with *ōphthē*."[18] In a footnote Schrage refers to Genesis 12:7 and four further examples of such theophanies reported in Genesis. Like Fitzmyer and others, Schrage finds the LXX background of theophanies decisive and translates the verb accordingly in 1 Corinthians 15—Christ "appeared" or "let himself be seen." He deals with the parallel to *egēgertai* (1 Cor 15:4) by detecting a chiasm between active and passive elements in the formula: "(a) he died; (b) he was buried; (b) he has been raised; and (a) he appeared." The chiastic structure holds the formula together, as well the central affirmations, "he died" and "he has been raised," being confirmed, respectively, by "he was buried" and "he appeared."

We should agree with Fitzmyer, Schrage, and the other scholars and translations mentioned above that in all four instances in 1 Corinthians 15:5-8 *ōphthē* is to be translated "he appeared."[19] This leaves it open, however, to consider "he was made manifest by God" as a legitimate (theological) paraphrase of, or (theological) comment on, what we can call "Christophanies," even if it is not a strict translation (from a philological point of view). The *theological* paraphrase draws support from the *grammatical* category of the divine passive (in particular, 1 Cor 15:4). Theology cannot be totally separated from (biblical) philology.

In the LXX, *ōphthē* is used for what have been called "theophanies" (e.g., Gen 12:7; 17:1) and "angelophanies" (e.g., Exod 3:2; Judg 6:12). This has encouraged Fitzmyer, Schrage, and others to speak of "Christophanies" reported by 1 Corinthians 15:5-8 and similar passages in the New Testament (e.g., Luke 24:34).[20] Apropos of the Christophany to the more than five hundred faithful (1 Cor 15:6), Fitzmyer remarks, "One has to rule out a purely internal experience of these recipients of the appearance."[21] If this Christophany may not be reduced to "a purely internal experience," what does the New Testament witness encourage us to say about it and similar episodes? Let us begin with Paul and then take the discussion further.

## THE NATURE OF THE CHRISTOPHANIES

Among the various witnesses—some would say eyewitnesses[22]—to encounters with the risen Christ, Paul's is the only case where we can be confident of hearing that testimony directly from the person in question. He presents his encounter as closing a series of appearances: "Last of all he appeared to me" (1 Cor 15:8). Earlier in the same letter, Paul defends his apostolic authority through two questions: "Am I not an apostle? Have I not seen Jesus our Lord?" (1 Cor 9:1). Here the perfect indicative (*heōraka*) expresses "the present effect of Paul's earlier experience of encounter with the raised Christ at the moment of his missionary and apostolic commission on the way to Damascus."[23] As Collins puts it, "Paul's vision of the Lord . . . is the foundational warrant for his apostleship."[24] Apart from these two verses in 1 Corinthians, Paul *never again* speaks either of his having seen the Lord or of the Lord "[appearing]" to him.[25] While this encounter with the risen Jesus set Paul apart by conferring apostolic authority on him, it was never repeated; for the apostle, it was a once-and-for-all, foundational experience, which made him the last in the series of official witnesses to the resurrection (1 Cor 15:8).[26]

In another letter, Paul interprets his Damascus road experience as revelatory: it was a "revelation" (*apokalupsis*) of Jesus Christ as God's Son risen from the dead, a (foundational) revelation that commissioned Paul as an apostle (Gal 1:12, 16). Paul also uses the language of revelation in other contexts: for instance, he speaks of going up to Jerusalem with Barnabas and Titus "in response to a revelation" (Gal 2:1-2). To counter the impact of false apostles, he reluctantly speaks of "visions [*optasias*] and revelations [*apokalupseis*]." Although he uses both nouns in the plural, he presses on to recall only one personal experience, that of being taken up "to the third heaven" fourteen years earlier (2 Cor 12:1-4). While a deeply significant "revelation" characterized the Damascus road encounter, other episodes in Paul's life could also be called "revelatory."[27]

In his Letter to the Philippians, Paul describes the dramatic, personal change he experienced through encountering the risen Christ (Phil 3:2–4:1). But he speaks here not of "seeing" Christ but of "knowing" him (Phil 3:8, 10).

Elsewhere in the New Testament,[28] *ōphthē* is used in an ordinary way when Stephen recalls how Moses "appeared" or "came to" some of his fellow Israelites when they were quarrelling (Acts 7:26). In the book of Revelation, the use of this verb is anything but "ordinary." After the seventh trumpet sounded in heaven, God's temple was opened and the ark of the covenant "appeared" (perhaps better "was seen") within the temple (Rev 11:19). Then followed immediately the vision of the woman, the child, and the dragon: "A great sign appeared in heaven, a woman clothed with the sun. . . . She was pregnant and crying out in birth pangs . . . and another sign appeared in heaven, a great red dragon with seven heads" (Rev 12:1-3). All three "appearances" (the ark, the woman, and the dragon) happen "in heaven," even if the dragon is obviously an evil portent.

Then we should also recall the use in the New Testament of *ōphthē*, followed by the dative, to designate (a) appearances of angels (Luke 1:11; 22:43; Acts 7:30, with *opthentos* followed by the dative in 7:35, referring to the same appearance of an angel), and (b) the appearance "to them" (Peter, James, and John) of Elijah with Moses (Mark 9:4; Matt 17:3). Luke 9:31 uses the related participle (*opthentes*) to speak of Elijah and Moses "appearing in glory." In citing these passages about the "appearances" of (a) angels and (b) Elijah and Moses, my intention is to clarify language rather than to argue for the historicity of these episodes and their details. Nor do I want to press any comparison between Paul's experience of the risen Lord and any experiences of Zechariah in the temple (Luke 1:11); Peter, James, and John on the mountain (Mark 9:4); and Jesus in Gethsemane (Luke 22:43). Distinctions between various kinds of appearances should be respected and explored. The appearance of the angel to Zechariah, for instance, could be examined in the light of angelophanies in Genesis, the prophetic literature, and elsewhere (not least in Luke and Acts). But, in recalling the angelophanies and other appearances, I simply follow the example of Bauer-Danker, which cites these *ōphthē* events under the heading of "become visible, appear."[29]

Apart from one reference to an Old Testament theophany (Acts 7:2)[30] and the appearance of a Macedonian in a night vision to Paul (Acts 16:9), the central role of *ōphthē* in the New Testament comes in reference to appearances of Christ in the aftermath of his resurrection (Luke 24:34; Acts 13:31; 1 Cor 15:5, 6, 7, 8). In short, *ōphthē* was "used to identify visionary experiences of the risen Christ."[31] Ananias uses the related participle *ophtheis* to speak of "Jesus who appeared to you [Paul] on the road" (Acts 9:17). The risen Jesus himself says to

Paul, "I have appeared [ōphthēn] to you for this purpose, to appoint you to serve and to testify to the things which you have seen in me, and to those in which I will appear [ophthēsomai] to you" (Acts 26:16). Here and below, when dealing with the three accounts in Acts (in chs. 9, 22, and 26) of Paul's Damascus road experience, my interest is in exploring the language of "seeing" or "appearing" that Luke uses rather than in pressing claims about the historicity or otherwise of particular details.

Add here the use of ōphthē in a hymnic—or, more likely, a creedal—fragment in 1 Timothy: "He [Christ Jesus] appeared to messengers" (1 Tim 3:16).[32] Normally, aggelois has been translated "to angels," creating a question: How would we envisage the risen Christ appearing to beings of the other world, angels? But in the New Testament, no less than in the LXX, aggeloi can also designate human messengers: for example, John the Baptist (Matt 11:10; Mark 1:2; Luke 7:27), messengers sent by John (Luke 7:24), and Paul himself (Gal 4:14). Hence some major commentaries translate the phrase from 1 Timothy as "he appeared to messengers," understanding these to be witnesses who went on to proclaim the resurrection. The phrase puts together the individuals and groups that Paul lists in 1 Corinthians 15:5-8 as those to whom the risen Christ appeared.[33]

Clearly linked with this Christophany language are the many references to "seeing" the risen Christ: for instance, "he [the risen Christ] is going before you into Galilee; there you will see [opsesthe] him" (Mark 16:7; see Matt 28:7, 10). "Seeing" him on the mountain, the eleven disciples adored him (Matt 28:17). Mary Magdalene joyfully announces, "I have seen [heōraka] the Lord" (John 20:18). Barnabas explains that Saul "saw [eiden] the Lord on the road" (Acts 9:27). Thomas comes to faith because he has "seen" the risen Christ; those are blessed who come to faith without having "seen" Christ, as the original witnesses did (John 20:29; see 1 Pet 1:8). Likewise Paul (in 1 Cor 9:1) implies that the Corinthians have not experienced what he has experienced: his "seeing" (the risen Lord) should be distinguished from any other "coming to faith."[34] When the New Testament refers to some of the first disciples experiencing the risen Christ, the language of "seeing" predominates.[35] Their decisive experience of the risen Christ came through seeing him.

But was this (a) in some sense a seeing with their eyes when Christ became visible? Or was it (b) merely a seeing with their mind as Christ became interiorly visible in a divine self-manifestation? Kremer, while remarking that the power of God and the angels "to appear visibly is ascribed to the risen Christ," defends (a): "We ought not deny *ōphthē* any visual element, as though it were simply a formulaic term for revelation."[36] Collins endorses (b): "The traditional Jewish understanding of divine transcendence[37] . . . suggests that the use of this traditional language with regard to a manifestation of the divine did not imply physical sight."[38] For Collins, no less than for Kremer, it was Christ who at least immediately[39] made the appearances possible; he showed himself and "allowed himself to be recognized."[40]

In presenting his interpretation, Collins remarks that "in the biblical accounts of a manifestation of the divine, auditory [rather than visual] elements predominate."[41] But it is precisely because of this predominance of the auditory that those manifestations of God and angels in the LXX fail to prefigure precisely the *ōphthē* in Luke 24:34; Acts 13:31; and 1 Corinthians 15:5-8 (four times). When Gabriel "appeared" (*ōphthē*) to Zechariah, much is said on both sides (Luke 1:5-23). Likewise, at the transfiguration, when Elijah "appeared" with Moses, there were auditory elements in the sense that they "were talking with Jesus" (Mark 9:6). But the six references (just listed) to the appearances of the risen Christ—or seven if we include 1 Timothy 3:16— make no reference to anything that was said; the language is simply "visual" (he appeared or let himself be seen).

When we move beyond these six (or seven) occurrences of *ōphthē*, we find *ophtheis* (Acts 9:17) and two other passive forms of *ōphthēnai* and the active *eides* ("you have seen me") (Acts 26:16) used by Luke when reporting Paul's encounter with the risen Christ. In the context of the postresurrection appearances, further texts introduce the active voice of the same verb *horan* ("to see") (1 Cor 9:1; Mark 16:7; Matt 28:7, 10, 17; Luke 24:24, 39 [twice]; John 20:18, 20, 25 [twice], 27). Luke 24:37, 39 and John 20:12, 14 use, also in the active, another verb "to see" (*theōrein*), while John 21 uses the active voice of *phareroun* ("to show") (21:1 [twice]) and once the passive *ephanerōthē* (21:14). At the end of the story about the two disciples at Emmaus, "their eyes were opened and they recognized him [the risen Christ] and he vanished [*aphantos egeneto*] from their sight" (Luke 24:31). In reporting the appearances of the risen Jesus to Mary Magdalene, to two disciples, and to the eleven, the longer ending to Mark employs the passive voice of *theaomai* (Mark 16:11) and *phaneroō* (Mark 16:12, 14) and the middle voice of *phainomai* (Mark 16:9). Acts speaks of the risen Christ "presenting" (*parestēsen*) himself and "appearing" (*optanomenos*) (Acts 1:3), and being "allowed to appear" (*emphanē genesthai*) (Acts 10:40).

This last paragraph, far from pressing claims about historical details in the appearance narratives of the Gospels and Acts, aimed simply at establishing how they converged with Paul. In their choice of verbs, they witnessed to the Easter encounters as somehow being ocular and visual. In some narratives (classically in the Emmaus story of Luke 24), the disciples fail to recognize immediately the risen Lord. But such delayed recognition does not take away from the ways in which the Gospels and Acts use the language of sight in their Easter narratives.

The Easter stories of the Gospels also employ verbs expressing movement that suggest the risen Christ being seen. He "came to meet" two women (Matt 28:9); he "came near" two travellers and "walked" with them (Luke 24:15, 36). He "came" to the disciples (John 20:24, 26). The evangelists similarly introduce verbs of "presence": Jesus "stood among them" (Luke 24:36; John 20:19, 26) or "stood on the shore" (John 21:4). Unquestionably, one can and should raise this question: What would it be like for someone gloriously risen from the dead to "come" to others, to "meet" them, to "walk" with them, or to "stand" there before them? Nevertheless, such verbs imply that Jesus was seen by his disciples. Once again, in recalling these and other details from the Easter narratives in the Gospels, I do not want to read the details back into 1 Corinthians 9:1 and 15:5-8 (let alone into Gal 1:12, 16). My primary aim is to recall and clarify the language the evangelists adopted and relate it to Paul. In 1 Corinthians (and Galatians), Paul was using common language. Some clarity about that language might help us to sort out its relationship to what Paul and other New Testament witnesses had experienced.

All in all, when witnessing to the encounters with the risen Christ, the New Testament so privileges the language of seeing that Kremer seems justified in allowing for some "visual element" (see above). Nevertheless, the appearances did not imply *merely* physical sight or a *purely* ordinary seeing of an external object. As Paul implies, the post-resurrection appearances involved seeing a "spiritual" (*pneumatikon*) body and not some "physical" (*psuchikon*) body of this world (1 Cor 15:44).[42] It was a perception that led to recognizing someone who now

enjoys an exalted, heavenly existence: "Christ Jesus my Lord" (Phil
3:8, 10, 20), whose body is now "glorious" (Phil 3:21) and who now
incorporates (Phil 3:9) and will "transform" (Phil 3:21) others into his
risen life (Phil 3:11). John implies that "seeing" the risen Lord (John
20:18) presupposes his call and self-disclosure (John 20:16) and the
freedom to enter into a relationship of faith with him (John 20:27). It
brings the recipients to "know" him (John 21:12). John pictures this
freedom of faith through Mary Magdalene needing to "turn around"
once again (John 20:14, 16), this time spiritually and not merely physically, "before she can acknowledge the risen Lord."[43]

When we recall how Paul links "knowing" the risen Christ with
the hope of sharing in his glorious resurrection, we can agree with
Thiselton: "Christ's risen presence serves as God's eschatological
self-manifestation."[44] This is not to follow Willi Marxsen and others
who have identified the encounter promised in Mark 16:7 ("there you
will see him") with the Parousia.[45] In this and other references to the
postresurrection appearances, there is not a hint of those apocalyptic
images and signs (proposed in Mark 13:6-27 and elsewhere) that are to
accompany the Parousia. While anticipating and even inaugurating in
advance the end, the Easter appearances with their "seeing" do not yet
embody the final "seeing" of which Hebrews speaks: "Christ . . . will
appear [ophthēsetai] a second time, not to deal with sin, but to save
those who are eagerly waiting for him" (Heb 9:28; see Luke 17:22).

The language used by Paul, the Gospels, and further New Testament witnesses supports the following account of how they wanted
to express their experiences: (a) the appearances depended on the initiative of the risen Jesus, (b) were events of revelation, (c) disclosed
the eschatological and (d) christological significance of Jesus,[46] and
(e) called the recipients to a special mission through (f) an experience
that was unique[47] and (g) was not merely interior "seeing" but also
involved some exterior, visual perception.

The last point invites further reflection. Seeing the risen Jesus
called for a graced and enhanced power of perception. As Origen
put it, he "appeared after his resurrection not to all people but only
to those whom he perceived to have obtained eyes which had the
capacity to see the resurrection [i.e., to see him in his risen state]."[48]
Centuries later St. Thomas Aquinas stated that, on the one hand,
"the apostles could offer eyewitness testimony to the resurrection of
Christ." But, on the other hand, this was because "they saw Christ

alive after his resurrection with faith that works through eyes [*oculata fide*]."⁴⁹

Here we need to allow not only for a graced seeing on the part of the witnesses but also for the transformation in the One who is perceived. The resurrected Christ constitutes the beginning of the end of the world (1 Cor 15:20, 23), the realized presence of the new creation. Through his risen bodiliness, matter has been elevated to a final destiny that goes far beyond the bodiliness we experience in this world. "Exalted at the right hand of God" (Acts 2:33), Christ manifests himself as sharing in the divine mystery and is not to be manipulated, weighed, measured or in other ways treated like an ordinary object that takes up space in this world. He appears where and to whom he wills, and disappears when he wills (e.g., Luke 24:31). He now enjoys a "spiritual body," which Paul struggles to express in 1 Corinthians 15:12-58.

Those who accept this new state of the risen Christ should find little difficulty in acknowledging what it entailed: graced powers of perception on the part of those who "saw" him. To see the risen Christ required a transforming grace for the recipients of that experience. To see him they needed to be made in some sense like him. In all cases and, strikingly, in the case of Paul (and also, presumably, in that of James "the brother of the Lord" [1 Cor 15:7]), some healing grace was needed "before" (understood ontologically and not chronologically) they could see and believe in the crucified and risen Christ.

What I have just been arguing for does not purport to be merely exegetical comments on what Paul or any other New Testament author allegedly put in these terms. My argument exemplifies rather how pondering their witness leads us on to theological reflection and interpretation.

## DEALING WITH OBJECTIONS

The account just offered about the Christophanies or appearances of the risen Christ faces various objections. Let me take up three of them: the purported "appearances" in 1 Corinthians 15:5-8 (and elsewhere) are simply formulas to legitimate the authority of the recipients; the "appearances" were merely ecstatic, unreliable experiences; the "appearances" pointed only to internal phenomena, revelations to the mind of Paul and others of Christ's reality and status.

Those who have developed the thesis of "legitimation formulas" go far beyond what we have noted above: being a recipient of an appearance of the risen Christ conferred apostolic authority on Paul. Peter and other members of the Twelve had already been given some measure of authority by the earthly Jesus (Mark 3:13-19; 6:7-13; Luke 22:29-30). Now they were confirmed in those leadership roles by receiving one or more appearances of the risen Christ. Those who press the theory of "legitimation formulas" claim that the "appearances" were only a rhetorical device to confer authority on those competing for leadership in the emerging Church. In short, "appearances" were invented to underpin claims to authority.[50]

Schrage and others have drawn attention to fatal difficulties facing the "legitimation formula" theory. Paul lists among the Easter witnesses "more than five hundred" people. But there is not the slightest hint that this was a device to establish their *special* authority. The longest and, for many, the most beautiful account of a postresurrection appearance is the story of the risen Jesus joining Cleopas and his anonymous companion on the road to Emmaus (Luke 24:13-35). Yet there is no suggestion that Christ commissioned them to undertake some authoritative role. Finally, there is no reliable evidence that conflicts between leading early Christians—such as Mary Magdalene, Peter, and Thomas—triggered the invention (or at least the embellishment) of resurrection appearances.[51]

Those who want to explain or rather explain away the Easter "appearances" as (unreliable and highly subjective) ecstatic experiences point to Paul's account of being taken up to "the third heaven" (2 Cor 12:1-4) and try to identify this with his postresurrection encounter with the risen Christ (1 Cor 9:1; 15:8). But Paul writes here of an episode that took place "fourteen years" earlier: that is to say, around 42 A.D., and so years after his Damascus road encounter with Christ, which is dated at the latest to 38 A.D. Moreover, when "caught up into Paradise," Paul "heard" things that are "not to be told" and that "no human being is permitted to repeat" (2 Cor 12:4).[52] In 1 Corinthians 9:1 and 15:8, he recalls "seeing" Someone and certainly feels free to witness to that experience. There is a qualitative difference between the appearance that made him an apostle and these later experiences.

Some have proposed that the "appearances" were simply experiences of the Spirit and that, in particular, the "appearance" to the

more than 500 disciples (1 Cor 15:6) was simply a different tradition about the Holy Spirit descending on the 120 followers of Jesus
at Pentecost (Acts 2:1-13). But the traditions are radically different:
1 Corinthians 15:6 witnesses to a Christophany (with no reference
to the Holy Spirit); Acts 2, to the outpouring of the Holy Spirit (with
no Christophany). In general, Paul writes about the experience of the
indwelling Spirit (e.g., Gal 4:6) and various gifts of the Holy Spirit
(e.g., 1 Cor 12:1-13; 14:1-40). But he never identifies that common
experience of the Holy Spirit and the spiritual gifts with the once-and-
for-all encounter with the risen Christ that gave him his own special
mission (1 Cor 9:1; 15:8; Gal 1:12, 16).[53]

A third and final issue centers on the meaning of *horaō*. As we saw
above, this verb, which altogether occurs 449 times in the New Testament,[54] features centrally in the Easter witness. In their classical work,
James Hope Moulton and George Milligan proposed three categories
for appreciating the meaning of the verb: (a) see literally or with one's
eyes; (b) experience; and (c) see with the mind.[55] This scheme provides
part of the structure for the entry on the transitive uses of *horaō* set
out later in the Bauer-Danker lexicon: (a) "perceive by the eye," (b)
"experience," and (c) "perceive mentally."[56]

(a) Under "perceive by the eye," Bauer-Danker lists passages about
the Easter appearances that we have recalled above: for example,
"there [in Galilee] you will see him" (Mark 16:7), and "I have seen
the Lord" (John 20:18). In these and other similar cases of "seeing"
and "appearing" (or "becoming visible" or "letting himself be seen"),
personal nouns or pronouns are involved as subject and object (or
indirect object) of the verb: thus, "you" (Peter and the other disciples)
will see Jesus in Galilee (Mark 16:7); Mary Magdalene has seen the
Lord (John 20:18). This holds true of what we have recalled from
1 Corinthians 15—Christ appeared to Cephas and the others. To follow Bauer-Danker, in all such cases the risen and living Christ was,
at least in some sense, "perceived by the eyes" of Mary Magdalene,
Peter, and the further Easter witnesses. They perceived him, and not
merely some truth about him.

(b) Under "experience," Bauer-Danker cites Luke 3:6, a quotation from the LXX that illuminates the preaching of John the
Baptist and the baptism of Christ: "All flesh will see [*opsetai*] the
salvation of God." The lexicon could also have cited the words of
Simeon in Luke 2:30: "My eyes have seen [*eidon*] your salvation."

"Experience" conveys something of the new situation that has arisen with the birth of Jesus and the ministry of John (which culminated in the baptism of Jesus). Both cases include a "sensory" dimension. Simeon saw the Christ Child and took him in his arms; the general public ("all flesh") saw John engaged in his ministry and eventually baptizing Jesus himself. In these two cases, persons (Jesus and John) were there to be perceived by the eyes of other persons.

(c) It is the meaning of the third category in Bauer-Danker, "perceive mentally," that may raise questions about the Easter appearances. The lexicon examines first several cases (Acts 8:23; Heb 2:8; and Jas 2:24), in which some "sensory aspect [is] felt." To such cases, where *horaō* is used and some sensory aspect is felt, we can add Matthew 13:14-15 and Mark 4:12.

There remain, however, two cases in which Bauer-Danker recognizes that the "focus [is] on the cognitive aspect": Romans 15:21 (a quotation from the LXX of Isaiah 52:15, "those who have never been told of him shall see [*opsontai*], and those who have never heard [of him] shall understand"), and 3 John 11 ("whoever does evil has not seen [*heōraken*] God"). Bauer-Danker translates the first case, "they who have never been told (of Christ) shall look upon him." Here, however, I think the parallel between "shall see" and "shall understand" suggests not "looking upon him" but a less personal "complement." The context in Romans 15 implies "seeing" in the sense of understanding and accepting the truth of the gospel that Paul has been commissioned to preach.[57] It is not, as in the Easter appearances, a question of "seeing him." As regards 3 John 11, Bauer-Danker refers to 1 John 3:10 ("no one who sins has either seen [*heōraken*] him [the Son] or known him"). The lexicon proposes this translation: "no one who sins has become conscious of him and known him." Raymond Brown is a more helpful guide here. Instead of being concerned with literally perceiving with one's eyes God (3 John 11) or Christ (1 John 3:10), or not doing so, these matching passages are saying that those who commit sins are not Christians. The author of the two Epistles phrases this in terms of never having seen Christ or never having seen God. Those who sin prefer darkness to light; they deny the truth and are alienated from God; they have no true Christian experience of God.[58]

To sum up this lexical examination, apart from the two cases—Romans 15:21 and 3 John 11 (taken together with 1 John 3:10), which focus on the cognitive aspect—*horaō* regularly includes a sensory aspect: that is to say, some kind of perceiving by the eyes.[59]

## CONCLUSION

*That* Jesus lives and *that* we can hope to live with him is more important than *how* we know this. But how we know this—which means knowing this in dependence upon the first witnesses to the life, death, and resurrection of Jesus—is still vitally important. I am grateful to my correspondent for prompting me into examining once again the expressions of the first witnesses as to how they came to know that Jesus had been raised from the dead, or how it was "manifested" or "shown" to the first Christians that Jesus had been "woken from the sleep of death." Obviously, some accounts of *how* they came to know this will put into doubt *that* they did so and could then confidently witness that they had done so. This article has limited itself to clarifying what they expressed about the major experience through which they came to know that Jesus had been "woken from the sleep of death": the appearances. The full story of how they came to know this would involve examining much more and, not least, further details of the appearance narratives, the discovery of the empty tomb, and the gift of the Holy Spirit.

Finally, this chapter has put the case for acknowledging that the postresurrection appearances of Jesus involved some kind of ocular, visual element. The language used by Paul and other New Testament witnesses seems to imply that. Nevertheless, one should never forget that the Apostles' Creed and the Nicene-Constantinopolitan Creed do not profess faith in any account of the Easter encounters. They confess Jesus' glorious resurrection from the dead, without including particular details either about the experiences of the apostolic witnesses or about the way(s) in which they expressed what they had experienced.

# 5

# Peter as Witness to Easter

Four years after it appeared in German, Martin Hengel's *Saint Peter:
The Underestimated Apostle* was published in English in 2010.[1]
This learned book has established itself as a significant contribution
on Peter and his role in the emergence of Christianity. It belongs not
only with such earlier landmark works as Oscar Cullmann's *Peter:
Disciple, Apostle, Martyr,* and the ecumenical study *Peter in the New
Testament,*[2] but also with recent studies by authors like Christian
Grappe and Rudolf Pesch.[3]

Hengel argues that "the historical and theological importance
of the fisherman from Bethsaida has been generally underestimated
within both evangelical [i.e., Protestant] and Catholic exegetical cir-
cles." He applies his wide learning to establish Peter's "overarching
importance" for all four Gospels and, more generally, for Jewish *and*
Gentile Christianity.[4] Peter proved "the apostolic foundational figure"
in the emerging Church. The key texts for Hengel's argument are
Jesus' promise to Peter in Matthew 16:17-19 and, to a lesser extent,
the promise in Luke 22:31-32, along with the commission in John
21:15-17.[5] Yet Hengel, like so many earlier and later writers, has little
to say about the resurrection of Jesus and Peter's decisive function as
Easter witness. In Hengel's study (and elsewhere), it is that witness
which continues to be "generally underestimated."

In this chapter I will first discuss the work of Hengel, Pesch,
and Grappe, and then illustrate a pervasive inattention to the role of
Peter as witness to the resurrection. That will prepare the ground for
exploring—exegetically, historically, and theologically—the importance of the Easter function of "the fisherman from Bethsaida."[6]

## THREE VIEWS OF PETER

*Martin Hengel*

Hengel spends over one hundred pages arguing for the fullness of Peter's power that was exercised in proclamation and leadership for the emerging Church. Apropos of Matthew 16:17-19, he elucidates the nickname that functioned as an honorific name, *Kêphā* as "Rock";[7] insists that, as the one who alone has "the power of the keys," the Matthean Peter was not simply the "typical disciple";[8] and argues that long before Matthew wrote his Gospel, Peter was already *the* foundational, apostolic figure in the Church.[9] In particular, he was *the* great witness to the teaching and activity of the earthly Jesus; shortly after the martyrdom of Peter, his disciple Mark wrote a gospel that transmitted the witness of Peter.[10] Luke and, even more, Matthew were to draw on Mark and maintained "the overarching importance of Peter," an importance reflected not only in John but also in Acts and in such Pauline letters as Galatians and 1 Corinthians.[11]

When reaching these and other conclusions about Peter, Hengel draws magisterially on a great range of ancient and modern authors and generally establishes his case convincingly. He did not persuade me over a few items, like his late dating of Matthew's Gospel (around 95 A.D.). But these are minor issues, with my questioning centering on what was said (or rather not said) about the resurrection of the crucified Jesus. Hengel names Peter as "the decisive apostolic witness"[12] but—normally— without stating that the heart of this witness concerned the unique divine action in raising Jesus from the dead and making his glorious existence the beginning of the end for all history and of a new life for a transformed world.

Hengel refers to the appearances of the Resurrected One and what he did for the disciples (in the plural) by giving them "the experience of the forgiveness of their guilt."[13] Then he mentions Peter "as the first to see the Resurrected One," a vision that meant "both forgiveness and a new acceptance."[14] I had expected Hengel to say much more than that, by appreciating the appearance of the risen Jesus to Peter, who was named in the ancient "summary of the Gospel" in 1 Corinthians 15:5 not by his personal name "Simon" but as "Cephas." This marked the beginning of Peter's role as "the Man of Rock," who witnessed to the heart of the Christian Gospel, the utterly startling resurrection of Jesus from the dead.[15]

When characterizing Peter as "the recipient of the first appearance (protophany) of the Resurrected One,"[16] Hengel nowhere cited or even referred to Matthew 28:9-10 (where Mary Magdalene and "the other Mary" are the first to encounter the risen Jesus) or to John 20:11-18 (where Mary Magdalene alone is the recipient of the first appearance). May anyone, without further discussion, simply assume that Peter was the first to see the risen Lord? For Hengel this question proved even more pertinent since he spent pages arguing persuasively for the centrality of Peter in Matthew's Gospel. If Matthew made Peter as foundational apostolic witness even more central than Mark had done, why did that evangelist introduce Mary Magdalene and her companion as the first persons to whom the risen Jesus appeared? The "rival" claims of Peter and Mary Magdalene to be recipients of the protophany need to be explored.[17] I cannot avoid the suspicion that when the resurrection of Jesus is quietly taken for granted and its dramatic importance is not (fully) appreciated, the question of who received the protophany can also become quite secondary.

Glibly assigning Hengel's silence to male chauvinism would find no support from the way in which, when treating later in his book the family of Peter and other apostolic families, he happily drew on Richard Bauckham's *Gospel Women*, a work that champions the female disciples of Jesus.[18] It was rather a certain reluctance to recognize the full importance of Christ's resurrection and its first dramatic disclosure that seems to have affected Hengel. Rightly making much of Peter's new name, he took "Rock" to describe "the entire thirty-five years" of the apostle's activity, from "his call to his martyrdom in Rome."[19] But receiving a foundational appearance of the risen Christ stood out among the many items that made up the whole story—from call to martyrdom.

Some lecturing in Rome (at the Pontifical Biblical Institute) helped prompt Hengel's study of Peter. Hence it is no surprise to find him singling out Matthew 16:18-19, Luke 22:31-32, and John 21:15-18 as texts that impress "anyone who visits St. Peter's Basilica in Rome," and point "back to the reality of the special, unique 'apostolic service' that the Man of Rock performed for the growing church."[20] Hengel is not alone in privileging the three texts from Matthew, Luke, and John. Rudolf Pesch names them as the three "classical texts" establishing Peter's primacy.[21] But what of three other texts that, as we shall see, connect even more clearly the service of the Man of Rock with the resurrection of Christ: Mark 16:7; Luke 24:34; and 1 Corinthians 15:5?

## Rudolf Pesch

As Hengel would do five years later, Pesch dedicates pages to the origin, age, and meaning of Matthew 16:16-19 but includes further scholars (such as Jürgen Roloff) in the discussion. Did these verses derive from the earthly Jesus himself (a few scholars), from Peter's Easter encounter with Jesus (Pierre Grelot), from an early Christian tradition, and/or from the evangelist himself (the majority of commentators)?[22] Like Hengel and other recent scholars,[23] Pesch associates the Gospel of Mark with Peter. This allows him to call Peter *the* "eyewitness and servant of the word" (Luke 1:2).[24] This authoritative eyewitness could hand on and guarantee the tradition about the earthly Jesus' teaching and activity. The authority of Peter stood, above all, behind the passion story in Mark's Gospel.[25]

As Hengel would do, Pesch simply states, without pausing to examine the case of Mary Magdalene, that Peter was the first to see the risen Jesus.[26] Likewise, Pesch does not clearly recognize the full import of Peter's seeing the risen Lord. A chapter on the authoritative roles of Peter lists six areas: authority for the mission, for exorcising and healing, for teaching, for discipline, for reconciliation (the "binding and loosing"), and for leadership.[27] In the section on teaching, Pesch spends less than one page on Peter as the one who received the first Easter appearance" and "formulated Easter faith."[28] Something similar happens when Pesch sketches Peter's connection with various steps in the process of the Church's emergence: "Israel's rejection of Jesus; the Last Supper; the condemnation of Jesus; the renewal of fellowship with the Risen One; the restoration of the 'figure of the Twelve'; Pentecost; the opening and ratification of the Gentile mission."[29] The unique divine act that was Jesus' resurrection from the dead towers over the other events; we will also see how Peter's authoritative role as witness to the risen Christ towers over his other roles.

Pesch does his exegetical work on Peter carefully and is constantly persuasive. But he fails to acknowledge the huge significance of the resurrection as the beginning of the new creation, a significance that shapes Peter's primacy as Easter witness. One finds a similar gap in the longer book by Christian Grappe, a professor of New Testament on the Protestant Faculty of Theology at Strasbourg.

## Christian Grappe

In *Images de Pierre aux deux premiers siècles*, Christian Grappe explores nine images of Peter: as disciple, martyr, repentant sinner, pastor, writer, the receiver of revelations who guaranteed the tradition, the confessor of faith who became the destroyer of heresy, the foundation (the Rock) who founded communities, and the first disciple who became the necessary point of reference.[30] The classic ecumenical study, *Peter in the New Testament*, listed seven images: missionary fisherman, pastoral shepherd, martyr, recipient of special revelation, confessor of the true faith, magisterial protector, and repentant sinner.[31] That study noted the extensive presence of Peter in the Christian Apocrypha, gnostic works, and other postbiblical sources,[32] but did not draw on this material for its study of Peter. The scope of Grappe's work, however, involves him in examining the Apocrypha, the gnostic writers (who claimed to receive further revelations), and such mainline second-century writers as Ignatius, Justin, Irenaeus, and Clement of Alexandria.

Grappe recognizes the significance of the witness to Christ's resurrection coming from Peter as being the first recipient of an Easter appearance. Unlike Hengel and Pesch, he recalls the "rival" cases of Mary Magdalene and James, and spends pages on what both the New Testament and second-century sources say about Mary's encounter with the risen Jesus.[33] Yet it was Peter's role as the first, official witness to the resurrection, expressed in the early confession of faith (1 Cor 15:5), that underpinned his central significance.[34] Like Pesch, Grappe understands Mark 16:7 to refer to the primary appearance to Peter.[35] Hence three texts testify to the protophany to Peter (Mark 16:7; Luke 24:34; 1 Cor 15:5), unlike the three "classical texts" (Matt 16:18-19; Luke 22:31-32; John 21:15-17) that do not invoke the resurrection and the risen Lord's appearance to Peter, or at least do not emphasize that primary appearance as such.

Yet Grappe, like Hengel and Pesch, does not seem to appreciate the enormous impact and significance of Christ's resurrection from the dead. He "downsizes" the resurrection and so downsizes the significance of Peter precisely as Easter witness (see his nine images above). This is to underplay the utterly amazing, world-shattering act of God, the resurrection of Christ, which inaugurated the transformation of the universe and the final kingdom of God. From this resurrection flows the power that will resurrect and transform human beings and their world (1 Cor 15:20-28). This makes the resurrection of the crucified Jesus the focal point of the Gospel, which established the identity of Peter as *the* Easter witness. Proclaiming the resurrection of Jesus, Peter at the head of other Easter witnesses could guarantee its trustworthiness and bring into being the fellowship of Christians.

## LACK OF ATTENTION TO PETER AS EASTER WITNESS

Traditionally, both those who champion the Petrine ministry and those who reduce or even denigrate it have generally shared the same conviction about the central texts to be studied in the New Testament. On October 17, 1978, Pope John Paul II expressed this wide consensus when, in the address that opened his pontificate, he cited Matthew 16:18-19, Luke 22:31-32, and John 21:15-17 and stated, "We are completely convinced that all modern inquiry into the Petrine ministry must be based on these three hinges of the gospel."[36] Two of these three texts are situated in the pre-Easter situation: the first text promises Peter "the keys of the kingdom of heaven" and the power to "bind" and "loose"; in the context of Jesus' imminent death, the second text promises that the faith of Peter will not fail and that he will "lend strength" to the other disciples. On the far side of the resurrection, the third text establishes Peter as the pastor who must shepherd Christ's "lambs" and "sheep." These three classic texts have featured persistently in the defense of the Petrine/papal primacy (as well as in debates about and opposition to that primacy). They point to the function(s) of Peter instituted, or at least promised, by the pre-Easter Jesus.

These three texts about Peter have been repeatedly cited when examining or legitimating the pastoral ministry of Peter (and his successors) for the universal Church. Let me cite several examples. The first (Matt 16:18-19) and the third (John 21:15-17) of the "big three" texts feature prominently in the First Vatican Council's teaching on the Petrine primacy,[37] while the second (Luke 22:31-32) of these three texts turns up in the Council's statement on the pope's infallible magisterium.[38] More than a century later, in its first report on "Authority in the Church" (Venice, 1976), the Anglican-Roman Catholic International Commission (ARCIC) mentioned only three biblical texts when it came to discuss "conciliar and primatial authority" with their attendant "problems and prospects": Matthew 16:18-19; Luke 22:31-32; John 21:15-17 (no. 24).[39] In its second statement on "Authority in the Church" (Windsor, 1981), ARCIC listed a range of Petrine texts from the New Testament (nos. 2–9), paying particular attention to the "big three" texts, each of which it mentioned twice.[40] The same three texts received the primary emphasis when Pope John Paul II presented the bishop of Rome's "ministry of unity" in his encyclical of May 25, 1995, *Ut unum sint*, even if he added at once, "It is also significant that according to the First Letter of Paul to the Corinthians the Risen Christ appears to Cephas and then to the Twelve" (no. 91).[41] The Windsor statement from ARCIC had likewise remarked in passing on this "special appearance" of the risen Jesus to Peter, noting that it is also attested by Luke 24:34 (no. 3).[42] But both the Windsor statement of 1981 and John Paul's encyclical of 1995 privilege the "big three" texts when they reflect on the ministry of Peter (and his successors).

To conclude this picture of these three texts persistently taking attention away, or at least implicitly away, from Peter's role as Easter witness, let me mention two further authors: Jean-Marie-Roger Tillard and John Michael Miller. While being a valuable ecumenical work on Peter and the papacy, Tillard's *The Bishop of Rome* refers on only two pages to Peter as Easter witness.[43] Miller identifies the scriptural foundation for the Petrine ministry, notes in that section the apostle's role as witness to the risen Lord, but makes very little of it.[44] The twenty-one theses on the Petrine ministry of the pope with which he concludes his study refer to Christ's incarnation and divine sonship but include nothing about Christ's resurrection and the ministry of proclaiming it.[45]

In theology and in official teaching but, as we shall see, not in the New Testament, Peter as Easter witness has been left almost completely off the table. What if we take up a possibility offered by Paul, Mark, and Luke for interpreting the Petrine ministry: namely, an interpretation based on understanding Peter's primary (but not exclusive) role in the emerging Church to be that of spreading and gathering the community through the power of his Easter message?[46]

## THE TESTIMONY OF PAUL, MARK, AND LUKE

### The Testimony of Paul

In 1 Corinthians 15:3-5, we have a formula of Christian proclamation that Paul may have received as early as his stay in Damascus after the meeting with the risen Lord that radically changed his life and gave him his apostolic vocation.[47] The three verses run:

> I handed on to you as of first importance what I in turn had received:
> *that* Christ died for our sins in accordance with the scriptures,
> and *that* he was buried,
> *that* he has been raised on the third day in accordance with the scriptures,
> and *that* he appeared to Cephas, then to the twelve.

The fourfold repetition of "that" (*hoti* in Greek) emphasizes "each element in turn."[48] The two key affirmations are "that he died" and "that he has been raised"; in both cases, a further affirmation "confirms" what the formula proclaims. We know that "he died," because "he was buried." We know that "he has been raised," because "he appeared to Cephas, then to the twelve." Burial underlines the reality of the death. The resurrection reverses the burial and so indicates an empty tomb.[49]

The protophany to Peter is not the only appearance of the risen Christ to be reported. Paul adds at once an appearance "to the twelve," which presumably involved a second appearance to Peter, and also adds appearances to "more than five hundred" followers of Jesus, to James (presumably the brother of the Lord, who had not "believed" in him [John 7:5]), "to all the apostles" (with the "apostles" constituting a wider group than "the twelve"), and lastly to Paul himself (1 Cor 15:6-8). So the whole passage testifies to appearances to three individuals (Cephas, James, and Paul) and to three groups ("the twelve," the "more than five hundred" followers, and "all the apostles"). It is not totally clear where the pre-Pauline formula ends. A few scholars hold that the formula ends with "he appeared," while many maintain that the formula includes the name of "Cephas" and perhaps also "the twelve." Otherwise the formula would be left hanging at "he appeared," and with the inevitable question unanswered: "To whom did he appear?" Whatever one's view about this, it is clear that Paul depends on previous tradition(s) for his information about the names of those to whom the risen Jesus had appeared. It is also clear that, in writing to the Corinthians to whom Cephas had most probably also preached (see 1 Cor 1:12; 3:22; 9:5),[50] Paul wants to affirm harmony in the apostolic proclamation of the resurrection and in the faith it had evoked: "Whether then it was I or they, so we proclaim [Easter kerygma] and so you have come to believe [confession of faith]" (1 Cor 15:11).

According to the kerygmatic (and creedal) formula cited by Paul (1 Cor 15:3-5), Cephas was the first disciple (or at least the first male disciple) to whom the risen Lord appeared. We will see below how a similar formula in Luke 24:34 upholds the protophany to Simon Peter. The testimony offered by Paul in 1 Corinthians 15 allows us to draw this conclusion: by witnessing to his foundational Easter experience, Peter as Cephas offered firm and rocklike witness to the very center of Christian faith, the resurrection from the dead of the crucified Jesus.

## The Testimony of Mark

When transmitting the witness of Peter, Mark makes him serve as an "inclusion" that frames the whole Gospel. At the start Jesus calls Simon (Mark 1:16-18), to whom he soon gives the name of "Peter" (Mark 3:16). Then at the end of the Gospel, in an open and empty tomb, an interpreting angel says to Mary Magdalene and her two companions: "Go, tell his disciples and Peter that he [Jesus] is going ahead of you to Galilee; there you will see him" (Mark 16:7).

Joel Marcus agrees with many scholars in holding that "and to Peter" echoes the tradition that Jesus appeared first to Peter,[51] and, at the same time, suggests a double entendre on the part of the evangelist. "On the one hand, the women are to announce the news *especially* to Peter, the first disciple to be called," "the first to recognize Jesus' messiahship," and the one who would soon "be granted the first resurrection appearance." On the other hand, the women were "to proclaim the message *even* to Peter," whose opposition to Jesus' coming fate "earned him the epithet 'Satan'" (Mark 8:33) and who three times denied knowing Jesus (Mark 14:66-72).[52]

While acknowledging that 1 Corinthians 15:5 reports the protophany to Peter, Frederick Lapham claims that "nowhere in the Gospel record is there any hint that Peter was the *first* witness of the

Resurrection."[53] To be sure, Mark's Gospel presents three women as those who discovered the empty tomb and heard from an angel the astonishing news of the resurrection. But they did not see the risen Jesus himself. Yet Marcus and other scholars, pace Lapham, find Mark hinting that it is Peter who will soon be granted the first appearance of the risen Lord. Moreover and quite clearly, Luke adds his witness that—at some moment after visiting the empty tomb (Luke 24:12),[54] a visit that led Peter to "wonder" but not yet to believe in the risen Christ—the protophany was granted to Simon Peter (Luke 24:34).

## The Testimony of Luke

At the end of the Emmaus story, Luke quotes a traditional formula: "The Lord was really raised, and he appeared [ōphthē] to Simon" (Luke 24:34), a formula that converges with what we have seen in 1 Corinthians 15:4-5 (Christ "has been raised" and "appeared [ōphthē] to Cephas").[55] Seemingly, Luke introduces the early formulation about the appearance to Simon Peter to head off any impression that the Emmaus appearance is the primary one. The evangelist defers to the tradition of a first appearance to Peter. Even before Cleopas and his companion return, Peter's testimony to his meeting with the risen Lord has brought to Easter faith "the eleven" and "those who were with them" (Luke 24:33). Simon's encounter with the living Jesus has shifted the community in Jerusalem from their incredulity and persuaded them that the message which the women brought from the angels about the resurrection (Luke 24:9-11) is "really" true. The report from Emmaus and the subsequent appearance of the Lord reinforce and clarify this Easter faith but do not create it for the first time.

Luke has prepared his readers for this role of Peter as agent of faith in the resurrection of Jesus. This is the thrust of what Jesus promises at the Last Supper, even while foretelling Peter's denial: "I have prayed for you that your own faith may not fail; and you, when once you have turned back, strengthen your brothers" (Luke 22:32).[56] The primary appearance of the risen Lord to Simon Peter enables the apostle to play just that role. He "turns back" and "strengthens" his fellow disciples by the power of his Easter faith. The connection between Luke 24:34 and 22:32, as Robert Tannehill points out, "is reinforced by the fact that they are the only places in Luke where Peter is called

Simon after the formal indication in 6:14 that Jesus gave Simon a new name." Tannehill adds, "Simon is warned and charged with responsibility in 22:31-32, and he begins to fulfill that responsibility by bearing witness to the risen Jesus before Jesus' other followers."[57]

Testimony from Paul, Mark, and Luke converges to support a primary appearance to Peter. Yet, at first glance, they and other New Testament authors do not seem to contain any story of this protophany of the risen Christ. Do we then look in vain for a vivid narrative of an appearance to Peter that could be like that of Jesus appearing to Mary Magdalene (John 20:11-18)?

## THE STORY OF AN APPEARANCE TO PETER

Like others, Andrew Lincoln is open to the idea that Luke knew of a postresurrection miracle involving Peter and a great haul of fish but, given the evangelist's "exclusively Jerusalem-oriented ending," inserted the story earlier—in the context of the call of Peter and other first disciples (Luke 5:1-11). Peter's words ("go away from me, Lord, for I am a sinful man") make good sense if they originally came after his denials during the passion and on the occasion of his meeting the risen Lord.[58] In modern times it has been Raymond Brown who, appealing to this Lukan passage and other passages, has stood out for arguing that a primary appearance to Peter at the Sea of Tiberias in Galilee lies behind the catch of fish in John 21:1-14 and the rehabilitation of Peter in John 21:15-17.[59] Where Luke 5 relates the haul of fish to the calling of Peter, John 21 relates it to his installation as leader.

Brown recognizes, of course, the prima facie difficulty that Peter has six companions in John 21, whereas Luke 24:34 ("the Lord appeared to Simon") and 1 Corinthians 15:5 ("he appeared to Cephas") seem to suggest an appearance to Peter alone. Yet the presence of "silent" companions in the appearance to Peter cannot be simply excluded. After all, Paul speaks of an appearance to himself (1 Cor 15:8), and Luke three times indicates that others were present when the apostle met the risen Jesus on the road to Damascus (Acts 9:7; 22:9; 26:13). Like Paul's companions on the road to Damascus, Peter's fishing companions, apart from the Beloved Disciple whom the evangelist may well have added to the narrative, do not play an important part in the story of the risen Jesus appearing on the shore, and then disappear entirely in the dialogue that rehabilitates Peter. As

Lincoln was to suggest (see above), Brown observes that the rehabilitation scene, "made to correspond to Peter's denials, is more intelligible in the context of Jesus' first appearance to Peter."[60]

Brown also proposes that elements from the story of the appearance to Peter "have been preserved in fragments from the Synoptic description of Jesus' ministry."[61] He cites three possible places for finding such postresurrectional material: Peter's walking on the water (Matt 14:28-33), Peter as the foundation rock of the Church (Matt 16:16b-19), and the call of Peter and miraculous catch of fish (Luke 5:1-11). An Easter location for some of the themes in these three passages is possible. As regards the third, it is more than possible and even quite probable that some of its elements originally belonged to a story of the risen Christ appearing to Peter when the latter was fishing.[62]

Having reached some exegetical conclusions (about Peter being a primary Easter witness) and a plausible view of where the appearance of the risen Lord to Peter took place (at the Sea of Tiberias), we need to face a central question already mentioned above: Was Mary Magdalene chronologically the first to see Christ risen from the dead?

## MARY MAGDALENE AS EASTER WITNESS

All four Easter narratives found in the Gospels feature Mary Magdalene at the discovery of the empty tomb and always name her in first place, whether she has two other women as companions (Mark 16:1-8), only one woman companion (Matt 28:1-10), more than two other women companions (Luke 24:1-11), or seemingly goes alone and returns alone to the tomb (John 20:1-2, 11-18). According to Matthew (28:9-10), along with her solitary woman companion ("the other Mary"), Mary Magdalene encounters the risen Jesus and, after having been commissioned by an "angel of the Lord" to tell the "disciples" to keep the rendezvous in Galilee (Matt 28:7), is now commissioned a second time and by the risen Jesus himself to tell "my brothers" to keep the rendezvous. John 20:11-18 pictures her alone when the risen Lord appears to her and instructs her to tell "my brothers" that he is "ascending" to the Father.[63] According to the (second-century) appendix to Mark's Gospel, the risen Jesus "appeared first" to Mary Magdalene; she then "told those who had been with him" that Jesus "was alive," but they would not believe her (Mark 16:9-11). In all the

Easter texts, this is the only place that it is formally stated that the resurrected Christ *first* appeared to anyone.[64]

The Gospels converge in presenting Mary Magdalene as *the* primary and preeminent witness to the discovery of the empty tomb. What of her being the recipient of the first appearance of the risen Christ (Matt 28:9-10; John 20:11-18)—something explicitly asserted by Mark 16:9, apparently in dependence on John 20:11-18?[65] Any answer here must reckon with the fact that neither Mary Magdalene nor any other women are mentioned by Paul in the list of three individuals to whom the risen Jesus appeared (1 Cor 15:5-8): Cephas, James, and Paul himself. Paul also lists three groups: "the Twelve," more than five hundred "brothers," and "all the apostles." While women did not belong to the first group, they were presumably represented in the crowd of over five hundred "brothers and sisters" or "fellow Christians," and could well have numbered among "all the apostles." At the end of Romans, Paul names among his collaborators Andronicus and Junia (a married couple?) as "distinguished among the apostles" (Rom 16:7).[66] Understanding "apostles" to extend beyond "the Twelve," Paul makes room for women among the apostles for two reasons: they could be witnesses to the risen Christ (for this qualification of apostleship, see, e.g., 1 Cor 9:1) and sent on mission for Christ, like Epaphroditus (Phil 2:25; 4:18).[67] The concluding chapter of Romans opens by praising Phoebe and Prisca, includes further positive remarks about other women, and shows how comfortable Paul is with the prestige and leadership roles of women (Rom 16:1-16).

Did Paul know the tradition of an appearance to Mary Magdalene? It could be that he was aware of appearances in Galilee but not of appearances in Jerusalem, where Mary Magdalene met the risen Lord. If Paul knew about that meeting, why then did he not name Mary Magdalene in 1 Corinthians 15:5-7? He might have suppressed her name as an Easter witness, since he was sensitive to the fact that the testimony of women was, more or less, not accepted in Judaism and the community in Corinth included Jewish as well as Gentile Christians. However we construe the "silence" of Paul in 1 Corinthians 15, we cannot allege that the early Church as a whole placed little or no value on women's testimony. Otherwise we cannot convincingly account for the preeminence of Mary Magdalene and other (named) women both as witnesses to the empty tomb (all four Gospels) and as

those who bore to the other disciples the angelic message about Jesus'
resurrection (the Synoptic Gospels).

Two of the Gospels—Matthew and, at greater length, John—testify to a protophany to Mary Magdalene. For at least one good reason, we can hold that this tradition is early and historically reliable.
It runs counter to the "trend" to assign the first appearances to Peter
and other male disciples.[68] With her "I have seen the Lord" (John
20:18), Mary emerged as equal to Peter and other male disciples in
her witness to the resurrection. Did the appearance of the risen Jesus
to her precede chronologically that to Peter? Matthew and John (*pace*
Paul, Luke, and perhaps Mark) would encourage this conclusion,
which has been long favored by the liturgical language used for her
feast on July 22.

Some have pointed to conflicts between Mary Magdalene and
Peter,[69] which are found in gnostic and other apocryphal works of the
second and third century and which speak of the risen Christ appearing to her, communicating new revelations, and creating her authoritative role that male leaders in the Church then suppressed.[70] This
material—even though it seems a later, odd spin-off from, rather than
a reliable guide to, what was happening in mainstream Christianity—
has been used to argue for serious divisions in the early Church over
apostolic authority.[71] Here one should recall that, from the late first
century to the end of the second century, such writers as Clement of
Rome, Ignatius of Antioch, Justin Martyr, and Irenaeus have various things to say about issues and problems in the early Church, but
nothing at all to say about any debates over women legitimately transmitting apostolic revelation and tradition, and, in particular, nothing
to say about any conflict between Mary Magdalene and Peter. Clement goes out of his way to praise women like Esther and Judith for
what they had done for their people (*1 Clement 55*), while Irenaeus
famously places Jesus' mother as the New Eve alongside her son as the
New Adam. The appendix to Mark (16:9-20), which many scholars
date to the first half of the second century, has nothing to say about
any debates over the testimony and authority of women. Rather, it
highlights the role of Mary Magdalene as primary Easter witness
and the male disciples' failure to accept her testimony. If serious divisions existed in mainstream Christianity over the separate authority
of Mary Magdalene and of male disciples headed by Peter, why does
none of this conflict show up in the work of writers from Clement to

Irenaeus? The case for such gender conflict during the early years of
Christianity is, as Philip Jenkins shows, quite weak.[72]

Apropos of Mary Magdalene in her role as Easter witness, many
cite Hippolytus of Rome referring in the third century to the women
at the tomb of Jesus as "apostles," which developed into Mary Magdalene often being called *apostola apostolorum* (the apostle of the
apostles). Soon after the Council of Chalcedon in 451, Pope Leo the
Great named her a figure of the Church (*personam Ecclesiae gerens*).
In the following century, Pope Gregory the Great referred to her as
"another" Eve, since she announced to the other disciples life and not
death.[73] But, in emerging Christianity, it was Peter who had taken the
primary role as official proclaimer of the Lord's resurrection.

## Peter as Easter Witness

Peter functions as bridge figure for Luke, being the last disciple to be
named in the Gospel (Luke 24:34) and the first to be named in the
Acts of the Apostles (Acts 1:13). In Luke's second work, Peter has
significant things to do: for instance, taking the initiative to find a
substitute member for the Twelve after the defection of Judas (Acts
1:15-26); conferring, along with John, the gift of the Holy Spirit (Acts
8:14-17); performing miracles by healing the sick and even raising the
dead (Acts 3:1-10; 5:15-16; 9:32-42); or playing a key role in admitting Gentiles into the Christian community without imposing on them
the observance of the Torah (Acts 10:1–11:18; 15:1-29).

But the major function of Peter is that of being, right from the
day of Pentecost and along "with the eleven" (Acts 2:14) and "all" the
other disciples (Acts 2:32), the leading, public witness to the resurrection of Jesus from the dead.[74] Just as Peter's "turning back" and witnessing to the resurrection had "strengthened" his "brothers" (Luke
22:32), so his witness to the risen Jesus now reaches out to those who
have come to Jerusalem from the wider world. He speaks with and
for a college or official group of Easter witnesses in announcing the
good news: "This [crucified] Jesus God raised up, and of that all of
us are witnesses" (Acts 2:32). Peter stands "with the eleven" (Acts
2:14) and proclaims a resurrection of which "*we* are witnesses" (Acts
3:15). For Luke, Peter leads the others in being the example par excel-
lence of an authoritative eyewitness (to the risen Lord) and minister
of the (Easter) word (Luke 1:2). The first half of Acts presents various

dimensions of the leadership role that Peter exercised in the life of the early Church. But the heart of the matter was his preeminence among the official witnesses to the resurrection of Jesus (e.g., Acts 3:13-15; 4:10; 5:30-32).

Neither Luke nor any other New Testament author allows us (1) to separate Peter from Mary Magdalene, the Twelve, Paul, and other Easter witnesses. Nor do they encourage us (2) to reduce the Petrine function simply to that of being a witness to the resurrection. Nor do they permit us (3) to isolate Peter's experience of the post-Easter Jesus from all that has gone before. The watershed of Easter does not invalidate or cancel what has happened to Peter through his closeness to Jesus and leadership of the Twelve. If Peter holds a special leadership role in the early Church, this is associated not only with his function as *the* Easter witness but also with a position he has already enjoyed during Jesus' ministry. Nevertheless, it is Easter that brings Peter the new, worldwide function of being the leading Easter witness as missionary, shepherd, and rock—an activity that eventually leads to his final "witness" as martyr.

Understanding and interpreting this Petrine function primarily (but not exclusively) in the light of the Easter appearance to him looks attractive from the point of view of the liturgy and of God's self-revelation. First, this interpretation links Peter expressly with the center of the Church's life of worship, the resurrection of the crucified Jesus. Not only baptism and the Eucharist but also all the sacraments focus on and draw their power from the paschal mystery. Second, this vision of his function expresses Peter's relationship with the climax of divine self-revelation: the resurrection of the Crucified One, through which Jesus was revealed as the effective Messiah, Lord, and Son of God. Highlighting what the New Testament reports about Peter's role as Easter witness moves us to the center of our christological confession. The events of the first Good Friday and Easter Sunday form the highpoint of the saving self-communication of the tripersonal God, which was proclaimed by Peter and eventually enshrined in the Creed of the Church.

Prioritizing Peter's role as Easter proclaimer has a further theological advantage. Those who follow Vatican II in setting the (prophetic) service of the word ahead of the (priestly) sacramental ministry and the (kingly) shepherding and leading of the Christ's flock should be attracted to my account of the Petrine function.[75] This account attends primarily (but not exclusively) to the prophetic service of the word in witnessing to the resurrection (on the basis of Peter's meeting with the risen Jesus).

When prioritizing Peter's Easter witness, we need to recall that the New Testament does not offer a single, monolithic tradition about him. He can be depicted as fisherman or missionary (e.g., Mark 1:16-18; Luke 5:10), shepherd (e.g., John 21:15-17), rock (e.g., Matt 16:18), repentant sinner (e.g., Mark 14:72), and martyr (e.g., John 21:18-19; see 13:36). We can relate these different images to that of Easter witness. In the opening chapters of Acts, Peter's missionary "fishing" takes the form of proclaiming the resurrection. The shepherding vocation comes to him from the risen Christ. Peter's role as "rock" receives its legitimacy from the crucified and risen Jesus, who is "the living stone," "the cornerstone," and "the stone of scandal" (1 Pet 2:4-8). Peter's repentance has its context in the passion, death, and resurrection of Jesus (Luke 22:61-62; 23:49; John 21:15-17); he will suffer martyrdom in the service of the risen Lord (John 21:18-19). In short, the different images of Peter and traditions about him converge on his function as Easter witness. In the words of Raymond Brown and his colleagues, "The important tradition about Peter having been the first of the major companions of Jesus' ministry to have seen the Lord after the resurrection" provided "very likely" the "original context for much of the New Testament material about Peter."[76]

## PETER AND THE POPE

As regards the way Peter's leadership should be or was in fact handed on, the New Testament contains no explicit directions. The Acts of the Apostles contain nothing about Peter's later life. They describe Paul's coming to Rome (Acts 28:11-31) but not his martyrdom there. John's Gospel points to Peter's martyrdom (John 21:18-19) but does not specify how or where it took place.[77] Nevertheless, Rome was the city where Peter and Paul suffered death for their Master.[78] The Church of Rome came to be recognized as exercising a unique responsibility for all the communities of Christians. As successor of Peter, the bishop of Rome was acknowledged to be called in a special way to do two things. He was *both* to proclaim the saving truth revealed by Christ *and* to keep all Christians united in their faith.[79]

Here, "called in a special way" does *not* mean "called as the only one" or "called exclusively." Peter's role of leadership did not isolate him from the other apostles. Paul and the other apostolic missionaries also witnessed authoritatively to the good news, centered on the resurrection of the crucified Jesus, and set themselves to maintain unity among the churches. Likewise, the special responsibility of the Bishop of Rome to uphold the truth about Christ and preserve Christian unity is a function also exercised with other bishops (and, indeed, all Christians).

What light could my presentation of Peter's primary role throw on the nature of the papacy? From his primary role as Easter witness, let me briefly draw five conclusions for the ministry of the bishop of Rome.

(1) The Church was founded on *all the apostles* (Eph 2:20), the official witnesses to Jesus Christ. They proclaimed the resurrection of the crucified Savior, admitted all nations into the new community, and authoritatively guided the emerging Church. In this college of witnesses, Simon Peter stood out as *the* foundational witness to Jesus' resurrection. His new name, "Cephas," suggested his special function. To him alone was addressed the promise: "On this rock I will build my Church."

(2) The mission given to Peter and the other apostles was partly but not totally handed on to their successors, the bishop of Rome and the other bishops. I say "not totally," because certain functions died with the apostles. Under the risen Christ and through the power of the Holy Spirit, they were called to preach the resurrection of the Crucified One and so bring the Church into existence. Once achieved, this founding of the Church could never be repeated. Pope, bishops, and other believers bear—in different ways—the common responsibility of nourishing Christian life and mission and so keeping the Church in a flourishing existence. They are all called to maintain the good state of the community but not to found (or refound) the Church.

Hence, the words "on this rock I will build my Church" do not apply to the bishop of Rome in precisely the way they apply to Peter. In the case of the pope, the meaning would rather be, "on this rock I will preserve my Church in existence."

(3) Nevertheless, the mission given to Peter and the other apostles was partly handed on to their successors. Let me sketch some details of this succession.

The Bishop of Rome has a relationship to his fellow bishops that is *like* that of Peter to the other apostles. Together they share the major responsibility for spreading the good news of the risen Christ, leading the Church with authority, and maintaining the sacramental life of the community. In the life of the Church, the bishops with the pope are the primary preachers, pastors, and celebrants of the liturgy.

Among all the bishops, the bishop of Rome, like Peter, has a special role of leadership to serve the whole Church with love (John 21:15-17) and through suffering (John 21:18-19). His special service aims at maintaining the true faith and unity of all Christians.

(4) Christian Grappe, Raymond Brown, and his colleagues, in listing "repentant sinner" among the major images of Peter (see above), drew attention to the shadow side in the chief apostle's exercise of his ministry. Rather than being surprised at human weaknesses and limitations in the ministry of Peter's successors, we should expect them. Even after the resurrection and the coming of the Holy Spirit, Peter could at least on one serious occasion appear to limit true Christian freedom (Gal 2:11-21).[80] Among all the disciples, only Peter is reported to have confessed his sinfulness so strikingly: "Simon Peter . . . fell down at Jesus' knees, saying: 'Depart from me, for I am a sinful man, O Lord' " (Luke 5:8).

The conclusion from this seems clear. The shadow side of the papacy, far from ruling out the Petrine succession, belongs to it. We should not be surprised if, like Peter, the bishop of Rome at times fails in the way he exercises his special function of leadership for the whole Church.

(5) In this chapter I have shown how Peter fulfilled his ministry, primarily but not exclusively, through being *the* official witness to Christ's resurrection from the dead. This suggests that among the various titles exercised by the bishop of Rome the primary one could be recognized as being *the* proclaimer of the Lord's victory over death. I need to work this out in a little detail.

The pastoral jurisdiction and teaching function of the pope, defined by the First Vatican Council (1869–1870), can be contextualized by recalling the Petrine ministry of being the primary witness to the risen Christ. Vatican I described the papal office as a "perpetual principle and visible foundation of the *unity*" that belongs to the bishops and the whole Church.[81] It is above all through being the primary, official proclaimer of the central truth, "Jesus is risen," that the pope expresses and supports this unity. Vatican I went on to describe the goal of papal primacy: "By preserving unity, both in communion and the profession of the same faith, the Church of Christ may be one flock under one supreme shepherd."[82] Now the Church as a community of believers brings together those who confess Jesus as risen Lord and through sharing this faith are bound in love to each other. Their faith and communion are served by the pope (as primary teacher and pastor) proclaiming through word and deed *the event* that more than anything else founded the community of believers: the resurrection of the crucified Christ (along with the outpouring of the Holy Spirit).

The Second Vatican Council's Dogmatic Constitution on the Church (*Lumen gentium*) put "preaching the Gospel" ahead of pastoral and liturgical roles as the most important duty of bishops (no. 25). No less than the other bishops, the bishop of Rome must fulfill this duty, which in a 1975 apostolic exhortation Pope Paul VI called "the pre-eminent ministry of teaching the revealed truth."[83] One might reasonably comment that "the Gospel" to be preached and "the revealed truth" to be taught primarily concern and essentially derive from the resurrection of the crucified Jesus.

In recent decades, contacts between Catholics and other Christians have highlighted more and more the need to find real *unity* in confessing the *truth* of faith. How best can we describe that unity and truth? The central truth of Christian faith can be formulated by saying, "The crucified Son of God is risen from the dead to give us the Holy Spirit." The Easter mystery says it all. It is the basic truth to be maintained and passed on by Christians. They are baptized into Christ's death and resurrection (Rom 6:3-11) to live together as God's new Easter people.

What more could we expect from the Bishop of Rome than that like Peter he strengthen the whole Church's faith in Christ's resurrection? How could he better serve the unity of an Easter people than by proclaiming insistently the event that brought the Church into existence: the resurrection of the crucified Jesus followed by the coming of the Holy Spirit? To be sure, the pope must also lead the Church with loving authority and celebrate the sacraments. But his great task for all the world is to announce through word and deed the news that lies at the heart of Christianity: Jesus is risen.

A Lutheran-Catholic report on which I have drawn observes that "no matter what one may think about the justification offered by the

New Testament for the emergence of the papacy, this papacy in its developed form cannot be read back into the New Testament."[84] In general, one can only agree with this statement. Nevertheless, there is one yearly ceremony in which, by proclaiming the resurrection, the pope strikingly symbolizes and even parallels Peter's central function as Easter witness. Each year millions of people see on television or follow by radio the pope's Easter broadcast. In many languages he announces to the city of Rome and the world the glorious news that gave rise to Christianity: "Christ is risen. Alleluia!"

Of course, we should respect the great differences between our cultural and historical setting in the twenty-first century and that in which nearly two thousand years ago Peter carried out his ministry. Nevertheless, one need not strain to find some parallel between what the pope does at Easter and what Luke pictured happening at Pentecost. In Jerusalem, Peter stood up to announce Jesus' resurrection to "Parthians, Medes, Elamites, and residents of Mesopotamia, Judea and Cappadocia, Pontus and Asia, Phrygia and Pamphylia, Egypt and the parts of Libya belonging to Cyrene, and visitors from Rome, both Jews and proselytes, Cretans and Arabs" (Acts 2:8-11). Today the television cameras catch the faces of those who have come to Rome from all over the world, so that they can stand in St. Peter's Square on Easter Sunday and hear from Peter's successor the great news that has forever changed human history: "This Jesus God raised up, and of that we are witnesses" (Acts 2:32). Peter's witness to the resurrection lives on strikingly in the pope's Easter proclamation. In that special way, the bishop of Rome visibly serves and strengthens the Church's faith by reenacting before all the world the primary role of Peter as fundamental witness to Jesus risen from the dead.[85]

# PART THREE

# 6

# The Priesthood of Christ and Followers of Other Faiths

From the second half of the twentieth century and into the third millennium, numerous Roman Catholics and other Christian writers have taken up the theology of religions. Divergent views have prompted serious debates in many languages. But, in all that literature, as far as I can see, no one has set out to reflect on other faiths in the light of the priesthood of Jesus Christ. Without alleging that his priesthood should be seen as *the* major approach to be adopted in this field, nevertheless, I believe, as will be argued below, that the theme of his priesthood pulls together some or even much of what Christian thinkers would, or at least should, want to deal with when reflecting on other living faiths. But so far the light that Christ's priesthood throws on those other faiths remains an untold story.

## KARL RAHNER, JACQUES DUPUIS, AND OTHERS

Before exploring what the priesthood of Christ can contribute to a theology of religions, let me illustrate the general neglect of this theme by first sampling the work of two leading authors in this area: Karl Rahner (1904–1984) and Jacques Dupuis (1923–2004). Both shaped what many Catholics and other Christians have thought about the followers of other religions. Rahner, along with Yves Congar and various theologians in Asia, prepared the way for the relevant teaching of the Second Vatican Council (1962–1965). But neither Rahner nor Dupuis introduced Christ's priesthood into their theology of religions.

Starting from a lecture he delivered in April 1961, "Christianity and the Non-Christian Religions,"[1] Rahner often returned to this and closely related themes, in essays included in *Theological Investigations*[2] and in *Foundations of Christian Faith.*[3] Yet he never reflected on other religions and their followers—or, for that matter, on the offer of divine salvation to all human beings—in the light of Christ's priesthood. It would have been surprising if he had done so, since in all his writing he did not have much to say about that priesthood.

The relatively little that Rahner wrote about Christ's priesthood turned up in spiritual writing directed toward those about to be ordained to the priestly ministry or already exercising that ministry. Both in Germany and in Rome, Rahner often gave eight-day retreats, based on the *Spiritual Exercises* of St. Ignatius, to young, German-speaking candidates for the priesthood. Many of these meditations were eventually edited and printed in 1965, and in the same year translated and published in English.[4] Rahner closed the section of the retreat that corresponded to the "second week" of the *Exercises* with a meditation on the priesthood. The opening page dealt briefly with the priesthood of Christ, about which Rahner made two points. First, from the moment that the Word takes on a human existence, he is "essentially God's high priest."[5] Here Rahner followed St. John Chrysostom and others in the Christian tradition when firmly stating that the priesthood of Christ and its exercise began with the incarnation.[6] Secondly, Rahner understands that Christ as priest "pours out God's love" on "the whole world" and "makes possible the holy conversation" between "God and the whole world."[7] Linking "the whole world" with the exercise of Christ's priesthood might, in another context, have led Rahner to reflect on the followers of other religions and the followers of none. But, given the audience for whom he was developing the meditation, he moved at once to speak of "our priesthood," "our priestly existence," and "our priestly life."[8]

In a 1967 book, published the following year in English,[9] Rahner wrote of the greatness and the burden of the priesthood. Addressed chiefly to his fellow priests, the chapters originated in ordination sermons, jubilee sermons, retreat conferences, essays, lectures, and prayers. Once again he did not focus on the priesthood of Christ himself. The book includes a chapter on "Christ the Exemplar of Priestly Obedience" and a "Prayer for the Right Spirit of Christ's Priesthood" (which began by calling Christ "high priest of all human beings").[10] Yet, in both the chapter and the prayer, Rahner directed his attention to those exercising ordained ministry in the Church and did not set himself to explore the priesthood of Christ himself, let alone connect that priesthood with the religions of the world. In some related publications listed at the end of the book, we find that Rahner maintained steadily the same primary focus: on the life and ministry of ordained priests rather than on Christ's own priesthood.[11]

Finally, Rahner retrieved some conferences that he had given in 1961 to candidates for priestly ordination, and published them in 1970.[12] The conferences were intended to encourage his hearers to understand more deeply and accept more devoutly the priestly way of life. For Rahner, ordained priesthood embodied selfless, loving service of others and of God's coming kingdom. Once again the focus of the book allowed only for incidental references to Christ's own priesthood and certainly not for any drawing of lines between that priesthood and world religions. Even when Rahner spoke of the "continuation of Christ's priesthood," he was primarily concerned to show how Catholic priests unite a prophetical calling with a cultic role.[13]

From the end of the 1960s and right through the 1970s, Rahner continued to write about the priestly office and the spirituality of priests. But he developed his reflections without first establishing any detailed theology of Christ's high priesthood, from which he could then draw some conclusions about the work and spiritual life of those who share in that priesthood through ordination.[14]

Jacques Dupuis, at greater length than Rahner, constructed over many years a theology of religions. This work climaxed with *Toward a Christian Theology of Religious Pluralism* and *Christianity and the Religions*.[15] In both books he discussed the "mediation" exercised by Christ,[16] but he did not characterize that mediation as "priestly." It was only once in either of the books that he ever spoke about Christ as "priest" or "high priest," and that was in a passage where he was concerned with Melchizedek, "the type of him who will be the eternal High Priest."[17]

From his first publication in 1960, right through to 2003, Dupuis often wrote about various christological questions and eventually published *Who Do You Say I Am? Introduction to Christology*.[18] But in no book or article did he ever explore the nature of Christ's priesthood as such. Hence, so far from being able to shape in any sense his theology of religions, the high priesthood of Christ never entered his reflections. At best, like Rahner, he only touched on it, and that was when reviewing books on ordained priesthood (four in 1971, one in

1975, and one in 1978) and publishing four brief articles on the same topic (two in 1971, and one in both 1975 and 1979).[19]

Rahner, Dupuis, and other specialists in the theology of religion, as I found, failed to explore possibilities offered by Christ's priesthood being exercised for the benefit of all humankind. Perhaps, I fondly imagined, theologians who write on that priesthood—or at least a few of them— might apply some of their conclusions to the situation of those who follow "other" faiths or follow none at all. Then I discovered to my astonishment how very few theologians, both in the past and in modern times, have investigated the priesthood of Christ.[20]

One of those very few to do so recently has been Robert J. Sherman. But he declines to accept and examine what Christ's priesthood could mean for the wider world. Christ's "priestly mediation and intercession," he writes, are "what make Christian worship possible in the first place. Christ is *our heavenly high priest, the head of the church*, enabling all who minister or worship in his name."[21] But does Christ exercise his priesthood only for members of the church who assemble for Christian worship? Do the baptized monopolize the attention of Christ as "our heavenly high priest," so that he is not high priest for all other human beings, many of whom may never have heard his name? Without argument, Sherman seems to have instinctively limited the beneficiaries of Christ's priestly office to the members of the church.

After examining Rahner, Dupuis, Sherman, and other modern theologians, I came to two negative conclusions. First, those (many) who write on other faiths do not introduce the priesthood of Christ into their discussion. Second, those (very few) who write on Christ's priesthood have not appreciated the possibilities it offers for a theology of religions. What story would I now propose about the high priesthood of Christ and the light it sheds on the revealing and saving self-communication of God to those of other faiths?

## HEBREWS, PAUL, AND JOHN

### Hebrews

The Letter to the Hebrews stands apart by containing the only explicit biblical narrative of Christ as priest and by portraying him extensively in the exercise of his high priesthood. The vision of Christ as eternal high priest makes its first appearance in Hebrews and seems a self-consciously avant-garde interpretation of Christ's life, death, and exaltation. Written between 60 and 95 A.D. (more plausibly before 70) and sent to Italy (Rome?) from Ephesus (Heb 13:23-24), Hebrews is an anonymous sermon aimed at encouraging a particular community, which had earlier suffered considerable hardships (10:32-34), to maintain their faith and hope. They may be facing further persecutions (13:3). Some of them could be already "slipping away" (2:1), in danger of letting their hearts become "hardened by sin" (3:13), being threatened by "strange teaching" (13:9), and even abandoning their faith in Christ (3:12; 6:4-6; 12:25). Certain individuals are already staying away from the liturgical meetings of the community (10:25).[22]

All these particular circumstances leave us with this question: Does Hebrews, while expounding the priesthood of Christ, envisage its impact affecting only a specific Christian community or, perhaps, other such communities suffering from similar challenges? From such particular "scraps," can we create a compelling narrative of Christ as high priest who exercises a universal office and offers salvation to the whole world?

Priesthood and sacrifice are correlative terms—something taken for granted by the author of Hebrews (8:3). The priestly practices outlined in sections of the Pentateuch that he recalls involved offering sacrifices of animals. When he mentions for the first time the *priestly* identity of Christ, he links it at once to Christ's *sacrificial* activity: he became "a merciful and faithful high priest to expiate the sins of the people" (2:17). In the context, "people" points, at least immediately, to the descendants of Abraham and Sarah and not to the human race in general. Nevertheless, the author of Hebrews envisages a group that is much broader than the group he addresses, a particular community that is being "tested" (2:18).

The horizon that the letter proceeds to open up will be as large as the whole human race. The author lists three qualifications that made Jesus the high priest of the new dispensation: "Every high priest is [1] taken from among human beings [*anthrōpōn*] and [2] appointed on behalf of human beings [*anthrōpōn*] with respect to the matters pertaining to God, [3] in order to offer gifts and sacrifices for sin" (5:1). In other words, as high priest Christ has been (1) chosen from among human beings, and (2) not self-appointed, but called by God to represent them (3) in the sacrificial offering he makes, in particular for the expiation of their sins.

Through taking on the human condition in the incarnation (1:1-4), the Son of God satisfied the first condition. As high priest he could represent (all) human beings, precisely because he shared their condition, including growth, suffering, and death (5:5-9). The opening verses of chapter 5 address explicitly the (three) requirements that qualified Christ for his role as high priest. Elsewhere, Hebrews fills out the (first) priestly requirement of "being taken from among human beings." As "high priest" he could "sympathize" with "our weaknesses" by being tested/tempted in all ways (4:15). In "the days of his flesh," he prayed, and did so in painful and threatening situations (5:7). He grew, was tested, and was made perfect through suffering (2:10, 18), above all through enduring death (2:9, 14; 5:7), a death by crucifixion (6:6).

Jesus shared and shares humanity with all human beings, who are "the children" of the one God and Father, "for whom and through whom all things exist." As "originator" of their salvation, Christ goes before his "brothers and sisters" to deliver them from being enslaved to the fear and power of death (2:10-15). This passage will specify these "brothers and sisters" as "the descendants of Abraham" (2:16). Nevertheless, it is "sharing" the same human "flesh and blood" (2:14), through being created by the one divine Father, that makes the one human family, who have been delivered by the high priestly work of Christ. He became high priest not only for the descendants of Abraham but also for all who belong to the human family.

While death and exaltation proved the defining moment of Christ's priesthood, a priestly self-offering characterized his whole human existence (10:5-7). From the start, Hebrews links his priestly activity of purifying sin (1:2-4) with the incarnation, through which he entered into solidarity with all human beings. The incarnation allowed the Son of God to become a high priest for everyone.

This global perspective also builds on the priest-king Melchizedek, who blesses Abraham (Gen 14:17-20) and is called a "priest forever" (Ps 110:4). The mysterious person of Melchizedek provides a figure who is both prior to and superior to the (Jewish) Levitical priests. After three times attributing to Christ an eternal priesthood "according to the order of Melchizedek" (5:6, 10; 6:20), the author of Hebrews comes clean, so to speak, with his strategy: the priesthood of the mysterious priest-king was earlier and greater than the Levitical priesthood (7:1-28). Since the Scriptures do not mention Melchizedek's ancestors, birth, or death, he "remains" a priest forever (7:3), unlike the Levitical priests who all died and could not continue in office forever. Abraham gave Melchizedek a tenth of the spoils from a victory over "the kings" and received a blessing from him, thus showing how Melchizedek was greater than Abraham and his descendant Levi (the head of the priestly tribe). With the cornerstone of Melchizedek in place, Hebrews presses on to argue that, being a "priest forever according to the order of Melchizedek," Christ is superior to any Levitical high priest. He "holds his priesthood permanently" and "always lives to make intercession" for those who "approach God through him" (7:24-25). Thus Christ is not only a priest for everyone (see above) but for always. His priesthood is exercised for all people and for all time (and beyond).

As high priest, Christ functions as the "mediator of a new covenant" (9:15; 12:24). The new covenant provides a linchpin, without which Hebrews would fall apart. This definitive commitment of God is interpreted against the background of the Mosaic covenant with the Jewish people but stands in contrast with it as the "better" or fully efficacious covenant (8:7-13). But does this covenant brought about by Christ the high priest apply to the whole human race? At first glance, it appears to be limited to Christian believers.

Christ's sacrifice, Hebrews declares, has opened a new and living way into the presence of God and allows his followers to move in hope toward the inner shrine of heaven, where Jesus their "forerunner" and high priest belongs forever (10:19-20). They can continue to appropriate Christ's self-offering, knowing that he constantly "appears in the presence of God" on their behalf (9:24; see 6:20). Christ's priestly journey into the heavenly sanctuary has ended with his sitting at the right hand of God (1:3). But, for his followers, his priesthood continues forever, inasmuch as he "lives always" to "make intercession" for those who "approach God through him" (7:25). But what of all "the others"?

Sometimes Hebrews seems comprehensive in its proposals about the beneficiaries of Christ's priestly work. Jesus, it announces, "tasted [i.e., experienced] death for everyone" (2:9). Yet it can also propose that he "became the source of eternal salvation [only?] for all who obey him" (5:9). Receiving the offer of salvation prompts believers into following Jesus on the journey of faith. What then of those who, through no fault of their own, have never heard of Jesus and thus are not in a position to repent of their sins, to "obey" him, be delivered from death, and enjoy in glory the presence of God? It seems that for Hebrews salvation is available only to those who know of Christ's priestly work and can approach God's "throne of grace" to "receive mercy" for past sins and find grace for present and future "need" (4:10). Is the possibility of salvation through the new covenant restricted to those who consciously approach the royal throne of God through Jesus the high priest (7:25)?

A roll call of heroes and heroines of faith (11:1–12:1) does not list any Christians but only those who lived before Christ and hence could not consciously have accepted redemption coming through his priestly work. Not surprisingly, Hebrews proposes in chapter 11 an "open" version of faith: "the reality of things hoped for" and "the proof of things not seen. By this [faith] the elders [our ancestors] received approval. By faith we understand that the universe was fashioned by the word of God, so that from what cannot be seen that which is seen has come into being" (11:1-3). A further verse adds two (rather general) requirements to this "open" account of faith: "Without faith it is impossible to please God; for whoever would approach him must believe that he exists and that he rewards those who seek him" (11:6).

The opening three verses of Hebrews 11 highlight faith but say little about its content. The passage hints at the future. Divine promises (presumably of some eternal inheritance) have aroused the hope of human beings and their trust that God will keep these promises, which concern future things that are "not seen." Faith also involves a conviction about the past. One understands by faith the unseen origin of the world: it was "fashioned by the word of God." Just as people of faith rely on the word of God about the *genesis* of the universe, so too do they rely on the word of God's promise when considering the *goal* of the world and of their own existence. Both in their view of the past and their hope for the future, the lives of those who have faith are intertwined with the life of the invisible God.

This account of faith makes no mention of Christ. He will appear later, when the list of heroes and heroines of faith reaches the figure of Jesus, "the pioneer and perfector of faith" (12:2). The opening verses of Hebrews 11 have invoked "the elders" or "ancestors," people whom God honored for their persevering faith. Then follow examples of those who have lived on the basis of faith, with particular attention paid to Abraham, Sarah, and Moses. Some of those who exemplify faith (Abel, Enoch, and Noah) existed prior to Abraham, Sarah, and the formation of the chosen people. One figure of faith is "Rahab the prostitute," an outsider who belonged to the story of the conquest of the promised land (Josh 2:1-24; 6:22-25).

Hebrews 11:6 lets us glimpse the shape that the faith of outsiders can take. "Pleasing God" means doing the divine will, in particular, through deeds of kindness and service of others (13:16, 20-21). Such conduct need not depend upon a conscious relationship with Christ the high priest. A faith that "pleases" God is a possibility open to all. Likewise, "approaching" God in prayer does not necessarily depend upon an awareness of the priestly intercession of the exalted Christ. That intercession functions, whether or not worshippers are conscious of the priestly presence of Christ when they draw near to God in prayer. These and further aspects of Hebrews 11:6 spell out an "open" account of faith. Salvation through such faith is offered to all people and offered on the basis of the self-sacrificing priesthood of Christ, even if they are not (or are not yet) in a position to follow him in conscious obedience on the pilgrimage of faith.[23]

When pursuing the biblical witness to the relationship between the priestly work of Christ and the salvation offered to all people, Hebrews is the standout. It is the one New Testament book that gives him the title of "priest" (six times) or "high priest" (ten times). Nevertheless, strands of teaching from other New Testament authors also illuminate the priesthood of Christ and not least its impact on the whole human race.[24] Let me limit myself to Paul and John.

## Paul and John

Paul writes of the risen Christ who "intercedes for us" at the right hand of God (Rom 8:34). Hebrews was to take this language further by characterizing the permanent intercession as Christ being "a priest forever" (7:22, 24). Without applying the title "priest" to Christ, the apostle expounds themes about Christ's priesthood and, in particular, its universal significance.[25] In Romans, immediately after establishing that "all" human beings, Jews and Gentiles alike, "have sinned and fallen short of the glory of God" (3:23), Paul introduces sacrificial, priestly imagery to present Christ as the means for wiping away the

sins of humanity (3:25).[26] He then elaborately contrasts the surpass-
ing work of Christ for human salvation with the universal effects of
Adam's disobedience. Obviously using them as synonyms, the apostle
passes from speaking of "all" (5:12) to speaking of "the many" (5:15),
and then back to "all" (5:18) and, finally, back to "the many" (5:19).
For Paul, "the many" (*polloi*) is equivalent to "all" (*pantes*). In 2 Corinthians, the apostle simply uses "all": "One has died for all, therefore
all have died. And he died for all, so that those who live might live
no longer for themselves" (2 Cor 5:14-15). The priestly redemption,
effected by Christ's death and resurrection, has a universal impact.

In the seven letters commonly recognized as coming directly from
Paul (Romans, 1 and 2 Corinthians, Galatians, Philippians, 1 Thessa-
lonians, and Philemon), he never speaks of Jesus specifically as priest.
He attributes other titles to Jesus: above all, Christ/Messiah, Lord,
and Son of God. In the first of the Pastoral Epistles (which most scholars would not attribute in their present form to Paul), Jesus is called
"the one mediator between God and human beings, who gave himself
as a ransom for all" (1 Tim 2:5).[27] The verse points us toward two
other works of the New Testament. First, Hebrews also calls Christ
"mediator" and does so three times when it presents his priestly work
as being that of "the mediator of the new/better covenant" (Heb 8:6;
9:15; 12:24). Second, Mark's Gospel represents Jesus as the Son of
Man who came "to give his life as a ransom for many" (10:45). Here
"the many" is equivalent to "all" in 1 Timothy.

Even more than Paul, John's Gospel gets close to giving Jesus the
title of "priest," through applying to him priestly imagery and themes.[28]
In particular, the evangelist presents the high priest as clinching the
debate about killing Jesus with words that express simultaneously "a
criminal human calculation and a divine plan of redemption."[29] What
Caiaphas says enjoys prophetic value rooted in the priestly nature of
his office: "It is better to have one man die for the people than to
have the whole nation destroyed." As John comments, these words
reveal a central truth about Jesus as priest and victim: he was about
to die for the sake of and on behalf of the whole people, and that
people would include not only Israel but also all the scattered children
of God (11:49-52). The plan of Caiaphas to do away with Jesus had
unwittingly set in motion a "universal plan of salvation to produce
one people of God."[30]

Surely this strikingly universal passage from John about Christ as priest and victim should nourish *any* Christian theology of religions. But it remains sadly absent in current theologies of religion.

## SAMPLING THE TRADITION: PIUS XI AND
### *SACROSANCTUM CONCILIUM*

After sampling the New Testament on the significance of Christ's priesthood and its universal significance, we can investigate, albeit much more briefly, how the Christian tradition understood that priesthood. Reflections might be drawn from St. Augustine, other church fathers, St. Thomas Aquinas, Martin Luther, John Calvin, the seventeenth-century French School, and Blessed John Henry Newman. Let me limit myself to Pope Pius XI and the Second Vatican Council's Constitution on the Sacred Liturgy, *Sacrosanctum concilium.*

Luther, among other earlier writers, had recognized an intimate association between Christ's universal kingship and priesthood.[31] In the Feast of Christ the King, instituted by Pius XI in 1925, the preface addresses God the Father in the following words:

> You anointed Jesus Christ, your only Son, with the oil of gladness, as the eternal priest and universal king. As *priest* he offered his life on the altar of the cross and redeemed the human race by this one perfect sacrifice of peace. *As king* he claims dominion over all creation, so that he may present to you, his almighty Father, a universal kingdom: a kingdom of truth and life, a kingdom of holiness and grace, a kingdom of justice, love, and peace.[32]

Christ is being celebrated as king, but the preface (and, to some extent, the prayer over the gifts and the prayer after communion), without any special pleading, also attend to the priesthood of Christ. If distinguishable, the kingship and priesthood of Christ are inseparable; both extend to the whole "human race" and to "all creation." The preface calls him "eternal priest" and "universal king."[33] But it could have switched the adjectives and called him "universal priest" and "eternal king." Both his priesthood and his kingship are universal in their scope and eternal in their duration.

In the first document it promulgated (in 1963), Vatican II quoted (without giving the reference) a passage from Pius XII's 1947 encyclical, *Mediator Dei*.[34] Significantly, replacing "the Word of God" with a title that evokes Hebrews, *Sacrosanctum concilium* stated, "Jesus Christ, the High Priest of the New and Eternal Covenant, when he assumed a human nature, introduced into this land of exile the hymn that in heaven is sung throughout all ages. He unites the whole community of humankind with himself and associates it with him in singing the divine canticle of praise" (art. 83; translation mine). Earlier, the same constitution had taught that the risen Christ is present "when the Church prays *and sings*" (art. 7; emphasis added). Now, the same document summed up this singing as "one divine canticle of praise," led by the incarnate, high-priestly cantor. He associates with himself not only the church but also "the whole community of humankind" in singing a heavenly hymn that he has brought to earth. This picture brilliantly presents Christ the high priest as joining with himself, in virtue of his incarnation, all human beings without exception, including millions who will go through life without ever hearing his name. Without consciously knowing this, they belong to his cosmic chorus and are constantly affected by his priestly work.

## CHRIST'S PRIESTHOOD AND "THE OTHERS": SIX SYSTEMATIC POINTS

After sampling some items from the Scriptures and tradition, how would I propose relating systematically Christ's priesthood to the followers of other religions? What significance could that priesthood have for a theology of religions? Let me propose six points.

First, Christ's priesthood is made possible by his assuming a human existence (see Rahner and Hebrews above), through which he has become part (the supreme part) of creation and head of the human community. In its Declaration on the Relation of the Church to Non-Christian Religions (*Nostra aetate*), Vatican II named "stemming from the one stock which God created" as the initial reason for recognizing how all human beings form one community (art. 1). What makes Christ's priesthood possible—namely, his created humanity—is precisely what binds him to all people of all places and times. It is that created humanity which, from the outset, constitutes him in his universal priesthood.

To be sure, the institution of the Eucharist will prove a further decisive moment in constituting Christ as high priest.[35] But the Eucharist *also* embodies a cosmic, universal significance that involves all human beings and the whole created world. In a lyric passage, Pope John Paul II recalled how he had celebrated "Holy Mass in chapels built along mountain paths, on lakeshores and seacoasts": "I have celebrated it on altars built in stadiums and city squares. . . . This varied scenario of celebrations of the Eucharist has given me a powerful experience of its universal and, so speak, cosmic character." Echoing a famous work by Pierre Teilhard de Chardin (1881–1955),[36] the pope added:

> Even when it is celebrated on the humble altar of a country church, the Eucharist is always in some way celebrated *on the altar of the world*. It unites heaven and earth. It embraces and permeates all creation. The Son of God became man in order to *restore* all creation, in one supreme act of praise, to the One who made it out of nothing. He, the Eternal High Priest who by the blood of his Cross entered the eternal sanctuary, thus gives back to the Creator and Father all creation redeemed.[37]

What then "is accomplished in the Eucharist" is nothing less than "the world, which came forth from the hands of God the Creator," now returning "to him redeemed by Christ." The Eucharist "embraces" all creation and hence the entire human race. Christ, the invisible minister actively present at every celebration of the Eucharist, intends to accomplish through it the redemption of all human beings, Christians and non-Christians alike.

In the passage we have cited from John Paul II's encyclical, he did not link the priesthood of Christ with the followers of other religions. Yet to the extent that the Eucharist "embraces" the whole of creation, it involves all men and women and effectively links them with Christ the eternal high priest.

Second, from the time of Paul (1 Cor 15 and then Rom 5) and St. Irenaeus (in the second century), Christian theology, liturgy, art, drama, and legends have associated Christ with every man and every woman through two corporate figures: the first Adam of the Genesis story and Christ as the New or Last Adam.[38] The figures of Adam and Eve symbolize the human condition in its glory and misery. A hymn by a Latin poet Venantius Fortunatus (d. around 610), *"Crux fidelis"* ("faithful cross"), links two trees, the tree in the middle of the garden of Eden and the tree on Calvary, in one great drama of creation, fall, and redemption. The preface for the Feast of the Holy Cross or Exaltation of the Cross (September 14), a feast that goes back at least to the seventh century, declares, "Death came from a tree, life was to spring from a tree." Some imaginative writers and artists have also linked Adam and the Second Adam through the symbol of gardens: from the garden of Eden, over which Adam and Eve presided, to the garden of Gethsemane, the garden where Christ was buried and after his resurrection met Mary Magdalene (John 19:41-42; 20:11-18), and, finally, the garden of the heavenly Jerusalem that Christ as the slain and risen Lamb will illuminate (Rev 21:23; 22:1-2). Adam and Christ featured frequently in popular medieval drama. The Mystery Plays highlighted the connection between the two Adams by the practice of having the same actor portray both Adam and Christ.[39]

In connecting Adam and Christ, no work of literature has surpassed "Hymn to God My God in My Sickness," written by John Donne shortly before he died:

> We think that Paradise and Calvary,
> Christ's cross and Adam's tree, stood in one place.
> Look, Lord, and find both Adams met in me;
> As the first Adam's sweat surrounds my face,
> May the last Adam's blood my soul embrace.[40]

Donne recalls here an old and enduring legend that told the story of the tree from which Adam and Eve took the forbidden fruit and how it came to be used as the tree on which Christ died. According to a related legend, Calvary was the place where Adam was buried; accordingly, the Church of the Holy Sepulchre contains an "Adam Chapel." Christian artists at times placed his skull—and, occasionally, even his skeleton—at the foot of the cross. The New Adam died above the grave of the first Adam. Some artists pictured Adam and Eve standing together in a sarcophagus under the cross and looking up at the crucified Christ. A few representations have the figure of Adam holding a chalice to receive the first drops of blood falling from Christ on the cross.[41] The chalice symbolizes Adam's priesthood and links him (and Eve) with the defining moment in the exercise of Christ's priesthood, his death and exaltation.

One might recognize a prefiguring of this association by interpreting Adam and Eve as the priests of creation. In the Priestly tradition, being created in the image and likeness of God and as the crown of creation, the primeval couple have "dominion" over other created beings (Gen 1:26-31). Then follows a different tradition (often called Jahwist) of their being created in a garden (Gen 2:4b-25), which involves some ancient temple imagery. In this tradition, instead of being created earlier, animals and birds are created after Adam and brought to him to be named. Even if the text does not explicitly call Adam a "priestly king," that can describe his responsible place in creation and the stewardship he exercises. In particular, being created in the divine image, he resembles the coming Christ and qualifies to be understood as a priestly mediator of God's original covenant with humankind. But then, in disobediently eating of the fruit of the tree of knowledge of good and evil, Adam and Eve break their covenantal relationship and suffer the consequences (Gen 3:1-24).[42]

Acknowledging priestly overtones in the creation stories colors the meeting between Adam and the New Adam. We face a meeting between priests, one in which everyman and everywoman, represented by Adam and Eve, are blessed by the New or Last Adam. Such an elaboration of an Adam Christology provides a setting for recognizing how the priesthood of Christ had and continues to have its impact on the entire human race.

Eastern icons depicting Christ's passage down into the "limbo of the Fathers" and meeting with Adam and Eve—such as the sublime one in the monastery of Chora (Istanbul)—show large crowds of people standing behind them. In liberating and raising Adam and Eve, the Second Adam raises all humanity. To be sure, such icons do not expressly present Christ as the high priest, but they do not exclude reading the scene as a meeting between priests, which embodies a redemptive impact on the entire human race and the cosmos. Whatever use might be made of Eastern icons, the original priesthood of Adam (and Eve), which a fully deployed Adam Christology could incorporate, opens the way to appreciate how the exercise of Christ's priesthood (and, one should add, its sacramental enactment in the Eucharist) affects every human being, whether or not they ever become aware of this.

Thus, an Adam Christology, I would argue, opens up possibilities for a theology of religions, possibilities that have not yet been taken up. Dupuis moved in that direction by presenting creation as a cosmic event in which God made a universal covenant with humanity through

Adam and Eve. Although the Genesis story does not explicitly speak of a covenant relationship, Dupuis followed St. Irenaeus in recognizing a covenant given to the human race under Adam. Three further covenants followed: under Noah, under Moses, and, finally and supremely, under Christ.[43] Being involved in the making of the first covenant invested Adam, the representative of the human race, with some kind of priestly character.[44] But Dupuis did not pursue that line.

Third, John Henry Newman famously incorporated something of an Adam Christology in his hymn "Firmly I Believe and Truly." But it is elsewhere that we should look—to a sermon by Newman on Christ's priesthood and to one of his letters that offers hints about a primordial priesthood of all human beings, a priesthood that links them with Christ the high priest.

On April 6, 1851, when Newman chose to preach on the priesthood of Christ, he dwelt on a theme dear to Luther, Christ's priestly service for sinners, and applied the theme very broadly in the light of John 1:29 ("the lamb of God who takes away the sins of the world"). "What is a priest?" Newman asked. "See how much it implies: first the need for reconciliation; it has at once to do with sin; it presupposes sin. When then our Lord is known to come as priest, see how *the whole face of the world* is changed." Newman underlined the universal character of Christ's priestly service: "The Son of God offers for *the whole world*, and that offering is himself. He who is high as eternity, whose arms stretch through infinity, is lifted up on the cross for the sins of *the world*." Here Newman was even clearer about the universal scope of the beneficiaries of Christ's priestly sacrifice. Like Hebrews, Newman took up the language about Christ being "a priest forever according to the order of Melchizedek," but, unlike Hebrews, he applied it to the permanent sacrifice of the Mass: it is not "done and over; it lasts."[45]

Two decades later, in the aftermath of the First Vatican Council's definition of papal primacy and infallibility, William Gladstone questioned whether Catholics in the United Kingdom could remain loyal to their country. In an 1874 response to the prime minister, Newman famously portrayed conscience as taking precedence over any authority, papal or secular. He expressed this precedence by making use of the triple office of priest, prophet, and king: "Conscience is the aboriginal Vicar of Christ, a prophet in its information, a monarch in its peremptoriness, a priest in its blessings and anathemas, and, even though the eternal priesthood throughout the Church could cease to be, in it [the human conscience] the sacerdotal principle would remain and would have a sway."[46] Here Newman presented the triple office as if it were a spiritual genetic code that preexisted any institutional structures, and highlighted in particular "the sacerdotal principle" as intrinsically shaping the human spirit.

Naming the universally present human conscience a "sacerdotal principle" or "priest in its blessings and anathemas" could lead us to take a lead from Rahner and coin a new expression, the "sacerdotal principle," in which all human beings participate. Let me explain. Rahner famously introduced the term "supernatural existential" to describe the situation created for human freedom by the redemptive work of Christ. Even before they freely accept (or reject) grace, human beings are positively preconditioned from within by the divine self-communication offered to all in and through Christ. Hence "the expressly Christian revelation" is "the explicit statement of the revelation of grace," which all human beings already experience "implicitly in the depths" of their being.[47]

Likewise, "the sacerdotal existential," adumbrated by Newman, is the priestly condition in which all human beings participate. As "the aboriginal Vicar of Christ," it is "constituted" by the redemptive work of Christ. Through the sacerdotal existential, which is their conscience, human beings are positively preconditioned from within to share through baptism in the priesthood of Christ (and in his office as prophet and king). But they already experience that priesthood in the depths of their being and through the voice of conscience.

One might express this by saying that all human beings are, from their conception and birth, already priests (as well as prophets and kings/pastors). The sacerdotal existential suggests the way in which Christ's priestly work has already shaped them even before they ever have the chance of responding to what that work brings them in the offer of God's grace.

Fourth, the priesthood of Christ involved him not only in being tried and tested but also in becoming vulnerable to lethal persecution.[48] Extreme vulnerability, as the Letter to the Hebrews recognized, belonged to his job description as priest. By assuming the human condition and becoming a priest, the incarnate Son of God made himself subject to suffering and violent death (Heb 5:7-8). Becoming a priest involved becoming a victim—a new and disturbing aspect of

Christ's priesthood. This becoming personally the victim took him quite beyond the job description not only of the Levitical priests (who sacrificed animals as victims) but also of Melchizedek (who offered some bread and wine and was held up by Hebrews as foreshadowing Jesus the high priest to come). Everywhere, suffering characterizes the human condition, and Christ's priestly vulnerability puts him in solidarity with every sufferer.

Christ the high priest drew near to all human beings in pain. His self-sacrificing death on Calvary between two criminals symbolized forever his solidarity with and priestly function for those who suffer and die, an identification with human pain expressed also by the criteria for the Last Judgment (Matt 25:31-46). The final blessings of the kingdom will come to those who, without necessarily recognizing Christ, have met his needs in people who suffer by being hungry, thirsty, strangers, naked, sick, or imprisoned. To articulate the world-wide presence of Christ priest and victim in all who suffer, we might say, *Ubi dolor, ibi Christus sacerdos et victima* (wherever there is suffering, there is Christ priest and victim).

Fifth, for Hebrews, the death, resurrection, and glorification of Christ characterized essentially his priesthood. But this did not mean that everything that came before, above all his public ministry, was a mere prelude to the real exercise of his priesthood. His wise teaching during that ministry should also be recognized as priestly. Mediating the divine revelation to people belonged (and belongs) essentially to the work of priests.[49] The role of Jesus as preacher/teacher entered essentially into the exercise of his priesthood, as Origen, Luther, the French School, and others emphasized.[50] He continues to exercise his priesthood by being "the light of the world" and the incarnate wisdom of God.

Hence we should acknowledge the active, if mysterious, presence of Christ the priest wherever religious truth is taught in any cultures, societies, and religions. As the Second Vatican Council stated, "The precepts and doctrines" of other religions "often reflect a ray of that Truth that enlightens all people" (*Nostra aetate* 2). That is to acknowledge the priestly role of Christ as universal mediator of divine revelation and wisdom. Such mediation belongs essentially to the exercise of his priesthood.

Sixth, in the exercise of his priesthood, the risen and exalted Christ sends the Holy Spirit into the Church and the world. In John's

Gospel, Jesus says, "When the Paraclete comes whom I will send you from the Father, the Spirit of truth who proceeds from the Father, that One will bear witness to me" (John 15:26). The evangelist associates the Spirit not only with witnessing to Jesus but also with new birth and life (3:5-8; 4:10, 14; 7:37-39), with truth and teaching (14:16-17, 26; 16:13-15), and with mission and the forgiveness of sins (20:22-23). Such witnessing, giving new life, teaching the truth, and commissioning on the part of the Spirit are ongoing activities that involve a constant sending of the Spirit by the eternal high priest. Or, to put it another way, the Spirit universalizes the priestly work of Jesus. We might say, *Ubi Spiritus Sanctus, ibi Christus sacerdos* (wherever there is the Holy Spirit, there is Christ the priest).[51]

In modern times few have done more to emphasize the universal presence and activity of the Holy Spirit than Pope John Paul II.[52] No individual and no culture or religion is simply outside the influence of the Spirit. The Holy Spirit, sent by Christ the high priest, is incessantly active everywhere and for everyone. Our reflections on the universal presence of the Spirit should factor in the universal presence of Christ in the eternal exercise of his priesthood.

Here then are six systematic ways of thinking about the followers of other faiths and indeed of all human beings, ways that draw inspiration from the priesthood of Jesus Christ. Like his kingship, that priesthood has no limits and will have no end. It throws much light on the situation and destiny of those who follow other faiths or who follow none. Yet, so far, in the theology of religions, the universal priesthood of Christ has remained an untold story. The theology of religions would, I believe, be greatly enriched by incorporating "the sacerdotal principle" that would honor the priestly activity of Christ for the good of all human beings.

# 7

# Jacques Dupuis and Religious Pluralism

In late 1997 Jacques Dupuis (1923–2004)[1] of the Gregorian University (Rome) brought out a 447-page theological reflection on Christianity and other religions.[2] Written originally in English, this book appeared almost simultaneously in French and Italian, and subsequently in Portuguese (1999) and Spanish (2000). In the spring of 1998, the Congregation for the Doctrine of the Faith (hereafter CDF) began an investigation of the book, which culminated in the *Notification* published on January 24, 2001. While stating that the "book contained notable ambiguities and difficulties on important doctrinal points, which could lead a reader to erroneous or harmful opinions," the CDF did not ask Dupuis to change a single line in his text but only to include the text of the *Notification* in "any reprinting or further editions of his book, as well as in all translations."[3]

The literature and documentation on *Toward a Christian Theology of Religious Pluralism* are vast. An article written by Dupuis himself for *Louvain Studies* took into account twenty reviews that had appeared in English and twenty-seven in French.[4] Some of these, such as the assessment by Terrence Merrigan in *Louvain Studies*, entered into critical dialogue with Dupuis in a way that was admirable; others, such as an equally long piece in *Revue Thomiste*, seemed an odd going back to a dead past.[5] In all, there were well over one hundred reviews in English, French, German, Italian, Portuguese, Spanish, and other languages, as well as articles in journals and chapters in books dedicated, in whole or in part, to a critical evaluation of Dupuis' views.[6]

Shortly after *Toward a Christian Theology of Religious Pluralism* appeared in October 1997, the publishing house of Queriniana (Brescia) asked Dupuis to write a shorter, more accessible version. This time he wrote in Italian, and after some delay the book was published in the fall of 2001.[7]

Clearly, Dupuis addressed a central question: How can Christians profess and proclaim faith in Jesus Christ as the one redeemer of all humankind, and at the same time recognize the Spirit at work in the world's religions and cultures—as was done by Pope John Paul II?[8] From a Christian perspective, what is the place in God's providence for the other religions, some of which predate the birth of Christ (e.g., Hinduism), and what beneficial contribution do they make toward the salvation of their followers? As revealer and redeemer, Jesus is unique and universal, but in practice the visible paths to salvation have remained many. What might the various religious traditions mean in the one divine plan to save humanity?

After Dupuis died on December 28, 2004, his views have continued to be cited, approved, or criticized. Most of those who write on Dupuis concentrate on his *Toward a Christian Theology of Religious Pluralism*; only a few also take into account his subsequent *Christianity and the Religions*, in which he clarified his "inclusive pluralism,"[9] qualified his language about the "complementarity" (between Christianity and other religions) by calling it "asymmetrical complementarity,"[10] dropped the terminology of the "Logos *asarkos*" and the "Logos *ensarkos*" (to speak rather of "the Word as such" and "the Word as incarnate"),[11] introduced some of the teaching of the Third Council of Constantinople (680–681) (to support his position about the actions of Christ's divine nature and human nature being "distinct" but inseparable),[12] and made other changes.

Keeping in mind a certain shift from Dupuis' longer 1997 book to what he published in his 2001 work,[13] let me set myself now to present and evaluate (in chronological order) some of the discussion that has appeared in English after 2004.[14] The (seven) interlocutors run from Terrence Merrigan in 2005 to Keith Johnson in 2011. When discussing theological method, the nature of interreligious dialogue, and other issues raised by Dupuis, some prove, as we will see, open to his proposals, while others remain somewhat negative. All the interlocutors illustrate the enduring significance of his work. But, like Dupuis himself, they continue to overlook two items of vital significance in this area: (a) the (efficient) causality of love exercised when the church prays for those of other religious faiths; and (b) the central role of Christ's priesthood.

This article aims to establish three conclusions. First, the debate over the views of Dupuis, far from dwindling away after his death, has continued vigorously. Some of the seven scholars chosen for this article have written at greater length (e.g., Gavin D'Costa); others, at less. But we need to cite a range of authors to have an adequate sense of the ongoing debate and the issues that remain alive. This account of the debate will also involve responding to certain misplaced criticisms made by some of the interlocutors. Second, when discussing the mediation of salvation, some, like Dupuis himself, have attended to the Church's activity in praying for "the others." But neither he nor anyone else has appreciated that, being inspired and fuelled by *love*, that prayer enjoys not merely moral and final causality but even some efficient causality. Third, the mediatorial activity of the Church draws on and remains subordinate to that of Christ (and his Holy Spirit). His high-priestly mediation is very significant for the theology of religions but remains universally neglected. Let me begin with a chapter written by Merrigan for a book in collaboration.[15]

## TERRENCE MERRIGAN ON THE CHURCH'S MEDIATION (2005)

Merrigan, who had not only in 1998 reviewed Dupuis' *Toward a Christian Theology of Religious Pluralism* but also in 2003 contributed to the Festschrift in his honor,[16] observes perceptively that his conflict with the CDF "represented a decisive moment in the contemporary Catholic understanding of religions." In the whole debate, Merrigan names as "the most significant issue" the precise role of the church "with respect to the salvation of those who do not belong to her." How does the church mediate salvation to non-Christians?[17]

Merrigan recalls Dupuis' position: the church is an effective instrument of salvation for its own members but for others exercises only "moral" and "final" causality by interceding for them. That position involved acknowledging an intrinsic mediatory value in non-Christian religions for the salvation of their followers. When presenting and defending his views on the church's limited mediatorial role for "the others," Dupuis enlisted the support of Yves Congar. Merrigan raises this question: Was Congar a clear ally in Dupuis' efforts to circumscribe the church's mediation of salvation to those "outside"?[18] Merrigan's close analysis of what Dupuis drew from Congar and how he interpreted those texts suggests a certain divergence. Unlike Dupuis and somewhat ambiguously, Congar defended a universal role for the church in mediating salvation "efficiently."[19]

As regards the mediatory value of other religions, Congar at a 1971 conference declined to conclude that "these religions are divinely legitimated *in themselves* and *as such*. Their value derives from the persons who live them."[20] Speaking at the same conference, Dupuis took a different line: "It is said that, though non-Christians are saved due to the sincerity of their subjective religious life, their religion has for them no objective salvific value. However, the dichotomy on which this restriction is based, is seriously inadequate. Subjective and objective religion can be distinguished; they cannot be separated." Dupuis went on to say that it is "theologically unrealistic to maintain that, though non-Christians can be saved, their religion plays no part in their salvation." This led him to this conclusion: "No religious life is purely natural," and "no historical religion is merely human."[21] Dupuis was to put this positively in his 1997 book: "In the overall history of God's dealings with humankind," the world's religions express "distinct modalities of God's self-communication to persons and peoples."[22] As Merrigan remarks, the controversial position expounded by Dupuis in 1997 was nothing more or less than "the working out" of what he had said in 1971.[23] From the 1970s one could also cite Dupuis' comments on the apostolic exhortation of Pope Paul VI, *Evangelii nuntiandi*, where he urged that the non-Christian religions should be seen not "merely as expressions of human aspirations towards God but [also] as embodying for their followers a first, though incomplete, approach of God to human beings."[24]

Merrigan, reflecting on the divergence between Congar and Dupuis, associates their interest in the *mediation* of salvation with the sacramental nature of the church.[25] Beyond question, the church is an instrument of salvation for non-Christians who do not and never will belong to her. We will see how the church's liturgical life is also effective for them.

Nevertheless, important as it is to recognize the church as universal sign and sacrament of salvation, it is even more important here to acknowledge the *priesthood* of Christ and its universal impact—something relentlessly ignored, as we will continue to see below, by those who reflect of the salvation of "the others." The sacramental work of the church must not be downplayed, but it depends upon and is incorporated into Christ's exercise of his priestly function, a function that not only involves the sacramental life of the church but also goes beyond it to affect all humankind. Vatican II's Constitution on the Sacred Liturgy, *Sacrosanctum concilium*, pictured strikingly the worldwide force of Christ's priesthood: "Jesus Christ, the High Priest of the New and Eternal Covenant, when he assumed a human nature, introduced into this land of exile the hymn that in heaven is sung throughout all ages. He unites the whole community of humankind with himself and associates it with him in singing the divine canticle of praise" (art. 83; translation mine).

In the Eucharist, the crucified and risen Christ, invisibly but really, lovingly presents to the Father his self-offering on behalf of all people and, mysteriously but truly, draws them into his own self-offering. In the celebration of the Eucharist, the administration of the other sacraments, and beyond, but supremely in and through the celebration of the Eucharist, Christ continues his high-priestly, mediating role not only for the faithful who take part in the liturgy but also for all human beings and, indeed, the whole created world. As Tom Torrance remarks, "When the Church at the Eucharist intercedes in his [Christ's] name for all mankind, it is Christ himself who intercedes in them."[26] Below we will return to the question of the mediation of the church's prayer exercised at common worship. But we should never forget that this mediation depends upon and remains subordinate to the priestly self-offering of Christ, who intercedes before the face of the Father for the baptized faithful *and* for the entire human race. The priestly intercession of Christ, if we want to apply to it Aristotelian-style language, is a supremely "efficient" and no "merely moral" cause.[27] Below I will take up again the significance of Christ's priestly ministry—something glossed over not only by Dupuis himself but also by his commentators and critics.

## MARA BRECHT ON THE HUMANITY OF CHRIST
### (2008)

Like Don Schweitzer (as we will see), Mara Brecht explores Dupuis' thinking about other religious traditions and Christianity's relationship to them within the context of his Christology. She writes, "Unless one reads his view of religious pluralism through the lens of his Christology, one mistakes its status."[28] Unlike any of the other six authors examined in this chapter, she also presents his theological method, which correlates Christian tradition and experience, before she evaluates his position on other religions.[29]

Where, as we shall see, Gavin D'Costa associates Dupuis with Karl Rahner, Brecht is at pains to show how Dupuis went beyond Rahner. She touches, for instance, on one point that sets Dupuis and Rahner apart.[30] Rahner persistently named Christ as "absolute Savior."[31] Whatever Rahner's reasons for this expression, Dupuis maintained a firmly Thomistic line: only God—who is totally necessary, utterly unconditioned, uncaused, and unlimited—is truly absolute. While Dupuis certainly never wanted to reduce Christ to being one Savior among many, he was sensitive to the limits involved in the historical incarnation of the Son of God, the created character of the humanity he assumed, and the specific quality of his redemptive human actions. Moreover, the incarnation itself was a free act of God's love and not unconditionally necessary. Dupuis could never apply to Christ the title of "absolute Savior," but called him "constitutive" for human salvation.[32]

Brecht aims, above all, to highlight the importance for Dupuis of Christ's humanity: "By reason of his humanity he is uniquely related to the whole human universe." This means that Christ's "claim and effect on humanity cannot be restricted to any earthly institution."[33] Although they do not make this connection, Brecht and Dupuis have Vatican II's Pastoral Constitution on the Church in the Modern World (*Gaudium et spes*) on their side. After retrieving the patristic theme about the incarnation ("by his incarnation, the Son of God has in a certain fashion united himself with every human being"), *Gaudium et spes* went on to teach that all human beings can share in Christ's "paschal mystery" (art. 22)—a striking statement about his "claim and effect on humanity" not being "restricted to any earthly institution," including the church.

While one should value Brecht's emphasis on Christ's humanity, she (and before her Dupuis himself) failed to attend to a significant consequence of the incarnation. By taking on the human condition, the Son of God could now exercise a priestly function for the human race. A straight line led from his assumption of humanity to his being the high priest for all men and women of all times and places.

## CATHERINE CORNILLE: FOUR THEMES (2008)

Catherine Cornille signaled her interest in the work of Dupuis by inviting him to contribute to a work she edited in 2002.[34] *The Im-pos-sibility of Interreligious Dialogue* shows that she has not lost that interest after his death.[35] She highlights four significant themes in his *Toward a Christian Theology of Religious Pluralism* and does not neglect modifications Dupuis subsequently introduced in *Christianity and the Religions*.

Firstly, she appreciates Dupuis' respect for the fullness of the reign of God to come. This means that, while recognizing "a privileged role for Christian revelation and the church," he regarded all religions "as oriented towards an ultimate state of realization that is beyond any one particular religion."[36] Second, she notes how Aloysius Pieris had employed the category of "complementarity" eight years before Dupuis used it in *Toward a Christian Theology of Religious Pluralism* (1997). But she recognizes the force of characterizing such complementarity as "asymmetrical," a modification that Dupuis introduced in *Christianity and the Religions* (2002). It reminds "us of the impossibility of reconciling religious commitment with a recognition of the radical equality of religions." Cornille quotes what Dupuis wrote in his 2002 book: "[It is] in this fidelity to personal, non-negotiable convictions, honestly accepted on both sides, that the interreligious dialogue takes place 'between equals'—in their differences."[37]

Third, Cornille observes that Dupuis faced religious pluralism within a Trinitarian framework, focusing primarily on the Holy Spirit. She writes, "Without denying the inseparability of the Spirit from the Son," Dupuis emphasized the distinctive role of the Holy Spirit in an economy of salvation.[38] Here Dupuis spelled out at much greater length what John Paul II taught about the presence and activity of the Holy Spirit in the cultures and religions of the world.[39] Fourth, Cornille wants to restore "empathy" in the context of interreligious dialogue. Hence she is attracted by what Dupuis wrote about the depth of religious experience and the struggle to express this in words. Empathy can help us understand and interpret what the "others" contribute to interreligious dialogue.[40] What she says in this connection makes me regret a little that she does not engage with Dupuis over what he proposed concerning interreligious prayer.[41] She examines mysticism and intermonastic dialogue,[42] but I would gladly have heard her reaction to Dupuis on interreligious prayer.

## GAVIN D'COSTA: A MAJOR CRITIC (2009, 2010)

Back in 1998, Gavin D'Costa published a lengthy review of Dupuis' *Toward a Christian Theology of Religious Pluralism*.[43] That review anticipated some of the comments and criticisms that D'Costa would later repeat and develop after the death of Dupuis in 2004. For instance, (1) he argued, "Dupuis is basically a Rahnerian. . . . Theologically, he carries on from where Rahner left off."[44] (2) He also linked the views of Dupuis (later called "inclusive pluralism" by Dupuis himself) with those of Paul Knitter,[45] even though he was aware that Dupuis strongly distanced himself from the pluralist paradigm of Knitter. (3) D'Costa claimed that Dupuis held that both Christ and the kingdom "can be severed from the Church." In other words, Dupuis "breaks the link between Christology and ecclesiology."[46] This strong language about "severing" and "breaking" the link between the kingdom of God and the Church seems quite incompatible with what Dupuis wrote about the Church as sacrament of the kingdom. He argued that, while not identical with the kingdom, the Church remains the efficacious sign of the reign of God already present in history.[47] As for any "breaking the link between Christology and ecclesiology" (or, to put this more concretely, between the risen Christ and the Church), Dupuis stated clearly that the Christ remains the head of the Church, with his reign extending beyond the Church: "The kingship of Christ extends not only to the Church but also to the whole world."[48] The generalizing and unqualified language used here by D'Costa seemed prompted by his disagreement with Dupuis over a specific issue: the extent of the mediatorial activity of the Church. We will come back to that shortly when examining two books in which he discussed the theology of Dupuis: first in 2009 and then in 2010.

In *Christianity and World Religions*, D'Costa, while critically expounding what he called the "structural inclusivism" of Karl Rahner,[49] introduces Dupuis and names him as a "neo-Rahnerian."[50] Although Dupuis, in both *Toward a Christian Theology of Religious*

*Pluralism* and *Christianity and the Religions*, refers to or quotes from Rahner more than any other modern theologian, did that make Dupuis a "neo-Rahnerian"? In all the years that I spent with Dupuis, I never heard him suggest that he belonged to Rahner's "school." Of course, he could have been a "neo-Rahnerian" without realizing it. We would need to compare and contrast in considerable detail the theology and, specifically, the theology of religions developed by Rahner and Dupuis to reach a truly justified conclusion about naming or not naming Dupuis as a "neo-Rahnerian" (see below in the next chapter).

In *Christianity and World Religions*, D'Costa comments that Dupuis did not endorse "the provisional status of other religions as salvific structures," and that this was "one reason" why the CDF questioned Dupuis' *Toward a Christian Theology of Religious Pluralism*. Presumably, D'Costa has in mind section IV of the *Notification* ("On the orientation of all human beings to the Church") and, in particular, number 7: "According to Catholic doctrine, the followers of other religions are oriented to the Church and are called to be part of her." This affirmation could appeal to *Lumen gentium* 15 ("all human beings are called to belong to the new People of God") and to what number 16 says about all people being "ordained" or related to the Church—language that reaches back through Pius XII's 1943 encyclical, *Mystici corporis*, to the theology of Thomas Aquinas.[51] This question, however, remains: What of those millions who—while being "ordained" to the Church and "called" to belong to her, nevertheless, for a variety of reasons (often not implying their sinful refusal of God's call)—did not come to Christian faith and baptism and eventually died as faithful followers of other religions? As far as they were concerned, the religions that they conscientiously practiced and through which the light and grace of Christ mysteriously came to them were not "provisional." These living faiths provided the permanent salvific structures for their entire existence. In section V of the *Notification* ("On the value and salvific function of the religious traditions"), the CDF speaks of "the elements of truth and goodness present in the various world religions," which "*may* prepare peoples and cultures to receive the salvific event of Jesus Christ" (no. 8; emphasis added). The CDF does *not* claim that such elements will infallibly prepare people to receive the gospel of Christ. This may happen, but obviously not always. Hence the CDF refrains from presenting as necessarily "provisional" what the adherents of other religions receive through the elements of truth and goodness and all that D'Costa calls "the salvific structures" of the other faiths.

Finally, in his 2009 book, D'Costa comes to the mediatorial activity of the Church and, in particular, to the mediation of salvation through liturgical prayer for all people. He recalls what Francis Sullivan had proposed about "the instrumental causality" being at work when the church prays for all people.[52] Dupuis questioned this and, appealing to Yves Congar, argued that "the causality involved is not of the order of efficiency but of the moral order and finality."[53] Against Dupuis, D'Costa cites number 6 of the CDF's *Notification on Toward a Christian Theology of Religious Pluralism*: "It must be firmly believed that the Church is sign and instrument of salvation for all people."[54] D'Costa rightly insists against Dupuis that it is through instrumental causality that the church's liturgical prayers mediate salvation. Merely moral or final causality do not describe adequately what such prayers involve.

Yet none of those involved in this debate (Sullivan, Dupuis, and then D'Costa) recognized that it is precisely the (efficient) *causality of love* that is at work. The church at worship prays for the salvation and well-being of all people, because she regards them with love. Here I obviously disagree with those who think of love as merely a subjective disposition and—unlike Dante Alighieri, Charlotte Brontë, Fyodor Dostoevsky, Pierre Teilhard de Chardin, and other classical authors—fail to acknowledge love as a powerful, efficient cause: the "love that moves the sun and the other stars," to quote the final words of the *Divine Comedy*.

D'Costa stood apart by quoting the bidding prayers of the Good Friday liturgy. But neither he nor Sullivan and Dupuis noticed what the Second Vatican Council did in restoring the "prayer of the faithful," an old tradition that had disappeared in the Roman liturgy, except on Good Friday. This prayer was restored after the gospel and homily, especially on all Sundays and holidays of obligation. The Constitution on the Sacred Liturgy explained, "By this prayer in which the people are to take part, intercessions are to be made for the holy Church, for those who lead us politically, for those weighed down by various needs, *for all human beings, and for the salvation of the entire world*" (*Sacrosanctum concilium* 53; emphasis added). It is through such loving prayer for all people that the church at worship proves to be God's instrument in mediating salvation to the world.

In a 2010 work in collaboration that ran to over six hundred pages, Gavin D'Costa engaged again with the views of Dupuis. When dealing with "pluralist arguments" and, in particular, with the writing of Knitter, D'Costa remarks, "This emphasis [Knitter's emphasis] on the Spirit as a way of endorsing other religions as God-given and inspired, without having to have an anonymous Christ present, is to be found in the works of [Roger] Haight, [Georges] Khodr, Knitter, and, with a twist, Dupuis."[55] "With a twist," an unusual expression to use in a theological context, presumably means "with a small variation." Whether or not the picture, of the Spirit present and Christ absent, accurately represents the views of Knitter, not to mention Haight and Khodr, the passage gravely misrepresents what Dupuis wrote in *Toward a Christian Theology of Religious Pluralism*. There he persistently upheld what cannot be separated, "the universal presence and activity of the Word and the Spirit."[56] For Dupuis, the activity and presence of the Son of God and the Holy Spirit are distinguishable but never separable. Picking up the image of St. Irenaeus, Dupuis insisted that the two "hands of God" are "paired hands"; while "distinct," they are "united and inseparable."[57]

D'Costa, having in his main text lined Dupuis up with the pluralist theologians,[58] in an endnote makes this acknowledgment: "Dupuis is admittedly critical of this tendency [Spirit present but Christ absent] in Knitter." Yet D'Costa presses on at once to say that Dupuis "is found guilty of ambiguity on this point in the Congregation for the Doctrine of the Faith's *Notification* on his book."[59] In the literal sense, "guilt" belongs to one's deliberate (and deliberately malicious) intentions. Where D'Costa states flatly that Dupuis was "found guilty of ambiguity," the CDF explicitly refrained from any judgment about Dupuis' intentions. It simply presented the Church's teaching so as to counter "erroneous or harmful opinions" that "could be derived from reading the ambiguous statements and insufficient explanations found in certain sections of the book," sections that were never named.[60] The CDF considered some of Dupuis' statements (which, however, it failed to specify) to be ambiguous but refused to attribute deliberate ambiguity to Dupuis himself.

When D'Costa refers above to "this point" (the theory of the Spirit being present but Christ being absent), he does not indicate which paragraph of the *Notification* he has in mind. But it is clearly number 5, which makes a positive statement and immediately appends a negative judgment: "The Church's faith teaches that the Holy Spirit, working after the resurrection of Jesus Christ, is always the Spirit of Christ sent by the Father, who works in a salvific way in Christians as well as non-Christians. It is therefore contrary to Catholic faith to hold that the salvific action of the Holy Spirit extends beyond the one, universal salvific economy of the incarnate Word." Here, as when the *Notification* speaks elsewhere about what is "contrary to Catholic faith," it cites no passages from Dupuis' book and does not offer any references to it. In fact (there are no passages that could be cited and no references that could be given), Dupuis never expressed the view (which maintains two "economies" of salvation) that is here (correctly) labeled as "contrary to Catholic faith." As we saw above, he insisted that the presence and activity of the Spirit and the Word are "united and inseparable." He never divided the divine "economy" of salvation into two separate "economies," the salvific economy of the incarnate Word and a more universal and extensive "economy" of the Holy Spirit.

Finally, D'Costa writes of Dupuis, "He also makes too sharp a distinction between the *Logos asarkos* and *ensarkos*, [an issue] also raised by the CDF."[61] Here D'Costa does not seem to be aware that Dupuis had changed his terminology. *Toward a Christian Theology of Religious Pluralism* distinguished the Logos *asarkos* (the Word of God as such and not, or not yet, incarnated) from the Logos *ensarkos* (the Word of God precisely as incarnated). Dupuis was surprised to find this distinction leading a few readers to imagine that he was "doubling" the Logos and speaking of two "Logoi" or "Words" (one *asarkos* and the other *ensarkos*). For "clarity's sake" he decided to put the distinction in terms of "the action of the Word-to-be-incarnate (*Verbum incarnandum*), that is, the Word before the incarnation," and "the action of the Word incarnate (*Verbum incarnatum*), either in the state of kenosis during his human life or after the resurrection in the glorified state."[62] He went on to distinguish, more briefly, between the action of the Word of God "before the incarnation" and "after the incarnation and resurrection," and, even more briefly, the Word "as such" and "as incarnate."[63]

When introducing such a "sharp" (that is to say, clean-cut and well-defined) distinction in Christology, Dupuis was following in the footsteps of St. Thomas Aquinas and his use of reduplicative statements (as, *qua*, insofar as, inasmuch as) in the christological section of

his *Summa theologiae*. The "inasmuch as" characteristic of a reduplicative statement indicates the manner in which a particular predicate
can be truthfully attributed to a particular subject. Thus Aquinas
distinguishes Christ "as subsistent subject" or divine agent, on the
one hand, from Christ "as man," on the other. As man, Christ is a
creature, is not eternal, and begins to exist.[64] It was by forgetting the
force of such reduplicative statements that two critics of Dupuis at
the CDF allowed themselves to say that the Word "as such" is the
Word incarnate.[65] This would mean that, by definition and hence
necessarily and always, the Word *is* the Word incarnate. We would
need then to rewrite John's prologue and make it read, "In the beginning was the Word incarnate, and the Word incarnate was with God,
and the Word incarnate was God." This would mean falling into the
error condemned by the CDF's own declaration issued on September
5, 2000: namely, that of "a metaphysical emptying of the event of
the eternal Logos's historical incarnation." That would reduce the
incarnation "to a mere appearing in history" of the Logos "already"
incarnated "from the beginning."[66] *Pace* D'Costa, Dupuis needed to
make a "sharp distinction" between the Word "before" and "after"
the incarnation, or between the Word "as such" and the Word "as
incarnate."

When D'Costa refers to an issue "raised by the CDF" (see above),
he gives no precise reference but presumably means number 2 in the
text of the *Notification*. After rightly noting "the unity of the divine
plan of salvation centred in Jesus Christ," it added a negative judgment: "It is therefore contrary to Catholic faith not only [a] to posit
a separation between the Word and Jesus, or [b] between the Word's
salvific activity and that of Jesus, but also [c] to maintain that there is
a salvific activity of the Word as such in his divinity, independent of
the humanity of the incarnate Word." Once again, the *Notification*
neither cited any passages from Dupuis' book nor offered any references to it. Did the CDF want to imply that Dupuis (mistakenly) held
these views but, for some undisclosed reason, refrained from providing the evidence? What in fact did he propose in *Toward a Christian
Theology of Religious Pluralism*?

As regards (a), Dupuis never separated the Word from Jesus. *Au
contraire*, he stated clearly that "the Word cannot be separated from
the flesh it has assumed." He wrote of "the divine Word and Jesus'
human existence" as being inseparable.[67] As regards (b), Dupuis never

alleged that "the Word's salvific activity" was or is "separate" from the salvific activity of Jesus. What he argued on the basis of John 1:9 was that "the saving action of God through the non-incarnate Logos (Logos *asarkos*)" continues "after the incarnation of the Logos" (John 1:14). He went on to explain that "the human action of the Logos *ensarkos*" does not "exhaust the action of the Logos." A "distinct" (but not separate) "action of the Logos *asarkos* endures," but not "as constituting a distinct economy of salvation, parallel to that realized in the flesh of Christ."[68] This is carefully chosen language: some activity of the Logos *asarkos* or Logos eternally as such is "distinct" and enduring (e.g., the work of conserving the universe and guiding all things through the divine providence). Yet such continuing activity does *not* constitute even a "distinct economy of salvation," still less a separate economy. One can relate the argument of Dupuis to the teaching of the Third Council of Constantinople and Thomas Aquinas.

Constantinople III defended the presence in Christ of a complete human nature with its complete human operations, and so upheld in him a duality of natures and a unity of agent.[69] Obviously, the Council's focus of attention was not precisely on distinguishing (1) the ongoing, postincarnation, *divine* operations effected by the incarnate Word of God from (2) the human operations of the same agent (whose actual human operations began with the incarnation). Nevertheless, the Council's insistence on the continuing presence in the *one* Christ not only of *two* wills but, more generally, of *two* "natural operations," which are to be distinguished and not blended or amalgamated, does not seem compatible with holding that the infinitely powerful, unlimited divine activity of the Logos is limited by, must "pass through," or is somehow determined or even "eclipsed" by his humanity assumed at the incarnation and glorified through the resurrection. In the incarnation the Son of God's divine nature does not lose any of its essential characteristics and, in particular, its operations that are strictly infinite and uniquely divine and in that sense transcend the finite operations of his human nature, even while being constantly related to it. A remark by Aquinas seems apropos here. He both championed the oneness of Christ's person *and* recognized that Christ's "divine nature [with its operations] infinitely transcends his human nature [with its operations]," while remaining always inseparable from that human nature.[70]

In the book examined by the CDF, Dupuis did not cite Constantinople III in support of his position about the divine activity of the incarnate Logos not being limited by his humanity. In *Christianity and the Religions*, he briefly drew attention to the importance of this council's teaching on the universal salvific activity of the divine Word "before" and "after" the incarnation.[71] In general, however, the highly relevant teaching of Constantinople III has hardly surfaced in the whole debate about the views of Dupuis. That teaching also supported some pertinent remarks by Thomas Aquinas about "the soul of Christ" and its operations, since and inasmuch as they are created, not being "almighty."[72]

What of the view that the CDF declared to be "contrary to Catholic faith"—namely, (c) maintaining "that there is a salvific activity of the Word as such in [surely it would be better to say "through"] his divinity, independent of the humanity of the incarnate Word"? The key word here is "independent." There can or should be no doubt about the "salvific activity of the Word as such," being exercised both "before" the incarnation and "after" the incarnation and resurrection. To allege otherwise would be incompatible with the doctrine of Constantinople III. But did Dupuis ever argue that this divine activity was/is "independent" of the humanity of the incarnate Word and the activity exercised through that humanity? He explicitly rejected such a vision: "The Word cannot be separated from the flesh it has assumed."[73] It was no wonder that the CDF could not refer to even one passage where Dupuis asserted that the activity of the Word was "independent" of the humanity that it had assumed at the incarnation.

I have taken issue with several criticisms that, somewhat in dependence on the CDF's 2001 *Notification*, D'Costa brought against Dupuis. Moreover, as we have seen, D'Costa, like others (including Dupuis himself), never attributed the mediation of grace either to the *love* at work in the church's liturgy or to the universal role of *priesthood* that the risen and exalted Christ continues to exercise.

## ILARIA MORALI ON AMBIGUITIES (2010)

Ilaria Morali, who studied with Dupuis at the Gregorian University (where she now teaches), begins her comments on his work by stating that the *Notification* issued by the CDF did not condemn him, recognized his "intellectual honesty," and expressed no judgment on

his "subjective thought."[74] She also differs from D'Costa by insisting
that "it would be an error to reduce or even to associate too closely"
the views of Dupuis with those "of such authors as Knitter or Hick."
She continues, "Dupuis's method of argumentation, and his tenacious
desire to remain firmly anchored in the Christian faith, set him light
years apart from the pluralists, who are much less concerned than he
about keeping their thought within the confines of orthodoxy."[75] By
proposing in an earlier work what he called "inclusive Christocentrism," he disagreed with "most pluralist authors" by holding that
Christocentrism and theocentrism do not constitute "two different
and [even] opposite points of view, but together constitute the very
character of Christian theology, which 'is theocentric insofar as it is
Christocentric, and vice versa.' "[76]

Morali agrees with the CDF that three positions defended by
Dupuis in his 1997 book do "admit of some ambiguity—likely inevitable, given his treatment of questions the *Notification* itself described
as hitherto unexplored. These ambiguities touch on [a] the interpretation of Christ's uniqueness, [b] the way of understanding the saving
action of the Spirit, and [c] the salvific value of religions."[77] Although
she mentions in an endnote the issue raised by the CDF over "the
orientation of all people to the Church,"[78] the mediation of salvation
through the church does not become an issue for her, as it does for
Merrigan and D'Costa. Apropos of the three positions with which she
has difficulties, Morali presses on at once to recall how Dupuis himself had admitted the "intentionally tentative" character of his book
and how he made a "gentle reply" to his reviewers: "I am the first to
be aware of this [the problematic character of my work]. It is in fact
my awareness that I desired clearly to express in the very same title of
the book: *Toward* a *Theology of Religious Pluralism*."[79]

Despite the ambiguities she detects, Morali judges Dupuis' work
to be "worthy of appreciation. He must be given credit for having
sought to delineate, in harmony with the data of faith, a way *toward*
a theology that could somehow incorporate the achievements of the
*praxis* of interreligious dialogue, of which he was a firsthand witness
for thirty years in India." Morali ends by evoking the traumatic experience of Dupuis in the final six years of his life, and paying tribute to
his greatness: "In the often harsh judgments that were made of him,
and that caused him great personal suffering (this author saw at first

hand the suffering they caused him), sufficient consideration was not given to the importance, psychological and spiritual too, that India had in his theological reflection, which beyond the objective ambiguities, was lived as a wholehearted search for truth in the faith."[80]

## DON SCHWEITZER AND THE CHRISTOLOGY OF DUPUIS (2010)

As the title of his book *Contemporary Christologies* indicates, Don Schweitzer presents the thought of Dupuis on "the religious others" within the context of studying fifteen modern Christologies.[81] Second, Schweitzer also differs from the other authors we discuss in this article, with the exception of Brecht, by clearly recognizing how Dupuis wrote *Toward a Christian Theology of Religious Pluralism* as the third work in a trilogy.[82] He is thus in a position to place and evaluate Dupuis' reflections on Christianity and world religions within the context of his complete Christology developed in a Trinitarian key. Third, unlike the other authors examined above, Schweitzer enters into some detail about Dupuis' dialogue with Hinduism.

Three points deserve to be retrieved from Schweitzer's discussion. Firstly, "the theological density" of the Christ event and the value of history for Christian faith cannot, according to Dupuis, be reconciled "with Hinduism's relativisation of the value of history and perception of the absolute as categorically beyond it." Hence Dupuis refuses "to follow an extensive tradition in India of seeking to enculturate Christology in Hindu terms"—a decision that Schweitzer respectfully questions. Yet Schweitzer acknowledges that this decision may well have resulted from Dupuis' "prolonged exposure to Hinduism's emphasis on the transcendence of Brahman to the *maya* (unreality) of history."[83]

Second, Dupuis, nevertheless, wins Schweitzer's appreciation for arguing that "one must begin inductively with one's own experience of a praxis of interreligious dialogue."[84] Third, the Christology of Dupuis proceeds inductively and deductively by uniting both history and doctrine or both an "ascending" and a "descending" approach.[85] The outcome is not a Christology "in Hindu terms" but a Christology "open to dialogue with Hinduism," which shows "how Christology can be enriched through dialogue with Hinduism."[86]

Schweitzer deserves credit for locating the views of Dupuis on other religions within his complete Christology. But, like Dupuis, he fails to recognize that any such complete Christology should involve being attentive to the mediating role of Christ's priesthood.

## KEITH JOHNSON ON UNDERMINING THE TRINITY (2011)

Keith Johnson entered the debate about Dupuis with a book that is a revised version of a 2007 doctoral dissertation defended at Duke University.[87] He repeatedly cites and draws on D'Costa, seven of whose works feature in the bibliography, but curiously fails to include him in the index of authors. Like Morali but unlike D'Costa, he respects the difference between the theology of Dupuis and the pluralist paradigm of Knitter.[88] He sums up adequately the way in which Dupuis proposed the doctrine of the Trinity as a basis for positively interpreting non-Christian religions.[89]

But, paying particular attention to Augustine's theology of the Trinity, Johnson charges Dupuis with making the Son unacceptably "subordinate" to the Father, threatening the unity of Christ's person, undermining the unity of the economy of salvation, and severing the economic and immanent Trinity.[90] Nevertheless, Johnson uses tentative language when spelling out the four charges: Dupuis "*may* solve the problem of subordinationism" but does so "by undermining the unity of two natures in one person." "The way Dupuis distinguishes kingdom and church *seems* to require a second parallel economy"; he "*implicitly* posits two economies." The Trinitarian Christology of Dupuis "*may implicitly* undermine the unity of the divine and human natures of Jesus Christ." This language of "may," "seems," and "implicitly" reaches its high point with the claim that Dupuis "*implicitly* severs the unity of the economic and the immanent Trinity."[91]

Johnson has the merit of arguing his case on the basis of a more accurate view of Augustine's theology of the Trinity that has been recently and rightly expounded by Michel Barnes and Lewis Ayres. Johnson presents Dupuis' views in terms of the Logos *asarkos* and the Logos *ensarkos*, terminology used in the 1997 book *Toward a Christian Theology of Religious Pluralism*,[92] but, while listing *Christianity and the Religions* in the bibliography, Johnson does not seem to be aware that Dupuis replaced this terminology in his 2002 book. Like

D'Costa, Johnson queries the sharp distinction Dupuis made between the two natures of Christ.[93] But classical christological doctrine—not least the teaching of Thomas Aquinas, as we saw above—requires a well-defined distinction.

It would take at least a full-scale article to debate Johnson's charges against Dupuis. Let me observe only what happens to his tentative language about what "may" be the case, what "seems" to be implied, and what is "implicitly" proposed by Dupuis. At the end of his book, any qualifications drop away, and, although he has produced no further evidence, Johnson now flatly claims, "I showed that Dupuis's proposal introduces subordinationism into the Father-Son relationship, undermines the unity of the economy of salvation, and severs [a verb adopted from D'Costa?] the economic and the immanent Trinity." Dupuis, we are now assured, uses "trinitarian claims to undermine Christian teaching regarding the person and work of Christ."[94]

Finally, Johnson understands that space for the views of Dupuis had been opened up because the Second Vatican Council remained "silent about the means through which salvific grace is mediated apart from the church."[95] Johnson is certainly not the only one to make this mistaken comment on the documents of the council. But, in *Lumen gentium Nostra aetate Ad gentes* and *Gaudium et spes* Vatican II did indicate how, through the Son of God and the Holy Spirit, grace is mediated beyond the visible Body of Christ.[96]

## Conclusions

How might one draw together the ways in which Merrigan, Brecht, Cornille, D'Costa, Morali, Schweitzer, and Johnson have continued a (posthumous) debate about Dupuis' interpretation of Christianity and the other religions? Some stand apart by discussing such significant questions as his theological method (Brecht) or his dialogue with Hinduism (Schweitzer). Some (e.g., Cornille and Morali) show themselves substantially friendly toward his investigation and proposals. Others prove to be substantially "hostile" (D'Costa and Johnson). All seven authors witness to the lasting significance and challenge of Dupuis' views.

Without intending to do so, Merrigan, Brecht, and D'Costa, in particular, can lead us to two approaches that, as far as I know, have not entered the debate about Christianity and the other living faiths and that take us beyond what Dupuis himself argued: (a) the causality of love involved in the church's praying for others; and (b) the central role of Christ's high priesthood. Let me explain.

(a) D'Costa and Merrigan raise the question, how does the church mediate salvation to "the religious others?" Does the church act as an "instrumental cause" or a "merely moral or final cause" in mediating grace to them? Recognizing how the church's prayer for "others," both within the strictly liturgical context and beyond, is inspired by love should prompt us into specifying the kind of instrumental causality at work. To do this, of course, presupposes acknowledging love to be a true, if mysterious, creative and efficient cause. The gift of God's love has drawn Christians into a network of loving relations not only with other Christians but also with those of other living faiths. When they meet for common worship and pray for "the others," Catholics and other Christians show that their faith is actively "working through love" (Gal 5:6).

(b) Brecht moves the focus away from the church to highlight the importance of Christ's humanity by which "he is uniquely related to the whole human universe" (see above). That implies the question, how does Christ mediate salvation to those who do not belong to the community of the baptized? I would propose answering this: he mediates grace to "the others" through his humanity, which enabled him to exercise forever a high-priestly role.

From the time of the Letter to the Hebrews, right down to the twentieth century, Christian theologians have repeatedly taught that the Son of God could not have exercised his priestly ministry unless he had truly taken on the human condition. His humanity was essential to his priesthood. We find that teaching developed, for example, by St. John Chrysostom, St. Augustine, St. Thomas Aquinas, John Calvin, Blessed John Henry Newman, and Tom Torrance.[97] Augustine developed this theme through his image of Christ as "the humble doctor": becoming *the priest* for the human family involved Christ in a radical self-humbling. Torrance distinguished between (1) the church rightly recognizing Christ's divine identity by adoring him "equally with the Father and the Holy Spirit"; and (2) a misguided reaction to Arianism that gave rise to some liturgical texts that reduced the place given to the human priesthood of Christ. Any such excessive reaction in defense of Christ's true divinity at the expense of his humanity entails losing a proper appreciation of his priesthood.[98] That priesthood stands or falls with his being fully and truly human.

It is supremely in and through the Eucharist that Christ lovingly presents to the Father his own self-offering on behalf of all people and draws them into that self-offering. In the celebration of the Eucharist and the administration of the other sacraments, Christ continues his high-priestly, mediating role not only for the faithful who share in the liturgy but also for all human beings. Dupuis and D'Costa, as we saw above, explore the mediation exercised by the prayers of the church when celebrating the Eucharist. But we should not forget that this mediation draws on and remains subordinate to the priestly self-offering of Christ, who intercedes before the Father for the baptized faithful *and the entire human race*. This universal, priestly intercession of Christ might lead us to coin a new axiom. Provided we insist that no one is "outside Christ," we should state, "Outside the priestly intercession of Christ there is no salvation."

In the theology of religions, as well as in theology in general, the high priesthood of Christ (along with the Letter to the Hebrews) has suffered from benign neglect. For a full-scale treatment of Christ's priesthood and other faiths, we would need to draw on what Hebrews, some voices in the tradition, and the Second Vatican Council said about that priesthood.[99] We would then be in the position to illustrate adequately how reflection on the exercise of Christ's priesthood would incorporate but go beyond what Dupuis proposed about the divine plan for the whole human race with its diversity of religions.

[Gavin D'Costa: an Addition and a Modification.

In a debate with Terrence Tilley, D'Costa also evaluated Dupuis' theology of religions: D'Costa, "Christian Orthodoxy and Religious Pluralism: A Response to Terrence W. Tilley," *Modern Theology* 23 (2007): 435–46; D'Costa, "Christian Orthodoxy and Religious Pluralism: A Further Rejoinder to Terrence Tilley," *Modern Theology* 23 (2007): 455–62; D'Costa and Tilley, "Concluding our Quaestio Disputata of Religious Diversity," *Modern Theology* 23 (2007): 463–68. Modifying what I have written below on pp. 139 and 167, D'Costa had read Dupuis' *Christianity and the Religions*; see his review in *New Blackfriars* 84 (2003): 310–11.]

# 8

# Jacques Dupuis and Karl Rahner

In a 1998 review of Jacques Dupuis' *Toward a Christian Theology of Religious Pluralism*, Gavin D'Costa argued that "Dupuis is basically a Rahnerian. . . . Theologically, he carries on from where Rahner left off."[1] After Dupuis died in 2004, D'Costa repeated this judgment about Dupuis. When critically examining what he called the "structural inclusivism" of Rahner in *Christianity and World Religions*, D'Costa introduced Dupuis and named him a "neo-Rahnerian."[2] In writing of interreligious dialogues, D'Costa stated that Dupuis at various points not only paralleled Rahner's thought but had also "developed" it.[3]

Elsewhere D'Costa has classified Dupuis differently. When dealing with pluralist arguments and, in particular, with the writing of Paul Knitter, D'Costa remarked, "This emphasis [Knitter's emphasis] on the Spirit as a way of endorsing other religions as God-given and inspired, without having to have an anonymous Christ present, is to be found in the works of [Roger] Haight, [Georges] Khodr, Knitter, and, with a twist, Dupuis."[4] "With a twist"—an unusual theological expression— presumably means "with a small variation." Whether or not the picture of the Spirit present and Christ absent accurately presents the views of Knitter, not to mention Haight and Khodr, the passage gravely misrepresents what Dupuis had written in *Toward a Christian Theology of Religious Pluralism*: the universal presence and activity of the Son of God and the Holy Spirit are distinguishable but never separable.[5] But, finally, in a 2013 essay "Christian Theology of Religions," D'Costa abandoned this attempt to link Dupuis with Knitter and other pluralists, and once again labeled Dupuis a "neo-Rahnerian."[6] Hence D'Costa's most recent (is it his final?) label for Dupuis is that of being a neo-Rahnerian.

As far as I know, however, no other theologian has labeled Dupuis a "Rahnerian" or "neo-Rahnerian." They had their chance to do so; there were well over one hundred reviews (in English, French, German, Italian, Portuguese, Spanish, and other languages) of *Toward a Christian Theology of Religious Pluralism*, as well as articles in journals and chapters in books, dedicated in whole or in part, to a critical evaluation of Dupuis' views.[7] But nowhere was Dupuis described as a Rahnerian or neo-Rahnerian. At most, what you find are remarks that associate Rahner and Dupuis as holding inclusive views in the theology of religions. They have developed similar ideas that justify our setting them side by side. Thus Francis Clooney wrote of "those inclusivist theologies in the great tradition of Karl Rahner, SJ, and Jacques Dupuis, SJ, that balance claims to Christian uniqueness with a necessary openness to learning from other religions."[8] Yet did Dupuis not merely stand side by side with Rahner but also depend on him in a way that would justify D'Costa's judgment?

## DIFFERENCES AND SIMILARITIES

Since Rahner was born in 1904 and Dupuis in 1923, they more or less belonged to successive generations. Rahner completed his higher studies in Austria, Germany, and Holland, whereas Dupuis completed his in Belgium, India, and Italy. Rahner's doctoral dissertation in theology at Innsbruck dealt with a patristic theme (the church born from the wounded side of Christ), whereas Dupuis wrote his doctorate (on Origen) for the Gregorian University (Rome). A common interest in the fathers of the church brought Dupuis and Rahner together. Moreover, over the years, Dupuis reviewed various works by Rahner: notably, seven volumes of his *Theological Investigations* and his 1976 classic, *Foundations of Christian Faith*. It was in 1983, the year before Rahner's death, that Dupuis published his last review of a book by Rahner.[9] Nevertheless, as he spent thirty-six years of his life in India and (even after being appointed to the Gregorian University in 1984) remained until his death in 2004 a member of the Calcutta Jesuit Province, the interfaith setting for Dupuis' work set him apart from Rahner, who passed most of his life in the traditionally Catholic countries of Austria and Germany.

Rahner was famously interested in and influenced by the philosophy of Joseph Maréchal and Martin Heidegger, and went on to
develop his own theological/philosophical anthropology. Some misguided latter-day critics dismiss Rahner as primarily a philosopher,
who dabbled in theology. Even such critics could never make such
comments about Dupuis. Of course, he grew to appreciate classical
Hindu philosophy and, unlike Rahner, enjoyed a close knowledge
of Hinduism in general. But the major strength from which he drew
came from his encyclopedic knowledge of modern theologians and of
the history of Christian doctrine. From 1960 to 2004, Dupuis published—in the *Clergy Monthly* (renamed in 1974 the *Vidyajyoti Journal of Theological Reflection*) and in the *Gregorianum*—562 reviews
of books, mainly written in (or translated into) English, French, and
Italian.[10] Decades of work as editor of those journals also involved
reading articles submitted by theologians working around the world.

A common, scholarly interest in publishing the doctrinal teaching
of the Catholic Church associated Dupuis and Rahner. In 1938, Josef
Neuner and Heinrich Roos brought out *Der Glaube der Kirche in
den Urkunden der Lehrverkündigung*, a compendium of documents
on the Catholic faith, gathered according to themes and arranged in
twelve chapters, each with a brief introduction. Rahner edited the subsequent six editions of this volume, until Karl-Heinz Weger took over
the eighth edition in 1971. In 1967 an English translation of the sixth
edition appeared.[11] Rahner also served as editor for the twenty-eighth
to the thirty-first edition (1952–1957) of *Enchiridion symbolorum,
definitionum et declarationum de rebus fidei et morum*, a work
launched by Heinrich Denzinger in 1854. While very many of the
same documents are published in both volumes, "Denzinger" differed
from "Neuner-Roos" by being arranged throughout in a chronological (and not a thematic) order and by publishing the documents in
their original languages (mostly Greek and then Latin).

After the Second Vatican Council (1962–1965), Dupuis and
Neuner (now a colleague teaching theology in India) set themselves
to prepare an updated collection of doctrinal documents, gathered
in twenty-three thematic chapters (each with their own introduction)
that followed an opening section on "symbols and professions of
faith." Assisted by eight other professors, Neuner and Dupuis produced in 1973 the first edition of *The Christian Faith: In the Doctrinal Developments of the Catholic Church*. Dupuis continued this

project, enlisting other colleagues in the work, which grew from the 711 pages of the original edition to the 1135 pages of the seventh edition.[12]

During the years of Vatican II, Rahner proved an outstanding and influential *peritus*, and, after the Council closed in December 1965, he contributed much to the analysis and dissemination of its teaching.[13] Dupuis wrote two popular articles on the Christocentrism of Vatican II,[14] was deeply involved with implementing in India the conciliar reform of the liturgy, and ensured that the Council's teaching was adequately represented in *The Christian Faith*. After his transfer to the Gregorian University, in 1985 he became editor of the *Gregorianum* and quickly made the journal a means for discussing and promoting the teaching of Vatican II.[15] Both before and after he transferred to the Gregorian University, Dupuis attended (as an interpreter) four of the bishops' synods held in Rome (1974, 1983, 1985, and 1987). A long article he published after the 1974 synod (on evangelization) showed how deeply committed he was to implementing Vatican II's teaching on the collegial coresponsibility of all the bishops "with Peter and under Peter."[16]

Thus far, in exploring the question of whether Dupuis could or even should be called a neo-Rahnerian, I have sketched some of the background data that either bring Dupuis and Rahner together (e.g., an effective desire to make the doctrines of the Catholic Church available and a deep commitment to the teaching of Vatican II) or set them apart (e.g., Rahner's philosophical concerns and strengths, on the one side, and the interreligious setting for much of Dupuis' academic life and his familiarity with Hindu thought, on the other). We could press ahead and invoke further relevant data. While both of them, for instance, revealed the impact of their Ignatian roots, Rahner differed from Dupuis by persistently publishing in the areas of Christian spirituality and preaching. But, since it is apropos of the theology of religions that D'Costa has applied to Dupuis a Rahnerian label, we should focus on that specific area and test the validity of D'Costa's judgment on *Toward a Christian Theology of Religious Pluralism*.

But to do that we need to remember that this book followed *Jesus Christ at the Encounter of World Religions* and *Who Do You Say I Am?* and so appeared as the third in a trilogy.[17] Unlike many commentators on Dupuis' thinking, Mara Brecht has recognized how his thinking about other living faiths and Christianity's relationship to them should be explored within the context of his integral Christology. She writes, "Unless one reads his view of religious pluralism through the lens of his [total] Christology, one mistakes its status."[18] Like her, Don Schweitzer clearly acknowledges how *Toward a Christian Theology of Religious Pluralism* was the third work in a trilogy. He is thus at pains to evaluate Dupuis' reflections on Christianity and world religions within the context of his complete Christology that Dupuis developed in a Trinitarian key.[19] Only that context will enable us to evaluate the accuracy of naming Dupuis a "neo-Rahnerian."

## EARLIER STATEMENTS

Even before examining *Jesus Christ at the Encounter of World Religions*, we should, however, recall some earlier statements by Dupuis (in 1971 and 1976) that foreshadowed what he would later elaborate. Terrence Merrigan has recalled a 1971 conference at which Dupuis and Yves Congar differed on the value of other religions in mediating salvation for their followers. Congar refused to say that "these religions are divinely legitimated *in themselves* and *as such*."[20] Speaking at the same conference, Dupuis took a different line: "It is said that, though non-Christians are saved due to the sincerity of their subjective religious life, their religion has for them no objective salvific value. However, the dichotomy on which this restriction is based, is seriously inadequate. Subjective and objective religion can be distinguished; they cannot be separated." Dupuis went on to say that it is "theologically unrealistic to maintain that, though non-Christians can be saved, their religion plays no part in their salvation."[21] This led him to this conclusion: "No religious life is purely natural," and "no historical religion is merely human."[22] In this debate with Congar, Dupuis argued that the objective reality of religions cannot be separated from the subjective experience of those religions, and that the religions embody something more than the merely human, so as to be in some sense divinely legitimated in themselves and as such.

Merrigan rightly recalled the 1971 conference and commented that Dupuis was more or less working out what he had already said at this conference when he wrote in 1997: "In the overall history of God's dealings with humankind," the world's religions express "distinct modalities of God's self-communication to persons and peoples."[23] Merrigan could also have cited some comments from Dupuis on Pope Paul VI's 1975 apostolic exhortation, *Evangelii nuntiandi*, which followed the 1974 synod on "Evangelization of the Modern World." Dupuis had attended the synod not only as an interpreter but also as secretary to Archbishop (later Cardinal) Lawrence Picachy of Calcutta, adviser to Archbishop Angelo Fernandes, and collaborator of Fr. Duraisamy Simon Amalorpavadass, one of the two secretaries for the synod.[24] After summarizing accurately and fully *Evangelii nuntiandi*, in his final pages Dupuis showed how this document failed to reflect the open attitude of the synod on a number of important issues: evangelization itself; particular churches and small communities; indigenous liturgy; catechesis and theology; *and non-Christian religions.* Apropos of the last point, he urged that these religions should be seen not "merely as expressions of human aspirations towards God but [also] as embodying for their followers a first, though incomplete, approach of God to human beings."[25] Here, even more clearly than at the 1971 conference, Dupuis prefigured what he would develop in his 1997 book.

In terms of the issue being explored in this chapter, neither in 1971 nor in 1976, when he espoused a more open view on the divine involvement in and salvific value of other religions, did Dupuis do so as if he were a neo-Rahnerian carrying on where Rahner had left off. At the 1971 conference, Dupuis was driven by dissatisfaction at what he heard from Congar. In his 1976 article, he showed how Pope Paul VI had failed to reflect the more open attitude toward "non-Christian religions," which Dupuis had heard expressed at the 1974 synod. Dissatisfaction with what Congar and Paul VI said and long experience of the religious "others" motivated Dupuis' remarks rather than any desire to take further the thought of Rahner.

## THE FIRST TWO WORKS OF A TRILOGY

In the opening volume of Dupuis' trilogy, the first part of the book explored some Hindu themes and the second part examined what is involved in confessing Christ as "one and universal." Rahner may be strongly represented in the bibliography,[26] but he appears in the text merely three times and then only briefly.[27] More attention is paid to Panikkar, whose positions Dupuis presents and, to some extent, questions.[28]

In *Jesus Christ at the Encounter of World Religions*, Dupuis discusses in one page "the inclusive paradigm" of Rahner, which holds together Christ's role as "God's definitive revelation and the absolute Saviour" with the efficacious "elements of grace" to be found in other religious traditions. It is through a commentary from Gavin D'Costa himself that Dupuis takes up Rahner; Dupuis ends the page by endorsing D'Costa's account and drawing from him a long quotation.[29] At this point Dupuis raises no objection to the language of "definitive" revelation and "absolute" Savior.

Three years later, in *Who Do You Say I Am?*, Dupuis inevitably introduced Rahner much more frequently: in fact, fifteen times. That book went, of course, beyond questions of Christ and other religions to present itself as a broad introduction to Christology, an area in which Rahner had developed important views through various essays in *Theological Investigations* and in the long christological section of *Foundations of Christian Faith*.[30]

In the course of summarizing several anthropological approaches, Dupuis presented Rahner's transcendental Christology with appreciation but drew attention to its limited biblical basis.[31] He cited Rahner's response to the question of divine immutability being qualified through the incarnation,[32] as well as Rahner's reflections on the human self-awareness and knowledge of Jesus.[33] Apropos of the human freedom of Jesus, Dupuis obviously found Rahner's argument congenial, quoting the same passage three times: "His [Christ's] humanity is the freest and most independent, not in spite of, but because of its being taken up, by being constituted as the self-utterance of God."[34]

In *Who Do You Say I Am?*, when Dupuis came to reflect on the situation of the followers of other faiths in the light of the person and work of Christ, he argued that "an open Christocentrism . . . represents the only way available to a Christian theology of religions truly worthy of the name."[35] When taking up, once again approvingly, D'Costa's *Theology of Religious Pluralism* and its presentation of Rahner's inclusive Christology, Dupuis repeated word for word, with only a few sentences omitted, what he had already written in *Jesus Christ at the Encounter of World Religions*.[36] There is no hint here of Dupuis wanting to develop further Rahner's inclusive thought and thus prove himself worthy of being named a "neo-Rahnerian."

## THE THIRD WORK IN THE TRILOGY

Three years later, in *Toward a Christian Theology of Religious Pluralism*, the longest discussion of Rahner's views comes in a section on "anonymous Christianity." Dupuis examines various objections to this notion and endorses a "brilliant" article by D'Costa when responding to the criticisms. Nevertheless, Dupuis does not personally appropriate the theme of "anonymous Christianity," when explaining how salvation through Christ reaches "the others."[37] He ends this section by remarking that "Karl Rahner has had his followers and sympathizers," names ten of them, but evidently does not want to take a place on that list.[38]

Elsewhere Dupuis endorses Rahner's clear distinction (but not separation) between the church, Christ, and the kingdom of God established in him, when expounding the role of the church as "the sacrament" of the kingdom.[39] But he finds difficulty when Rahner calls the other religions "lawful" up to a point and up to a time. This "weak expression" supposes "their provisional and transitory character."[40] Dupuis also expresses serious difficulties with Rahner's talk of the "absoluteness of Christianity" and of Christ as "absolute Saviour." His reason is "that absoluteness is an attribute of the ultimate Reality of Infinite Being, which must not be predicated of any finite reality, even the human existence of the Son-of-God-made-man. That Jesus Christ is 'universal' Saviour does not make him the 'Absolute Saviour,' who is God himself."[41]

Beyond question, there is a similarity between the inclusive views of Rahner and Dupuis: both hold that final salvation comes only through Christ, that God's saving will is effectively universal, that grace is everywhere present and operative (even if often hidden and unperceived), and that the other religions have a positive role for the salvation of their followers. But such similarity does not mean that the (slightly) later writer, Dupuis, in his three books published after Rahner's death showed himself, in any proper sense of the word, a "neo-Rahnerian."

Sometimes the prefix *neo-* can prove useful in mapping what has been retrieved and developed in Christian theology. Thus, for instance, a Panorthodox conference held at Athens in 1936 launched an attempt to develop an Orthodox theological synthesis by retrieving the teaching of St. Gregory Palamas (d. 1359). Some of the notable

Orthodox theologians in the twentieth century may be usefully classified as "neo-Palamite": George Florovsky (1893–1979), Vladimir
Lossky (1903–1958), Paul Evdokimov (1901–1970), John Meyendorff
(1925–1992), and Metropolitan Kallistos Ware (b. 1934).

We have noted serious differences between Rahner and Dupuis,
which militate against calling Dupuis a "neo-Rahnerian." We will
note further differences in the final section, which examines *Christianity and the Religions* (Italian original, 2001),[42] a book that significantly clarifies the views of Dupuis and introduces *for the first time*
in his publications the term "inclusive pluralism."[43]

## CHRISTIANITY AND THE RELIGIOUS

Right up to 2013, D'Costa has failed to list or refer to Dupuis' final
work, *Christianity and the Religions*. Nevertheless, without providing
any references, in 2009 D'Costa wrote of Dupuis calling his own position "inclusivist pluralism."[44] (Dupuis, in fact, used the term "inclusive
pluralism," without introducing the neologism "inclusivist.") How
did D'Costa learn of the expression that Dupuis, only at the end,
employed to describe his position? Had he in fact read *Christianity
and the Religions*, even if he did not refer to the book or even list it
in his bibliographies?

Here Dupuis differed, since he was always clear about the material
that drew (approvingly) from D'Costa and where he had found it. We
noted above how Dupuis in the first volume of his trilogy, *Jesus Christ
at the Encounter of World Religions*, quoted and endorsed what
D'Costa had written in a 1986 work, *Theology and Religious Pluralism*. In his final book, Dupuis once again made a "special mention"
of the same book for having shown how "the three basic positions
of exclusivism, inclusivism, and pluralism" derive from "contrasting
attitudes" toward "two basic axioms": "the universal salvific will of
God" and "the necessity of the mediation of Jesus Christ."[45] Right
through to that final work, Dupuis was perfectly clear when citing
D'Costa, and persistently did so with approval.

At the end, while continuing to express approval for what D'Costa
had written, Dupuis pulled further away from Rahner. Let me conclude with four points that illustrate the differences.

First, we have seen how in *Toward a Christian Theology of Religious Pluralism* Dupuis objected to Rahner's language about the

"absoluteness of Christianity" and about Christ being "absolute Saviour." In *Christianity and the Religions*, Dupuis not only repeated these objections but also continued to maintain some other terminology that also set him apart from Rahner. In *Toward a Christian Theology of Religious Pluralism*, Dupuis recalled how Rahner had talked of God being "definitively" communicated in Christ.[46] But, already in that book, Dupuis avoided following Rahner in using "definitive," and preferred to speak of Christ as being the "constitutive" Savior in whom God was "decisively" revealed.[47] In *Christianity and the Religions*, Dupuis saw no reason to change his language about Christ being "God's decisive revelation and constitutive [and not "absolute"] Saviour."[48]

Second, Dupuis had already joined Aloysius Pieris in raising an issue that lay outside Rahner's concerns: the "complementarity" between Christianity and other religious traditions.[49] In using this language, Dupuis never intended to claim that the revelation that reached its fullness in Christ needed to be filled out by other religious traditions. Rather, he used that term in *Toward a Christian Theology of Religious Pluralism* to indicate how some elements of the divine mystery can be vividly expressed by the practices and sacred writings found beyond Christianity. In prayerful dialogue with other traditions, Christians may "hear" something that enriches them spiritually.[50] They can receive as well as give, as the closing message of the 1977 international bishops' synod on catechetics recalled (no. 5). Nevertheless, to express Christian faith in the fullness of the divine self-revelation in Christ, it may have been better for Dupuis to have qualified from the outset the kind of complementarity he had in mind. In *Christianity and the Religions*, he called this complementarity "asymmetrical," an adjective that brings out the Christian belief that in Jesus Christ the divine revelation enjoys a unique fullness and that there is no gap to be filled by other revelations and traditions.[51] But, as found either in Dupuis' 1997 book or in that of 2001 (Italian original), his discussion of "complementarity" did not find a counterpart in Rahner's theology of religions.

Third, as D'Costa himself remarked in his 1998 review of *Toward a Christian Theology of Religious Pluralism*, Dupuis distinguished himself from Rahner through his thoroughgoing Trinitarian emphasis.[52] Dupuis remained concerned with the universal presence of the Word and the Holy Spirit, the two hands of God, as St. Irenaeus called them.[53] Rahner took up the presence of Christ in other living faiths, albeit a presence mediated in and through the Holy Spirit.[54] Nevertheless, D'Costa rightly recognized the Trinitarian nature of Dupuis' theology of religions, an emphasis that emerged even more strongly in his final work.

Fourth, Dupuis had already expressed "caution" about a distinction encouraged by Rahner: namely, that between "special" and "general" salvation history.[55] In *Christianity and the Religions*, Dupuis repeated even more strongly his misgivings about such a distinction.[56] It was attention to *the biblical witness* that fuelled these misgivings. In his 1997 work, Dupuis had already alluded briefly to the "permanence" and relevance for humankind of the divine covenants with Adam and Noah.[57] But his 2001 book shows how he now felt supported by the work of Adolfo Russo in holding the multiplicity of particular histories of salvation.[58] Russo had argued that, just as the Mosaic covenant remained "irrevocable," so too, in a similar (but not precisely the same) way, "those covenants that God has made with the other peoples of the earth, symbolically present in the Adam event, and more specifically in the story of Noah," are not rendered merely provisional or obsolete by the incarnation.[59] If D'Costa had read *Christianity and the Religions*, he could have seen that it was not a desire to remove any Rahnerian notion about "the provisional status of other religions as salvific structures" that prompted Dupuis into querying the "provisionality" of those faiths.[60] It was because he had been helped by Russo that Dupuis drew out the permanent implications of the biblical witness about the divine covenants made with Adam and Noah.

All in all, a careful examination of Dupuis' work on the theology of religions militates against calling him a neo-Rahnerian. Rather, while developing some views that find similar counterparts in Rahner's writing, he also differs from him in significant ways. Setting the two great theologians side by side, we find dissimilarity along with similarity. We do not throw light on Dupuis' theology by labeling him a "Rahnerian" or a "neo-Rahnerian."

# Notes

CHAPTER 1

1   See George Hunsinger, *How to Read Karl Barth: The Story of His Theology* (New York: Oxford University Press, 1991).

2   See Gabriel Flynn and Paul D. Murray, eds., *Ressourcement: A Movement for Renewal in Twentieth-Century Catholic Theology* (Oxford: Oxford University Press, 2012).

3   The fresh synthesis of evolutionary thought and religious faith offered by Pierre Teilhard de Chardin (1883–1955) made a wide impact once his works began to appear in English shortly after his death. As a result of the incarnation, the evolving universe now finds itself in a process of "christification." Rahner was one of the first among leading theologians to speak and write about Teilhard's views. De Lubac, another *ressourcement* theologian and *peritus* (or official adviser) at Vatican II, also wrote positively about Teilhard.

4   A widely used pre-Vatican II Christology, Jésus Solano, *Sacrae theologiae summa*, vol. 3 (Madrid: Biblioteca de Autores Cristianos, 1956), pursued an ontological Christology (without considering soteriology or the saving function of Christ), dedicated less than one page to the resurrection, and remained uninterested in Christ's mediating salvation to those of other living faiths or those of no faith at all.

5   A clarity that analytic philosophy can bring to some christological issues shows through T. V. Morris, *The Logic of God Incarnate* (Ithaca, N.Y.: Cornell University Press, 1986); Richard Sturch, *The Word and the Christ* (Oxford: Clarendon, 1991); and various chapters in Stephen T. Davis, Daniel Kendall, and Gerald O'Collins, eds., *The Incarnation: An Interdisciplinary Symposium on the Incarnation of the Son of God* (Oxford: Oxford University Press, 2002).

6   His influence on Pope John Paul II has, however, been exaggerated; see Brendan Leahy, "John Paul II and Hans Urs von Balthasar," in *The Legacy of John*

*Paul II*, ed. Gerald O'Collins and Michael A. Hayes (London: Continuum, 2008), 31–50.

7    Approaching Jesus through his beauty also involves retrieving teaching from St. Augustine of Hippo; for details, see Gerald O'Collins, *Jesus: A Portrait* (London: Darton, Longman & Todd, 2008), 1–15.

8    Walter Kasper, *Jesus the Christ*, trans. V. Green (Mahwah, N.J.: Paulist, 1976).

9    First published in 1911, this anthology reached its twenty-third edition the year Vatican II closed. Marie Joseph Rouët de Journel, *Enchiridion patristicum* (Barcelona: Herder, 1965).

10    While valuing greatly what Vermes did toward a balanced study of the Dead Sea Scrolls, I find much to debate in what he has written on Jesus: e.g., in his 2008 book, *Resurrection* (New York: Doubleday). See my *Believing in the Resurrection: The Meaning and Promise of the Risen Lord* (Mahwah, N.J.: Paulist, 2012), 20–22. Hence I would strongly query the claim made by his publishers that he was the greatest Jesus scholar of his generation. That accolade belongs rather to someone like Raymond Brown, Martin Hengel, or John Meier.

11    On attempts to explain (or rather explain away) Jesus as a Cynic philosopher, see Hans-Dieter Betz, "Jesus and the Cynics: Survey and Analysis of a Hypothesis," *Journal of Religion* 74 (1994): 453–75; and Philip Jenkins, *Hidden Gospels: How the Search for Jesus Lost Its Way* (New York: Oxford University Press, 2001), 54–81.

12    On the resurrection of Christ, see also Stefan Alkier, *The Reality of the Resurrection: The New Testament Witness*, trans. Leroy A. Huizenga (Waco, Tex.: Baylor University Press, 2013); Francis J. Moloney, *The Resurrection of the Messiah: A Narrative Commentary on the Resurrection Accounts in the Four Gospels* (Mahwah, N.J.: Paulist, 2013); and O'Collins, *Believing in the Resurrection*.

13    Eleonore Stump, "Aquinas' Metaphysics of the Incarnation," in Davis, Kendall, and O'Collins, *Incarnation*, 197–218.

14    Sarah Coakley, "What Does Chalcedon Solve and What Does It Not? Some Reflections on the Status and Meaning of the Chalcedonian Definition," in Davis, Kendall, and O'Collins, *Incarnation*, 143–63.

15    Caroline Walker Bynum, "The Power in the Blood: Sacrifice, Satisfaction, and Substitution in Late Medieval Soteriology," in *The Redemption: An Interdisciplinary Symposium on Christ as Redeemer*, ed. Stephen T. Davis, Daniel Kendall, and Gerald O'Collins (Oxford: Oxford University Press, 2004), 177–204.

16    See Gerald O'Collins, "Wisdom in the Universe: A Biblical and Theological Reflection," in *Is God Incarnate in All That Is?* ed. Niels H. Gregersen and Mary Ann Meyers (Minneapolis: Fortress, forthcoming).

17    See Clifton R. Clarke, *African Christology: Jesus in Post-missionary African Christianity* (Eugene, Ore.: Pickwick, 2011); Diane B. Stinton, *Jesus of Africa: Voices of Contemporary African Christology* (Maryknoll, N.Y.: Orbis Books,

2004); A. Alangaram, *Christ of the Asian Peoples: Towards an Asian Contextual Christology* (Bangalore: Bangalore Asian Trading Corporation, 2001).

18  Sergius Bulgakov, *The Lamb of God*, ed. Boris Jakim (Grand Rapids: Eerdmans, 2008).

19  Paul S. Fiddes, *Past Event and Present Salvation: The Christian Idea of Atonement* (London: Darton, Longman & Todd, 1989); for details and further literature, see Gerald O'Collins, *Jesus Our Redeemer: A Christian Approach to Salvation* (Oxford: Oxford University Press, 2007), 271–73.

20  Jacques Dupuis, *Toward a Christian Theology of Religious Pluralism* (Maryknoll, N.Y.: Orbis Books, 1997).

21  The proceedings launched against the book by the Congregation for the Doctrine of the Faith also helped to increase interest in Dupuis and his theology.

22  Jacques Dupuis, *Christianity and the Religions: From Confrontation to Dialogue*, trans. Phillip Berryman (Maryknoll, N.Y.: Orbis Books, 2002).

23  Daniel Kendall and Gerald O'Collins, eds., *In Many and Diverse Ways: In Honor of Jacques Dupuis* (Maryknoll, N.Y.: Orbis Books, 2003).

24  Gerald O'Collins, *Salvation for All: God's Other Peoples* (Oxford: Oxford University Press, 2008).

25  William R. Burrows, ed., *Jacques Dupuis Faces the Inquisition: Two Essays by Jacques Dupuis on* Dominus Iesus *and the Roman Investigation of His Work* (Eugene, Ore.: Pickwick, 2012).

26  Gerald O'Collins, *What Are They Saying about Jesus?* (1977; rev. ed., New York: Paulist, 1983); Giovanni Iammarrone, ed., *La Cristologia contemporanea* (Padua: Edizioni Messaggero, 1992); Edward T. Oakes, *Infinity Dwindled to Infancy: A Catholic and Evangelical Christology* (Grand Rapids: Eerdmans, 2011); and Francesca A. Murphy, ed., *The Oxford Handbook of Christology* (Oxford: Oxford University Press, forthcoming).

CHAPTER 2

1  Jürgen Moltmann, *The Way of Jesus Christ: Christology in Messianic Dimensions*, trans. Margaret Kohl (London: SCM Press, 1990), 38.

2  Gerald O'Collins, *Christology: A Biblical, Historical, and Systematic Study of Jesus* (Oxford: Oxford University Press, 1995); after several reprintings, Oxford University Press published an expanded and revised edition in 2009. The two editions will be cited as *Christology* (1995) and *Christology* (2009), respectively.

3  John P. Meier, *A Marginal Jew*, vol. 3, *Companions and Competitors* (New York: Doubleday, 2001).

4  How could this be otherwise? Over the years I have dedicated pages to the study of human experience, religious and otherwise, and have done so as recently as my *Rethinking Fundamental Theology: Toward a New Fundamental Theology* (Oxford: Oxford University Press, 2011), 42–55.

5    See Lewis Ayres, *Nicaea and Its Legacy: An Approach to Fourth-Century Trinitarian Theology* (Oxford: Oxford University Press, 2004); Ayres, *Augustine on the Trinity* (Cambridge: Cambridge University Press, 2010).

6    Gerald O'Collins and Michael Keenan Jones, *Jesus Our Priest: A Christian Approach to the Priesthood of Christ* (Oxford: Oxford University Press, 2010).

7    Augustine, *Letters 100–155*, trans. Roland Teske (Hyde Park, N.Y.: New City, 2003), 212–24. Some remarks of Augustine (214, 215, and 216) strongly tell against modern "explanations" of the "kenosis" involved in the incarnation (see Phil 2:7), as if it entailed the Word of God abandoning his divine powers or at least temporarily ceasing to exercise them.

8    See O'Collins, *Jesus Our Redeemer*, 266–67.

9    Burton L. Mack, *The Lost Gospel* (San Francisco: HarperCollins, 1993).

10   Robert W. Funk, *Honest to Jesus: Jesus for a New Millennium* (San Francisco: HarperSanFrancisco, 1996).

11   Funk, *Honest to Jesus*, 314.

12   Rudolf Schnackenburg, *God's Rule and Kingdom*, trans. John Murray (London: Burns & Oates, 1968), 95 (emphasis added).

13   John P. Meier, *A Majrginal Jew*, vol. 2, *Rethinking the Historical Jesus* (New York: Doubleday, 1994), 331.

14   Gerald O'Collins, "Jesus Christ the Liberator: In the Context of Human Progress," *Studia Missionalia* 47 (1998): 27, 32.

15   "The chief difficulty with O'Collins's position is its uneven relationship with modernity" (Wilson, 1138).

16   See, e.g., O'Collins, *Christology* (1995), 223; and O'Collins, *Christology* (2009), 227–28.

17   Gerald O'Collins and Daniel Kendall, "On Not Neglecting Hatred," *Scottish Journal of Theology* 47 (1994): 511–18. I am unaware of any response that we provoked; this lacuna serves to establish further our thesis that theologians of all kinds deplorably neglect hatred.

18   See, e.g., David Brown, "The Incarnation in Twentieth-Century Art," in Davis, Kendall, and O'Collins, *Incarnation*, 332–74.

19   See O'Collins, *Christology* (2009), 295; O'Collins, *Jesus Our Redeemer*, 37–42, 61–62, 110–15. Anthony Egan (on *Christology* [2009]) wanted to see me examine the "modern, literary, and secular images of Christ one finds in the controversial novels of authors like Nikos Kazantzakis" (Egan, 10).

20   O'Collins, *Jesus: A Portrait* (London: Darton, Longman & Todd, 2008).

21   See, e.g., O'Collins, *Rethinking Fundamental Theology*, 323–29.

22   Gerald O'Collins, "A Challenge for Theologians: Three Puzzling Positions," *America*, September 17, 2007, 23–24.

23   See Gerald O'Collins, *Jesus Risen: An Historical, Fundamental and Systematic Examination of Christ's Resurrection* (Mahwah, N.J.: Paulist, 1987), 94–98.

24   See Jon Sobrino, *Jesus the Liberator: A Historical-Theological Reading of Jesus of Nazareth*, trans. Paul Burns and Francis McDonough (Maryknoll,

N.Y.: Orbis Books, 1993); Sobrino, *Christ the Liberator: A View from the Victims*, trans. Paul Burns (Maryknoll, N.Y.: Orbis Books, 2001).

25  Gerald O'Collins and Daniel Kendall, *The Bible for Theology: Ten Principles for the Theological Use of Scripture* (Mahwah, N.J.: Paulist, 1997), 6; see 25–27.

26  O'Collins and Kendall, *Bible for Theology*, 25, 173–74.

27  O'Collins, *Christology* (2009), 47–52.

28  Gerald O'Collins, review of Richard Bauckham, *Jesus and the Eyewitnesses: The Gospels as Eyewitness Testimony* (Grand Rapids: Eerdmans, 2006), in *Heythrop Journal* 69 (2008): 309–10.

29  O'Collins, *Christology* (2009), 337–43.

30  Gerald O'Collins, "Vatican II and the Liturgical Presences of Christ," *Irish Theological Quarterly* 77 (2012): 9–16.

31  O'Collins, *Salvation for All*, 207–29.

32  At the Gregorian University (Rome), I directed the doctoral thesis of William Kelly, "Towards a Christology of Presence: Uncovering and Relating Themes from Scripture, Philosophy and Theology" (1996).

33  O'Collins, *Christology* (2009), 338.

34  O'Collins, *Christology* (2009), 354.

35  James L. Heft, ed., *Catholicism and Interreligious Dialogue* (New York: Oxford University Press, 2012).

36  O'Collins, *Christology* (2009), 328–33.

37  O'Collins, *Salvation for All*; and Gerald O'Collins, *The Second Vatican Council on Other Religions* (Oxford: Oxford University Press, 2013).

38  O'Collins, *Christology* (2009), 286–96.

39  O'Collins, *Christology* (1995), 275; O'Collins, *Christology* (2009), 291.

40  See Coakley, "What Does Chalcedon Solve?," in Davis, Kendall, and O'Collins, *Incarnation*, 143–63.

41  List of Reviews of *Christology: A Biblical, Historical and Systematic Study of Jesus*: Lewis Ayres, in *Tablet*, February 20, 2010, 28; Peter J. Bernardi, in *Horizons* 37 (2010): 353–54; Denis Carroll, in *Furrow* 47 (1996): 317–19; James D. G. Dunn, in *Epworth Review* 24 (1997): 133–34; Anthony Egan, in *Southern Cross*, June 23–29, 2010, 10; Earle Ellis, in *Southwestern Journal of Theology* 40 (1998): 125; Donal Flanagan, in *Doctrine and Life* 46 (1996): 187–88; Manuel Gesteira, in *Estudios Eclesiásticos* 72 (1997): 551–52; John Hadley, in *New Blackfriars* 86 (2005): 505–17; Charles Hefling, in *Anglican Theological Review* 79 (1997): 73–76; James L. Heft, in *Theological Studies* 57 (1996): 547–49; Leslie Houlden, in *Church Times*, October 27, 1995, 15; Robert P. Imbelli, in *Commonweal* 123, no. 2 (1996): 25–27; Dean M. Kelley, in *First Things* 60 (1996): 72; J. Peter Kenny, in *Australasian Catholic Record* 73 (1996): 120–23; Jean de Dieu Madangi, in *Estudios* Eclesiásticos 73 (1998): 365; James Massa, in *Crisis* 14 (1996): 44; James F. McGrath, in *Review of Biblical Literature* 12 (2010): 484–87; John McIntyre, in *Expository Times* 107 (1995–1996): 88; John McIntyre, *Shape of Christology*, 2nd ed. (Edinburgh: T&T Clark, 1998), 283–305; Robert Moloney, in *Milltown*

*Studies* 37 (1996): 132–35; George T. Montague, in *Catholic Biblical Quarterly* 59 (1997): 168–69; George Newlands, in *Journal of Theological Studies* 47 (1996): 782–84; Carey C. Newman, in *Choice*, January 1996, 8–9; Ann Nickson, in *Anvil* 14 (1997): 143; Patrick O'Connell, in *New Oxford Review*, September 1997, 31–32; John Parr, in *Theology* 99 (1996): 304–5; Pheme Perkins, in *America* 174, no. 10 (1996): 26–27; Timothy Caradoc Platts, in *Modern Believing* 37 (1996): 61; William L. Portier, in *Modern Theology* 14 (1998): 153–55; Lucien J. Richard, in *Catholic Library World* 80 (2010): 291; J. A. Riestra, in *Scripta Theologica* 28 (1996): 963–64; Anthony Saldarini, in *Bible Review*, October 1997, 10–14; Klyne R. Snodgrass, in *Bulletin for Biblical Research* 7 (1997): 255–58; John E. Thiel, in *Religious Studies Review* 23 (1997): 46–47; Humberto R. Treiyer, in *Andrews University Seminary Studies* 36 (1998): 303–5; Joseph Verheyden, in *Ephemerides Theologicae Lovanienses* 75 (1999): 474–75; Charles A. Wilson, in *Christian Century*, November 22–29, 1995, 1138. I remain grateful to all the reviewers. Hopefully this chapter goes some way toward completing the conversation they initiated.

## CHAPTER 3

1   Davis, Kendall, and O'Collins, *Redemption.*

2   O'Collins, *Jesus Our Redeemer.*

3   O'Collins, *Christology* (1995); in a revised and updated form, this book had a second edition (2009). In "Juridical Language in Soteriology: Aquinas's Approach," *Angelicum* 80 (2003): 309–26, Matthew Levering criticized my proposing love as the primary (but not exclusive) key to Christ's work "for us." He suggested that my approach endorsed the view that the crucified Christ *simply* revealed that God loves us, without showing how Christ accomplished a restoration (313). This criticism failed to notice how I insisted on the causality exercised by love being a "creative and re-creative activity" (*Christology* [1995], 289), and on the way that the divine self-revelation is always and necessarily transforming and redemptive (*Christology* [1995], 291).

4   O'Collins and Jones, *Jesus Our Priest.*

5   Without any reference to *Jesus Our Priest*, Garry Wills—in *Why Priests? A Failed Tradition* (New York: Viking, 2013)—rejects not only the Christian priesthood but also the priestly identity of Christ himself, arguing that the Letter to the Hebrews went astray in recognizing the priesthood of Christ. Once further reviews and other reactions appear, it will be worth examining critically and at length the case Wills proposes.

6   Reviews of *The Redemption* included Hans Boersma, in *Scottish Journal of Theology* 62 (2009): 109–12; Joris Geldhof, in *Ephemerides Theologicae Lovanienses* 82 (2006): 263–66; Gerard Loughlin, in *Theology* 110 (2007): 213–14; Raymond Moloney, in *Furrow* 56 (2005): 373–75; Anne Murphy, in *New Blackfriars* 87 (2006): 445–47; Susannah Ticciati, in *Journal of*

*Theological Studies* 58 (2007): 366–69; Sean Wales, in *Redemptorist Spirituality*, September 2007, 1. The reviews will be cited intratextually.

7    The claim that "none of the essays engage in conversation across disciplines" can hardly be sustained. Take, for instance, Brown's chapter, which engages in a conversation between theology, fine arts, and musicology.

8    Besides the symposium that produced *The Redemption*, three other symposia resulted in *The Resurrection* (1997), *The Trinity* (1999), and *The Incarnation* (2002), all published by Oxford University Press. A fifth symposium, promoted by the Templeton Foundation, brought together scientists and theologians on the theme of "light" and resulted in Gerald O'Collins and Mary Ann Meyers, eds., *Light from Light: Scientists and Theologians in Dialogue* (Grand Rapids: Eerdmans, 2012).

9    Peter Cornwell, in *Times Literary Supplement*, January 25, 2008, 30–31; Paul Crosbie, in *Furrow* 58 (2007): 313–15; Victor I. Ezigbo, in *Studies in World Christianity* 14 (2008): 98–99; Robert P. Imbelli, in *America*, October 8, 2007, 25; Andrew T. B. McGowan, in *Expository Times*, March 2008, 303–4; Christiaan Mostert, in *Pacifica* 22 (2009): 243–45; F. LeRon Shults, in *Journal of Reformed Theology* 2 (2008): 204–5. The reviews will be cited intratextually.

10   Ralph Martin, *Will Many Be Saved? What Vatican II Actually Teaches and Its Implications for the New Evangelization* (Grand Rapids: Eerdmans, 2012), xii.

11   Martin, *Will Many Be Saved?* 198.

12   On this and other Vatican documents concerned with the salvation of "others," see O'Collins, *Second Vatican Council*.

13   Glenn Siniscalchi, while sharing Martin's concern about making the Church at large more mission minded, ends both his reviews of *Salvation for All* (see below) by drawing from *Lumen gentium* 14 a summons to "all the church's children" that they should reach out to the millions of "others" and bring them the good news. To support his appeal for new evangelization, Siniscalchi, unlike Martin, interprets *Lumen gentium* appropriately.

14   This may leave open the possibility of producing an acceptable notion of "substitution," but, like Caroline Walker Bynum, I find talk about "substitution" and "representation" rather extrinsic terms that do not readily suggest personal participation. See, however, Henry L. Novello, *Death as Transformation: A Contemporary Theology of Death* (Farnham, U.K.: Ashgate, 2011), 36n41, and 66n121.

15   O'Collins, *Jesus Our Redeemer*, 139, 153–54.

16   George Thomas Kurian, ed., "Propitiation," in *The Testament Christian Dictionary* (New York: Random House, 2001), 632.

17   O'Collins, *Jesus Our Redeemer*, 136–37; see also my *Christology* (2009), 209–11.

18   Rik van Nieuwenhove, " 'Bearing the Marks of Christ's Passion': Aquinas' Soteriology," in *The Theology of Thomas Aquinas*, ed. Rik van Nieuwenhove and Joseph P. Wawrykow (Notre Dame, Ind.: University of Notre Dame Press,

2005), 290. Some years earlier, Matthew Levering in gentler tones had already taken issue with my interpretation of Thomas, in his "Israel and the Shape of Thomas Aquinas's Soteriology," *Thomist* 63 (1999): 65–82.

19    Brandon Peterson, "Paving the Way? Penalty and Atonement in Thomas Aquinas' Soteriology," *International Journal of Systematic Theology* 15, no. 3 (2013): 265–83.

20    Stephen Bullivant, *The Salvation of Atheists and Catholic Dogmatic Theology* (Oxford: Oxford University Press, 2012), 2.

21    Bullivant has in mind this passage of *Lumen gentium* 16: "Divine providence does not deny the helps necessary for salvation to those who, without any fault [of their own], have not yet reached an express acknowledgement of God, and, who, not without grace, strive to lead an upright life" (translation my own).

22    Bullivant, *Salvation of Atheists*, 115.

23    O'Collins, *Second Vatican Council*, 76–77.

24    These reviews were Timothy Bradshaw, in *Journal of Theological Studies* 60 (2009): 761–62; David Burrell, in *Tablet*, May 10, 2008, 26; Francis X. Clooney, in *Horizons* 36 (2009): 126–30; Catherine Cornille, in *Horizons* 36 (2009): 130–33; Gavin D'Costa, in *Theology Today* 66 (2009): 395–98; Ann Fritschel, in *Interpretation* 63 (2009): 430; Paul Griffiths, in *Horizons* 36 (2009): 133–38; Michael Ipgrave, in *Theology* 112 (2009): 449–50; Robert A. Krieg, in *Theological Studies* 71 (2009): 696–98; Peter Phan, in *Horizons* 36 (2009): 121–26; Glenn B. Siniscalchi, in *American Theological Inquiry* 3 (2010): 187–90; Siniscalchi, in *Downside Review* 129 (2011): 74–76. The reviews will be cited intratextually.

25    Let me list only my book chapters and do so in chronological order: "Christ and Non-Christians," in *Fundamental Theology* (New York: Paulist, 1981), 114–29; "Jesus the World's Redeemer," in *Interpreting Jesus* (London: Geoffrey Chapman, 1983), 133–69; "Saving Revelation for All Peoples," in *Retrieving Fundamental Theology* (Mahwah, N.J.: Paulist, 1993), 79–86; "Universal Redeemer," in *Christology* (1995), 296–305; "The Salvation of Non-Christians," in *Jesus Our Redeemer*, 218–37.

26    Martin also complained about the "remarkable methodology" adopted by my *explicitly* limiting myself to the "positive" elements in the divine stance toward the nonevangelized (*Will Many Be Saved?* 356n56). This complaint about my failing to tell the whole story (which in fact I expressly declined to do) was risky for him to make. As its subtitle indicated, his book promised to present "what Vatican II actually teaches" about the salvation of those who have not received the gospel. But he then limited himself largely to one (very important) article of *Lumen gentium* ignored (as we have seen) much relevant teaching found elsewhere in Vatican II, and spent well over a third of the book discussing (helpfully) the views of Karl Rahner and Hans Urs von Balthasar. Apropos of Vatican II's teaching, Martin himself clearly failed to tell the whole story.

27    Cornille remarked that, "while providing invaluable biblical data for reflection on the relationship between Christianity and other religions, the book

does not as such move the theological agenda forward" (Cornille, 133). But, firstly, if the book does for the first time provide such "invaluable" and comprehensive "biblical data," surely that moves forward the theological agenda? Henceforth any theologians who reflect on "the relationship between Christianity and other religions" should be expected to take on board the full biblical data. Secondly, Cornille did not set herself to evaluate the explicitly theological conclusions I drew in the concluding chapters. Did, for instance, my reflections on the universal *presence* of Christ and his Holy Spirit "move the theological agenda forward"? Her comments on these later chapters would have been very welcome.

28  Mark S. M. Scott, "Guarding the Mysteries of Salvation: The Pastoral Pedagogy of Origen's Universalism," *Journal of Early Christian Studies* 18 (2010): 347n1. Scott has since published a notable book on Origen; see his *Journey Back to God: Origen on the Problem of Evil* (New York: Oxford University Press, 2012).

29  Bullivant (see above) would not be happy about this proposal, since once again we have a Catholic theologian writing about the salvation of "non-Christians" and ignoring "the existence of millions of non-religious unbelievers."

30  O'Collins, *Salvation for All*, 76.

31  Wills, *Why Priests?*

32  See O'Collins, *Salvation for All*, 28–29.

33  O'Collins, *Salvation for All*, 39.

34  There *are* biblical hints about the value and truth of the religion of "outsiders" to be found, for instance, (a) in stories involving Abraham, Melchizedek, and Abimelech, (b) in Malachi's respect for the sacrifices of the nations, and (c) in the words attributed to Paul about "the God Unknown." See O'Collins, *Salvation for All*, 13–16, 48–53, and 158–60, respectively.

35  O'Collins, *Salvation for All*, 80–84.

36  On Rahner's use of "anonymous Christians" and "anonymous Christianity" and subsequent abandonment of that terminology, see O'Collins, *Second Vatican Council*, 55–57.

37  O'Collins, *Salvation for All*, 159 and 209n4.

38  See O'Collins, *Second Vatican Council*, 50–58; O'Collins, "The Priesthood of Christ and Followers of Other Faiths" (reprinted as ch. 6 below).

39  O'Collins, *Salvation for All*, 8–10.

40  O'Collins, *Salvation for All*, 34–36, 36–41, and 42–48, respectively. On the Scriptures possibly supporting the notion of many chosen peoples, see Mark G. Brett, *Decolonizing God: The Bible in the Tides of Empire* (Sheffield, U.K.: Sheffield Academic, 2008), 30, 73–74.

41  See further O'Collins, *Second Vatican Council*, 118–19.

42  O'Collins, *Salvation for All*, 204.

43  I wish to thank warmly Fr. Simon Wayte, MGL, for expertly tracking down many reviews for me.

## CHAPTER 4

1    Curiously, after translating *ōphthē*—in 1 Cor 15:5, 6, 7—as "he was seen by," in v. 8 Phillips translates the same word as "he appeared." Somewhat surprisingly, 1 Cor 15:6 (the only example selected from the four occurrences of *ōphthē* in these verses) is translated by Johannes P. Louw and Eugene A. Nida, eds., as Christ "was seen by" more than five hundred faithful, even though they have just explained "the subdomain of seeing" as "coming into the range of vision" or "appearing." *Greek-English Lexicon of the New Testament Based on Semantic Domains*, vol. 1 (New York: United Bible Societies, 1988), 277.

2    With the aim of elucidating Paul's language about seeing the risen Lord and the Lord's appearing, this paragraph has introduced examples from other (later) NT authors using various forms of *horaō*. The next paragraph will recall relevant passages from the (much earlier) LXX. We must examine later and earlier usage when investigating Paul's possible meaning(s).

3    Joseph A. Fitzmyer, *First Corinthians* (New Haven, Conn.: Yale University Press, 2008), 549.

4    In this and other OT theophanies, what God *says* is regularly to the fore rather than any details about the divine "appearance."

5    Normal Hellenistic language shows up in the appendix to Mark: Christ "appeared [*ephanē*] first to Mary Magdalene" (Mark 16:9; see also 16:12 and 14, which use the form *ēphanerōthē*).

6    Fitzmyer, *First Corinthians*, 549; in a partial list, Fitzmyer cites eighteen examples of this usage in the LXX.

7    Joachim Jeremias, *Eucharistic Words*, trans. Norman Perrin (London: SCM Press, 1966 ), 101–3. F. F. Bruce, clearly respectful of Jeremias' scholarship, translated *ōphthē* in 1 Cor 15 as "he let himself be seen," in *1 and 2 Corinthians* (London: Oliphants, 1971), 140.

8    Joseph H. Thayer, *Greek-English Lexicon of the New Testament* (Peabody, Mass.: Hendrickson, 1999; repr. of the 4th ed. of 1896), 452.

9    Fitzmyer, *First Corinthians*, 542.

10    Raymond F. Collins, *First Corinthians* (Collegeville, Minn.: Liturgical, 1999), 528, 535.

11    Anthony Thiselton, *The First Epistle to the Corinthians* (Grand Rapids: Eerdmans, 2000), 1198.

12    Wolfgang Schrage, *Der erste Brief an die Korinther* (Düsseldorf: Benziger Verlag, 2001), 4:47.

13    Daniel B. Wallace, *Greek Grammar beyond the Basics: An Exegetical Syntax of the New Testament* (Grand Rapids: Zondervan, 1996), 165n72. He refers not only to the four occurrences in 1 Cor 15 but also to Matt 17:3; Mark 9:4; Luke 1:11; 22:43; 24:34; Acts 7:2, 26, 30; 13:31; 16:9; 1 Tim 3:16. Besides the use of *ōphthē*, we should also recall the participle *ophtheis* (Acts 9:17) and the verbs *ōphthēn* (Acts 26:16) and *ophthēsomai* (Acts 26:16). In all three cases, the subject initiates the manifestation; the person mentioned in the dative—in all three cases Paul—is merely the recipient.

14  Friedrich Blass and Albert Debrunner, *A Greek Grammar of the New Testament and Other Early Christian Literature*, trans. and rev. Robert W. Funk (Cambridge: Cambridge University Press, 1961), no. 313; see also no. 101.

15  Walter Bauer, *A Greek-English Lexicon of the New Testament and Other Early Christian Literature*, 3rd ed., rev. Frederick William Danker (Chicago: University of Chicago Press, 2000), 719.

16  Acts 10:40, however, not only uses Hellenistic language (*emphanē*) rather than a Hebraism or what Fitzmyer (see above) calls "a semitized Greek verb" (*ōphthē*), but also names God as subject of the verb rather than Christ, as in 1 Cor 15. Thus Acts 10:40, while yielding a valid theological comment on 1 Cor 15:5-8, does not directly guide its translation. Similar Hellenistic language turns up in an apocalyptic addition in Matt 27:52-53, which speaks of "holy ones" emerging from tombs and "appearing [*enephanisthēsan*] to many people after his [Jesus'] resurrection."

17  Schrage, *Der erste Brief*, 4:47–48.

18  Jacob Kremer, who also examines the possibility of understanding *ōphthē* to be a divine passive, rejects it even more emphatically on the grounds that Christ is the subject of the verb: "Interpreting this phrase as a theological passive 'God caused him to be visible' founders on the fact that Christ is the subject." Jacob Kremer, "*horaō*," in *Exegetical Dictionary of the New Testament*, vol. 2, ed. Horst Balz and Gerhard Schneider (Grand Rapids: Eerdmans, 1991), 528.

19  When discussing 1 Cor 15:5-8, N. T. Wright also adopts the same translation, "he appeared." *The Resurrection of the Son of God* (Minneapolis: Fortress, 2003), 322–28.

20  Fitzmyer, *First Corinthians*, 550; Schrage, *Der erste Brief*, 4:54, 61.

21  Fitzmyer, *First Corinthians*, 550.

22  E.g., Bruce, *1 and 2 Corinthians*, 140; Richard B. Hays, *1 Corinthians* (Louisville, Ky.: John Knox, 1997), 257; Michael R. Licona, *The Resurrection of Jesus: A New Historiographical Approach* (Downers Grove, Ill.: IVP Academic, 2010), 323, 337, 349–55.

23  Thiselton, *First Epistle*, 668. Commentaries on 1 Cor 9:1 (in particular, Bruce, Collins, Fitzmyer, Schrage, and Thiselton) understand the verse to refer to the risen Jesus' appearance claimed by Paul in 1 Cor 15:8. As Collins says, the question ("Have I not seen Jesus our Lord?") "clearly makes reference to the event to which Paul alludes in 15:8" (*First Corinthians*, 334).

24  Collins, *First Corinthians*, 329. As Collins later states, "That Paul has seen the Lord has permanently established him as an apostle" (335).

25  In 2 Cor 4:6, Paul, although speaking in the plural ("our hearts"), may refer to his Damascus road encounter. But, while introducing "light," "shining," "glory," and "knowledge," he does not speak of his "seeing" the risen Christ: "It is the God who said, 'Let light shine out of darkness,' who has shone in our hearts to give the light of the knowledge of the glory of God on the face of Jesus Christ."

26   Daniel Kendall and Gerald O'Collins, "The Uniqueness of the Easter Appearances," *Catholic Biblical Quarterly* 54 (1991): 295–97.

27   Wilhelm Michaelis attempted to explain the Easter encounters simply as episodes of revelation, reducing the Easter encounters to a revelation by word (that we find repeatedly in the Jewish Scriptures) and playing down their eyewitness quality. But unlike the formula "the Lord appeared *and said*" (Gen 12:7; 17:1; 26:2, 24; 35:9), the postresurrection encounters echo only the first part of the formula ("he appeared") (Luke 24:34; Acts 13:31; 1 Cor 15:5-8 [4 times]), and there is no revelation by word in these six cases. Such revelation by word predominates with the great prophets, but in their case we never read that "the Lord appeared and said to them." The Old Testament background to which Michaelis appealed does not support his case. For full details and a complete rebuttal of his view, see Kendall and O'Collins, "Uniqueness of the Easter Appearances," 289–92.

28   Here this chapter moves its focus beyond Paul to examine the use (and possible meanings) of *ōphthē* and related forms of *horaō* in other NT texts. Neither Paul nor any other NT writer used such language in a kind of private "vacuum."

29   Bauer, *Greek-English Lexicon*, 719.

30   Stephen (as reported by Luke in Acts 7:2) speaks of God "appearing," whereas the relevant LXX passage (Gen 12:1) simply says that God "spoke" to Abraham.

31   Collins, *First Corinthians*, 334.

32   Wallace detects here hymnic material, in his *Greek Grammar*, 340–42.

33   Luke Timothy Johnson, *The First and Second Letters to Timothy* (New York: Doubleday, 2001), 233; Jerome D. Quinn and William C. Wacker, *The First and Second Letters to Timothy* (Grand Rapids: Eerdmans, 2000), 297, 315–48. Philip H. Towner considers a "reference to human messengers" possible but prefers to translate "angels" (*The Letters to Timothy and Titus* [Grand Rapids: Eerdmans, 2006], 281–82). I. Howard Marshall likewise notes the possibility of human "messengers" but prefers to translate *aggeloi* as "angels" (*The Pastoral Epistles* [London: T&T Clark, 1999], 526–27).

34   Kremer, "*horaō*," in Balz and Schneider, *Exegetical Dictionary*, 528.

35   For a complete account of the (visual) vocabulary used to express the risen Christ's appearances, see Joseph Hug, *La finale de l'Évangile de Marc* (Paris: Gabalda, 1978), 53–61.

36   Kremer, "*horaō*," in Balz and Schneider, *Exegetical Dictionary*, 528; see n. 23 above.

37   The New Testament endorses this transcendence by characterizing God as invisible (John 1:18; 5:37; 6:46; Col 1:15; 1 Tim 1:17; Heb 11:27; 1 John 4:12). While affirming that no one "can see" God (1 Tim 6:16), the New Testament also says paradoxically that Moses "persevered because he saw him [God] who is invisible" (Heb 11:27). This could also be translated, "persevered as though he saw him [God] who is invisible" (NRSV).

38 Collins, *First Corinthians*, 535. As regards "the traditional Jewish under-standing of divine transcendence," there could be exceptions: e.g., in his vision of the heavenly throne room, Isaiah says, "My eyes have seen the King, the Lord of hosts" (Isa 6:5).

39 I say "immediately," so as not to deny what was quoted from Schrage (see n. 17 above): "Ultimately it is God himself who brings about the appearances of Christ."

40 Kremer, "*horaō*," in Balz and Schneider, *Exegetical Dictionary*, 528.

41 Collins, *First Corinthians*, 535.

42 To be sure, in 1 Cor 15:42-44, Paul writes about the resurrection of the dead (in the plural). However, he moves at once to speak of Christ "the last Adam," who first had a "physical" and then a "spiritual" existence (1 Cor 15:45-49). Paul has already called the risen Christ "the first fruits of those who have fallen asleep" (1 Cor 15:20), thus implying some real analogy between the "spiritual body" of Christ and that of those who would be resurrected. See further O'Collins, *Jesus Our Redeemer*, 242–62.

43 Gerald O'Collins, *The Easter Jesus*, new ed. (London: Darton, Longman & Todd, 1980), 72; see also O'Collins, *Believing in the Resurrection*, 78–79, which also reflects on Mary Magdalene turning twice ("physically" and "spir-itually," respectively).

44 Thiselton, *First Epistle*, 1199.

45 Against this view see Gerald O'Collins, *Interpreting the Resurrection* (Mah-wah, N.J.: Paulist, 1988), 59–61; Schrage, *Der erste Brief*, 4:47n159.

46 Notice how, when citing the foundational appearance to him of the risen Jesus, Paul speaks of "Jesus our *Lord*" (1 Cor 9:1); this encounter also brought Paul a revelation of the *Son of God* (Gal 1:16).

47 To justify the claim that these appearances were unique and not repeatable, see Kendall and O'Collins, "Uniqueness of the Easter Appearances," 287–307.

48 Origen, *Contra Celsum*, trans. Henry Chadwick (1953; repr., Cambridge: Cambridge University Press, 1980), 2.65, p. 116.

49 St. Thomas Aquinas, *Summa theologiae*, 3a.55.2, *ad primum*. This laconic phrase might also be translated as "eyes/sight working through faith," or "with the eyes/sight of faith," or "with a faith that has eyes/sight."

50 On this view, see Kremer, "*horaō*," in Balz and Schneider, *Exegetical Diction-ary*, 528; Licona, *Resurrection of Jesus*, 339–43; Schrage, *Der erste Brief*, 4:49–51; Wright, *Resurrection of the Son*, 677–78.

51 See Gerald O'Collins and Daniel Kendall, "Mary Magdalene as Major Wit-ness to Jesus' Resurrection," *Theological Studies* 48 (1987): 631–46; Wright, *Resurrection of the Son*, 677–78.

52 On 2 Cor 12:1-4, see Licona, *Resurrection of Jesus*, 381–82.

53 See further O'Collins, *Jesus Risen*, 210–16; O'Collins, *Interpreting the Res-urrection*, 13–15; Wright, *Resurrection of the Son*, 324–25.

54 Quinn and Wacker, *First and Second Letters*, 297.

55 James H. Moulton and George Milligan, *The Vocabulary of the Greek Testa-ment* (London: Hodder & Stoughton, 1930), 455.

56  Bauer, *Greek-English Lexicon*, 719–20.

57  Various translations (e.g., NAB, NRSV, REB, and RSV) simply leave "see" here without an object. The NJB follows Bauer-Danker in translating "will see him."

58  Raymond E. Brown, *The Epistles of John* (New York: Doubleday, 1982), 403, 427–28, 720–21, 748.

59  A fuller lexical treatment would need to examine the related nouns: *horama* ("vision," used six times in the NT), *horasis* ("vision," "appearance," used three times in the NT), and *optasia* ("vision," used four times in the NT). With all three nouns, the "visions" are somehow "objective" and not mere figments of the imagination. In Acts 26:19, Luke uses *optasia* of Paul's encounter with the risen Christ on the Damascus road, describing it as a "heavenly vision" or "vision from heaven."

## CHAPTER 5

1  Martin Hengel, *Der unterschätzte Petrus: Zwei Studien* (Tübingen: Mohr Siebeck, 2006); Hengel, *Saint Peter: The Underestimated Apostle*, trans. Thomas H. Trapp (Grand Rapids: Eerdmans, 2010).

2  Oscar Cullmann, *Peter: Disciple, Apostle, Martyr; A Historical and Theological Study*, trans. Floyd V. Filson (London: SCM Press, 1962); Raymond E. Brown, Karl P. Donfried, and John Reumann, eds., *Peter in the New Testament: A Collaborative Assessment by Protestant and Roman Catholic Scholars* (Minneapolis: Augsburg, 1973).

3  Christian Grappe, *Images de Pierre aux deux premiers siècles* (Paris: Presses Universitaires de France, 1995); Rudolf Pesch, *Die biblischen Grundlagen des Primats*, Quaestiones disputatae 187 (Freiburg im Breisgau: Herder, 2001). See also Rudolf Pesch, *Simon Petrus: Geschichte und geschichtliche Bedeutung des ersten Jüngers Jesu Christi* (Stuttgart: Anton Hiersemann, 1980), 49–50 (on Peter as "witness of Easter faith").

4  Hengel, *Saint Peter*, 32, 36, 45, 53.

5  Hengel, *Saint Peter*, 30–31.

6  In "Peter as Easter Witness," *Heythrop Journal* 22 (1981): 1–18, I showed how earlier scholars, especially theologians, had widely neglected the priority of Peter's witness to the resurrection. This situation has hardly changed over the last thirty years. In *The Remembered Peter: In Ancient Reception and Modern Debate* (Tübingen: Mohr Siebeck, 2010), Markus Bockmuehl treats in a balanced fashion various Petrine themes but does not discuss Peter's witness to the resurrection. See, however, William Thomas Kessler, *Peter as the First Witness of the Risen Lord: An Historical and Theological Investigation* (Rome: Editrice Pontificia Università Gregoriana, 1998).

7  Hengel, *Saint Peter*, 20–25.

8  Hengel, *Saint Peter*, 25–28.

9  Hengel, *Saint Peter*, 28–36.

10 Hengel, *Saint Peter*, 36–48.
11 Hengel, *Saint Peter*, 48.
12 Hengel, *Saint Peter*, 82; see 99.
13 Hengel, *Saint Peter*, 43.
14 Hengel, *Saint Peter*, 44.
15 Hengel, *Saint Peter*, 22.
16 Hengel, *Saint Peter*, 29; see also 34, 44, 66 (n. 215), 88, 100. Hengel notes, however, the claim expressed in the Gospel of the Hebrews that the first appearance of the risen Jesus was to his "brother" James (*Saint Peter*, 9).
17 See O'Collins and Kendall, "Mary Magdalene as Major Witness," 631–46.
18 Richard Bauckham, *Gospel Women: A Study of the Named Women in the Gospels* (Grand Rapids: Eerdmans, 2002); see Hengel, *Saint Peter*, 108–10, 122.
19 Hengel, *Saint Peter*, 100.
20 Hengel, *Saint Peter*, 99. The key "appearance-to-Peter" texts (Luke 24:34; 1 Cor 15:5), which we will examine below, are notable for their absence in St. Peter's Basilica. Obviously, popes have not been very interested in linking their primacy to Peter *precisely* in his function as "first witness to the resurrection."
21 Pesch, *Die biblischen Grundlagen*, 60.
22 Pesch, *Die biblischen Grundlagen*, 21–26, 31–39.
23 See, e.g., Richard Bauckham, *Jesus and the Eyewitnesses: The Gospels as Eyewitness Testimony* (Grand Rapids: Eerdmans, 2006).
24 Pesch, *Die biblischen Grundlagen*, 39–41, 48.
25 Pesch, *Die biblischen Grundlagen*, 79.
26 Pesch, *Die biblischen Grundlagen*, 40, 41–42, 63, 79, 80, 87.
27 Pesch, *Die biblischen Grundlagen*, 85–91.
28 Pesch, *Die biblischen Grundlagen*, 87–88.
29 Pesch, *Die biblischen Grundlagen*, 57. Apropos of the origin of Christian faith in Jesus' resurrection, over the years Pesch changed his position in important aspects but continued to differ from my analysis of the emergence of Easter faith. See O'Collins, *Jesus Risen*, 110, 120; O'Collins, *Believing in the Resurrection*, 77, 83–85.
30 In her *Peter: Apostle for the Whole Church* (Columbia: University of South Carolina Press, 1994), Pheme Perkins refers to Peter as witness to the risen Christ only rarely (3, 8, 33); and, somewhat like Grappe, she presents Peter much more in such roles as exemplary disciple (who eventually suffers martyrdom), founder, universal apostle, and shepherd.
31 Brown, Donfried, and Reumann, *Peter in the New Testament*, 162–68. We should note that Peter as Easter witness does *not* explicitly feature among the seven images that conclude and summarize the study, even though the work has already examined the three key texts that concern Peter's witness to Christ's resurrection: 1 Cor 15:5 (pp. 33–36); Luke 24:34 (pp. 125–28); and Mark 16:7 (pp. 69–73).
32 Brown, Donfried, and Reumann, *Peter in the New Testament*, 21n47.
33 Grappe, *Images de Pierre*, 152, 201–5.

34 Grappe, *Images de Pierre*, 275.

35 Grappe, *Images de Pierre*, 155. Willi Marxsen and some others have understood Mark 16:7, along with 14:28, to refer, not to postresurrection appearances, but to the Parousia that will occur in Galilee. For references and a convincing list of reasons that tell against this explanation, see Christopher Bryan, *The Resurrection of the Messiah* (New York: Oxford University Press, 2011), 285; and Joel Marcus, *Mark 8–16* (New Haven, Conn.: Yale University Press, 2009), 1081.

36 Translated in *Origins* 8, no. 19 (1978): 292.

37 Heinrich Denzinger and Peter Hünermann, eds., *Enchiridion symbolorum, definitionum et declarationum*, 37th ed. (Freiburg im Breisgau: Herder, 1991), no. 3053; hereafter DzH. See also Josef Neuner and Jacques Dupuis, eds., *The Christian Faith: In the Doctrinal Documents of the Catholic Church*, 7th ed. (Bangalore: Theological Publications in India, 2001), no. 819; hereafter ND.

38 DzH 3070; ND 836.

39 Anglican Roman-Catholic International Commission [ARCIC], *The Final Report* (London: SPCK, 1982), 64.

40 ARCIC, *Final Report*, 81–85.

41 Translated in *Origins* 25, no. 4 (1995): 69.

42 ARCIC, *Final Report*, 82.

43 Jean-Marie-Roger Tillard, *The Bishop of Rome*, trans. John de Satgé (London: SPCK, 1983), 112–13.

44 John Michael Miller, *The Shepherd and the Rock: Origins, Development, and Mission of the Papacy* (Huntington, Ind.: Our Sunday Visitor, 1995), 12–49, esp. 31–33.

45 Miller, *Shepherd and the Rock*, 346–70, at 363 and 365.

46 As regards the Petrine Epistles, 1 Peter may have been written by Peter; the later 2 Peter almost certainly did not come directly from Peter. While mentioning Jesus' resurrection (1 Pet 1:3, 21; 3:21) and echoing the language of shepherding and martyrdom found in John 21:15-19 (see 1 Pet 5:1-4), 1 Peter has nothing clear to say about any appearance of the risen Christ to Peter. The reference to Peter as one who "shares" in Christ's "glory" (1 Pet 5:1) seems to refer to what will be revealed in the future, rather than to Peter having been the first (male) disciple to meet and witness to the risen Jesus. The text in 2 Peter 1:16-18 recalls Peter's experiencing, not the Christ's resurrection, but his transfiguration—a passage that second-century gnostics took up and developed (see Grappe, *Images de Pierre, passim*).

47 On 1 Cor 15:1-11, see Fitzmyer, *First Corinthians*, 539–57.

48 Bryan, *Resurrection of the Messiah*, 263.

49 On the empty tomb, see Bryan, *Resurrection of the Messiah*, 50–51, 264; and my *Believing in the Resurrection*, 80–99.

50 On Peter's visit and preaching in Corinth, see Hengel, *Saint Peter*, 66–78.

51 E.g., see Adela Yarbro Collins, *Mark: A Commentary* (Minneapolis: Fortress, 2007), 797, 801; and Francis J. Moloney, *The Gospel of Mark: A Commentary* (Peabody, Mass.: Hendrickson, 2002), 347n34. In *Peter in the New*

*Testament*, Brown, Donfried, and Reumann remarked that "many scholars have concluded from this verse [16:7] that Mark was aware of the tradition that Jesus had appeared first to Peter" (71).

52  Marcus, *Mark 8–16*, 1086.

53  Frederick Lapham, *Peter: The Myth, the Man and the Writings* (London: Sheffield Academic, 2003), 9; see 239. After this flat denial, curiously he then recognizes that "Luke does in fact record, in the Emmaus story, that the Lord had appeared to Simon (24.34)" (9n22).

54  On this verse, which current scholarship recognizes as belonging to the original text of Luke's Gospel, see François Bovon, *Das Evangelium nach Lukas* (Neukirchen: Neukirchener Verlag, 2009), 4:531–34; Joseph A. Fitzmyer, *The Gospel according to Luke X–XXIV* (New York: Doubleday, 1985), 1547–48; Daniel A. Smith, *Revisiting the Empty Tomb* (Minneapolis: Fortress, 2010), 115–18. Andrew T. Lincoln shows how, by adding the figure of the beloved disciple, John 20:3-10 elaborated on the tradition of Peter running to the tomb in Luke 24:12, in his *The Gospel according to St John* (London: Continuum, 2005), 489, 491, 495.

55  On Luke 24:34, see Bovon, *Das Evangelium nach Lukas*, 4:564; and Fitzmyer, *Gospel according to Luke X–XXIV*, 1569.

56  On this verse, see Bovon, *Das Evangelium nach Lukas*, 4:273–77.

57  Robert C. Tannehill, *The Narrative Unity of Luke–Acts: A Literary Interpretation* (Philadelphia: Fortress, 1986), 1:293.

58  Lincoln, *Gospel according to St John*, 514–15. On Luke 5:1-11 containing elements of the "lost" appearance to Peter, see Brendan Byrne, "Peter as Resurrection Witness in the Lukan Narrative," in Kendall and Davis, *Convergence of Theology*, 24–29.

59  Raymond E. Brown, *The Gospel according to John XIII–XXI* (New York: Doubleday, 1970), 1085–92, 1110–12. See also Brown, "John 21 and the First Appearance of the Risen Jesus to Peter," in *Resurrexit*, ed. Eduard Dhanis (Rome: Libreria Editrice Vaticana, 1974), 246–65.

60  Brown, *Gospel according to John*, 1087.

61  Brown, *Gospel according to John*, 1097.

62  Brown, *Gospel according to John*, 1087–92. On possible postresurrection elements in Matt 14:28-33, see Ulrich Luz, *Matthew 8–20*, trans. James E. Crouch (Minneapolis: Fortress, 2001), 317–23, at 318; and John Nolland, *The Gospel of Matthew* (Grand Rapids: Eerdmans, 2005), 595–603. On such postresurrection elements in Matt 16:16b-19, see Luz, *Matthew 8–20*, 353–77, at 356, 358; Nolland, *Gospel of Matthew*, 661–82. On probable postresurrection elements in Luke 5:1-11, see François Bovon, *Luke 1: Commentary on the Gospel of Luke 1:1–9:50*, trans. Christine M. Thomas (Minneapolis: Fortress, 2002), 166–72; and Joseph A. Fitzmyer, *The Gospel according to Luke I–IX* (New York: Doubleday, 1981), 559–70, at 560–62.

63  Matthew possibly knew this longer tradition about an appearance to Mary Magdalene but abbreviated it (Matt 28:9-10); see Bryan, *Resurrection of the*

*Messiah*, 329n82. Her prestige is hinted at: Matt 28:9 is the only text in the New Testament that speaks of Jesus "meeting" someone else.

64 On these texts, see (in Matt) Ulrich Luz, *Matthew 21–28*, trans. James E. Crouch (Minneapolis: Fortress, 2005) 590–608; Nolland, *Gospel of Matthew*, 1240–54; see (in Mark) Collins, *Mark*, 779–801; Marcus, *Mark 8–16*, 1079–87; see (in Luke) Bovon, *Das Evangelium nach Lukas*, 4:523–31; Fitzmyer, *Gospel according to Luke X–XXIV*, 1532–53; and see (in John) Lincoln, *Gospel according to St John*, 488–89, 491–96.

65 On Mark 16:9, see Collins, *Mark*, 808.

66 Some translate this phrase as "distinguished in the eyes of the apostles." See Joseph A. Fitzmyer, *Romans* (New York: Doubleday, 1993), 739–40.

67 On the qualifications and functions for "apostles" in the early Church, see Joseph A. Fitzmyer, *The Acts of the Apostles* (New York: Doubleday, 1998), 196–97.

68 See Luz, *Matthew 21–28*, 606.

69 In John's Gospel, when Mary Magdalene discovers the tomb of Jesus to be open, she goes at once to inform "Simon Peter and the other disciple, the one whom Jesus loved." Then they both run to inspect the tomb (John 20:2-10). This episode suggests closeness rather than conflict between Mary and Peter (and other male disciples).

70 Among these later apocryphal works, see, e.g., *The Gospel of Mary*, in *The Nag Hammadi Library in English*, 3rd ed., ed. James M. Robinson (Leiden: Brill, 1988), 523–27.

71 See O'Collins and Kendall, "Mary Magdalene as Major Witness," 640–43.

72 Jenkins, *Hidden Gospels*, 133–43.

73 Hippolytus, *De cantico* 24–26 (Corpus Scriptorum Christianorum Orientalium 264, 43–49); Leo, *De ascensione Domini sermo* 2.4 (*Sources Chrétiennes* 74, 280–81); Gregory, *De apparitione Christi Magdalenae facta* (Patrum opuscula selecta 2, hom. 25 [Innsbruck: Libreria Academica Wagneriana, 1892], 189).

74 On these passages about Peter's witness to the resurrection, see Charles Kingsley Barrett, *The Acts of the Apostles*, vol. 1 (Edinburgh: T&T Clark, 1994); Fitzmyer, *Acts of the Apostles*.

75 See, e.g., the order in which the 1964 Dogmatic Constitution on the Church, *Lumen gentium* expresses the triple *munus* (or office) of bishops: first, the teaching/prophetic role of the bishops, and then their priestly role in worship and their pastoral/kingly role in leadership (nos. 25–27).

76 Brown, Donfried, and Reumann, *Peter in the New Testament*, 165.

77 Charles Kingsley Barrett finds a reference to Peter's death by crucifixion in John 21:18-19. Barrett, *The Gospel according to John*, 2nd ed. (London: SPCK, 1978), 585. So too does Lincoln, in his *Gospel according to St John*, 318–19.

78 For the data, the debates, and bibliographies about Paul, Peter, and their martyrdom in Rome, see Frank Leslie Cross and Elizabeth Anne Livingstone, eds.,

"Paul, St" and "Peter, St," in *The Oxford Dictionary of the Christian Church*, 3rd rev. ed. (Oxford: Oxford University Press, 2005), 1243–46, 1269–70.

79 Among many publications on the bishop of Rome, see Tillard, *Bishop of Rome*; and James F. Puglisi, ed., *How Can the Petrine Ministry Be of Service to the Unity of the Universal Church?* (Grand Rapids: Eerdmans, 2010).

80 On Paul's conflict with Peter at Antioch, see Hengel, *Saint Peter*, 57–65.

81 DzH 3051; ND 818 (emphasis added).

82 DzH 3060; ND 826.

83 *Evangelii nuntiandi*, no. 67.

84 Brown, Donfried, and Reumann, *Peter in the New Testament*, 8.

85 See further William Henn, "The Church as Easter Witness in the Thought of Gerald O'Collins, S.J.," in Kendall and Davis, *Convergence of Theology*, 208–20.

## Chapter 6

1 Karl Rahner, "Christianity and the Non-Christian Religions," in *Theological Investigations*, vol. 5, trans. Karl-Heinz Kruger (London: Darton, Longman & Todd, 1966), 115–34.

2 In the twenty-three volumes of Karl Rahner's *Theological Investigations* (London: Darton, Longman & Todd, 1961–1992), the theme of Christ/Christianity and "the others" turned up frequently and was treated at chapter length in vols. 5, 6, 9, 12, 14, 16, 17, and 18.

3 Karl Rahner, *Foundations of Christian Faith: An Introduction to the Idea of Christianity*, trans. William V. Dych (New York: Seabury, 1978), 126–33, 138–75.

4 Karl Rahner, *Spiritual Exercises*, trans. Kenneth Baker (New York: Herder & Herder, 1965).

5 Rahner, *Spiritual Exercises*, 203–4.

6 O'Collins and Jones, *Jesus Our Priest*, 80, 241–43.

7 Rahner, *Spiritual Exercises*, 204.

8 Rahner, *Spiritual Exercises*, 204–9.

9 Karl Rahner, *Servants of the Lord*, trans. Richard Strachan (London: Burns & Oates, 1968).

10 Rahner, *Servants of the Lord*, 127–48, 213–16.

11 Rahner, *Servants of the Lord*, 217–18.

12 Karl Rahner, *Meditations on Priestly Life*, trans. Edward Quinn (London: Sheed & Ward, 1973).

13 Rahner, *Meditations on Priestly Life*, 103–6.

14 Karl Rahner, "The Point of Departure in Theology for Determining the Nature of the Priestly Office" and "Theological Reflections on the Priestly Image of Today and Tomorrow," in *Theological Investigations*, vol. 12, trans. David Bourke (London: Darton, Longman & Todd, 1974), 31–38, 39–60; Rahner, "The Spirituality of the Secular Priest" and "The Spirituality of the

Priest in the Light of His Office," in *Theological Investigations*, vol. 19, trans. Edward Quinn (Darton, Longman & Todd, 1983), 103–16, 117–38.

15  Dupuis, *Toward a Christian Theology*; Dupuis, *Christianity and the Religions*.

16  Dupuis, *Toward a Christian Theology*, 186, 307; this latter passage is repeated almost word for word in his *Christianity and the Religions*, 168–69.

17  Dupuis, *Toward a Christian Theology*, 37.

18  Jacques Dupuis, *Who Do You Say I Am? Introduction to Christology* (Maryknoll, N.Y.: Orbis Books, 1994); in this book Dupuis never mentions the christological title of "priest." For a complete bibliography of Dupuis' publications, see Kendall and O'Collins, *In Many and Diverse Ways*, 231–69.

19  For details, see Kendall and O'Collins, *In Many and Diverse Ways*, 236, 239, and 242 (for the reviews), and 235, 238, and 243 (for the articles).

20  For details of this perennial neglect of Christ's priesthood, see O'Collins and Jones, *Jesus Our Priest*, *passim*; our bibliography (294–96) shows how very few have written on that priesthood in modern times.

21  Robert J. Sherman, "Christ the Priest: The Son's Sacrificial Offering," in *King, Priest, and Prophet: A Trinitarian Theology of Atonement* (New York: T&T Clark, 2004), 218 (emphasis added).

22  On Hebrews, see Harold Attridge, *The Epistle to the Hebrews* (Philadelphia: Fortress, 1989); Craig R. Koester, *Hebrews* (New York: Doubleday, 2001); and Peter T. O'Brien, *The Letter to the Hebrews* (Grand Rapids: Eerdmans, 2010). For Hebrews' view of priesthood, see John M. Scholer, *Proleptic Priests: Priesthood in the Epistle to the Hebrews* (Sheffield, U.K.: Sheffield Academic, 1991).

23  See further O'Collins, *Salvation for All*, 248–59.

24  On the New Testament and Christ's priesthood, see O'Collins and Jones, *Jesus Our Priest*, 1–68.

25  O'Collins and Jones, *Jesus Our Priest*, 27–35.

26  1 John 2:2 speaks of Christ as "the means of expiating" not only "our sins" but also "the sins of the world." On this verse and Rom 3:25, see O'Collins and Jones, *Jesus Our Priest*, 30–31.

27  On this verse, see Johnson, *First and Second Letters*, 191–92; Quinn and Wacker, *First and Second Letters*, 165–66.

28  O'Collins and Jones, *Jesus Our Priest*, 24–26.

29  Albert Vanhoye, *Old Testament Priests and the New Priest*, trans. Bernard Orchard (Petersham, Mass.: St Bede's, 1986), 14.

30  Lincoln, *Gospel according to John*, 330–31.

31  O'Collins and Jones, *Jesus Our Priest*, 133–34.

32  Harold Winstone, ed., *The Sunday Missal* (London: Collins, 1975), 383. Emphasis added.

33  The Nicene-Constantinopolitan Creed professes that "his [Christ's] kingdom will have no end." Heb 7:24 could encourage us to say, "his priesthood will have no end."

34  "The Word of God, when he assumed a human nature, introduced into this land of exile the hymn that in heaven is sung throughout all ages. He unites

the whole community of humankind with himself and associates it with him in singing this divine canticle of praise" (art. 152). Pius XII, *Christian Worship: Encyclical Letter (Mediator Dei) of His Holiness Pius XII . . .*, trans. Canon G. D. Smith (London: Catholic Truth Society, 1959), 58.

35  See O'Collins and Jones, *Jesus Our Priest*, 19–24, 250–61.

36  Pierre Teilhard de Chardin, "The Mass on the World," in *Hymn of the Universe*, trans. Gerald Vann (London: Collins, 1965), 19–37.

37  The 2002 encyclical by John Paul II, "*Ecclesia de Eucharistia*," art. 8, in *Acta Apostolicae Sedis* 95 (2003): 437–38 (emphasis in original). [=*AAS*]

38  See O'Collins, *Jesus Our Redeemer*, 37–42.

39  See further Rosemary Woolf, *The English Mystery Plays* (Berkeley: University of California Press, 1980); and Brian O. Murdoch, *Adam's Grace: Fall and Redemption in Medieval Literature* (Cambridge: D. S. Brewer, 2000).

40  *John Donne*, edited John Carey (Oxford: Oxford University Press, 1990), 332–33.

41  See Gertrud Schiller, *Iconography of Christian Art*, trans. Janet Seligman (London: Lund Humphries, 1971), 2:131, 479. She quotes a legend about the death of Adam drawn from the Syrian *Cave of Treasures*. Apropos of the Christ's death on Calvary, Adam says to Seth: "There the Word of God will come and suffer and will be crucified up there at the place where my body lies, so that my skull will be wet with his blood. And in that hour I shall be redeemed and he will bring me back to my kingdom and restore to me my priesthood and prophetic status" (2:131).

42  Subsequently, Cain and Abel, the sons of Adam and Eve, act in a priestly way by making offerings to God (Gen 4:1-4). The fact that their children make priestly offerings suggests something priestly about Adam and Eve. In the story of the renewed relationship between God and human beings, Noah acts in a priestly way (see O'Collins, *Salvation for All*, 8–11). That story encourages reading in a priestly way the original relationship between God and Adam (and Eve).

43  Dupuis, *Toward a Christian Theology*, 32–33, 64, 78. Irenaeus passed over in silence other covenants: in particular, that with Abraham and Sarah (Gen 15:1-21).

44  In the Genesis story of the great deluge and its aftermath, Noah acts in a priestly fashion by building an altar to the Lord and making an offering; then God establishes a covenant that encompasses all humanity (Gen 8:20–9:17).

45  John Henry Newman, "On the Priesthood of Christ," in *Sermon Notes of John Henry Cardinal Newman 1849–1878* (London: Longmans, Green, 1914), 69–70 (emphasis added).

46  John Henry Newman, "A Letter Addressed to His Grace, the Duke of Norfolk on Occasion of Mr Gladstone's Recent Expostulation," in *Certain Difficulties Felt by Anglicans in Catholic Teaching Considered* (London: Longmans, Green, 1891), 2:248–49.

47   Karl Rahner, "Anonymous Christians," in *Theological Investigations*, vol. 6, trans. Karl-Heinz Kruger and Boniface Kruger (London: Darton, Longman & Todd, 1969), 393–94.

48   O'Collins and Jones, *Jesus Our Priest*, 248–50.

49   O'Collins and Jones, *Jesus Our Priest*, 3–4, 16–17.

50   O'Collins and Jones, *Jesus Our Priest*, 243–45.

51   O'Collins and Jones, *Jesus Our Priest*, 265–70.

52   For details, see O'Collins, *Salvation for All*, 227–29.

## CHAPTER 7

1    See Gerald O'Collins, "Jacques Dupuis," in *New Catholic Encyclopedia Supplement 2010*, ed. Robert L. Fastiggi (Detroit: Gale, 2010), 420–22.

2    Dupuis, *Toward a Christian Theology*.

3    For the full text of the *Notification*, see *AAS* 94 (2002): 141–45; translated in *Origins* 30, no. 38 (2001): 605–8. On the whole case of Dupuis and the CDF, see Gerald O'Collins, *On the Left Bank of the Tiber* (Leominster: Gracewing, 2013), 213–51.

4    Jacques Dupuis, " 'The Truth Will Make You Free': The Theology of Religious Pluralism Revisited," *Louvain Studies* 24 (1999): 211–63.

5    Terrence Merrigan, "Exploring the Frontiers: Toward a Christian Theology of Religious Pluralism," *Louvain Studies* 23 (1998): 338–59; Comité de redaction, " 'Tout récapituler dans le Christ': A propos de l'ouvrage de J. Dupuis, *Vers une théologie Chrétienne du pluralisme religieux*," *Revue Thomiste* 98 (1998): 591–630.

6    For a bibliography on *Toward a Christian Theology*, see Kendall and O'Collins, *In Many and Diverse Ways*, 270–81; for a shorter bibliography of reviews and reactions, see *Louvain Studies* 27 (2002): 406–10.

7    Jacques Dupuis, *Il Cristianesimo e le religioni: Dallo scontro all'incontro* (Brescia: Queriniana, 2001); Dupuis, *Christianity and the Religions*.

8    For details on this teaching of Pope John Paul II, see O'Collins, *Second Vatican Council*, 166–80.

9    Dupuis, *Christianity and the Religions*, 87–95, 255–58, 263.

10   Dupuis, *Christianity and the Religions*, 255–58; in a personal communication, I had suggested qualifying as "asymmetrical" what Dupuis meant by "complementarity."

11   Dupuis, *Christianity and the Religions*, 144–46.

12   Dupuis, *Christianity and the Religions*, 144; in a personal communication, I had pointed out how this council supported Dupuis' position about the human and divine actions of Christ.

13   I drew attention to these changes in "Christ and the Religions," *Gregorianum* 84 (2003): 355–60.

14   The discussion of Dupuis' views continues in other languages—e.g., in the following works in Italian: Alberto Cozzi, *Gesù Cristo tra le religioni: Mediatore*

*dell'originario* (Assisi: Cittadella, 2005); Fiorella Quirini, "La mediazione salvifica sacramentale di Cristo e della Chiesa secondo Jacques Dupuis," *Quaderni di Scienze Religiose* 24 (2005): 103–47; Adolfo Russo, *La Verità crocifissa: Verità e rivelazione in tempi di pluralismo* (Cinisello Balsamo: San Paolo, 2005); Mariano Crociata, ed., *Teologia delle religioni: La questione del metodo* (Roma: Città Nuova, 2006); Angelo Amato, *Gesù, identità del cristianesimo: Conoscenza ed esperienza* (Città del Vaticano: Libreria Editrice Vaticana, 2008); Giacomo Canobbio, *Nessuna salvezza fuori della Chiesa? Storia e senso di un controverso principio teologico* (Brescia: Queriniana, 2009); Paolo Selvadagi, *Teologia, religioni, dialogo* (Città del Vaticano: Lateran University Press, 2009); Gianni Colzani, *Missiologia contemporanea: Il cammino evangelico delle Chiese; 1945–2007* (Cinisello Balsamo: San Paolo, 2010); Ivan Macut, "La salvezza nelle religioni nel pensiero di Jacques Dupuis," *Città di vita* 66 (2011): 149–64. For help in gathering this (Italian) bibliography, I wish to thank Nunzio Capizzi.

15  Terrence Merrigan, "The Appeal to Congar in Roman Catholic Theology of Religions: The Case of Jacques Dupuis," in *Yves Congar: Theologian of the Church*, ed. Gabriel Flynn (Louvain: Peeters, 2005), 427–57.

16  Terrence Merrigan, "Jacques Dupuis and the Redefinition of Inclusivism," in Kendall and O'Collins, *In Many and Diverse Ways*, 60–71. For Merrigan's review, see note 5 above.

17  Merrigan, "Appeal to Congar," in Flynn, *Yves Congar*, 428–30.

18  Merrigan, "Appeal to Congar," in Flynn, *Yves Congar*, 436–39.

19  Merrigan, "Appeal to Congar," in Flynn, *Yves Congar*, 439–57.

20  Quoted in Merrigan, "Appeal to Congar," in Flynn, *Yves Congar*, 452 (emphasis in original).

21  Dupuis, as quoted by Merrigan, "Appeal to Congar," in Flynn, *Yves Congar*, 452, 453.

22  Dupuis, *Toward a Christian Theology*, 212.

23  Merrigan, "Appeal to Congar," in Flynn, *Yves Congar*, 453.

24  Jacques Dupuis, commenting on *Evangelii nuntiandi*, in *Vidyajyoti* 40 (1976): 230.

25  Merrigan, "Appeal to Congar," in Flynn, *Yves Congar*, 455–57. See Roger W. Nutt, "An Office in Search of Its Ontology: Mediation and Trinitarian Christology in Jacques Dupuis' Theology of Religious Pluralism," *Louvain Studies* 32 (2007): 383–407.

26  Tom F. Torrance, *Theology in Reconciliation: Essays Toward Evangelical and Catholic Unity in East and West* (Eugene, Ore.: Wipf & Stock, 1996), 134.

27  On Christ's priestly mediation of salvation to the world, see O'Collins and Jones, *Jesus Our Priest*, 226–29, 265–70.

28  Mara Brecht, "The Humanity of Christ: Jacques Dupuis' Christology and Religious Pluralism," *Horizons* 35 (2008): 54–71.

29  Brecht, "Humanity of Christ," 60–63.

30  Brecht, "Humanity of Christ," 70.

31  See, e.g., Rahner, *Foundations of Christian Faith*, 193–95, 204–5.

32  Dupuis, *Toward a Christian Theology*, 283. The issue here simply involves the use (or misuse?) in Christology of the term "absolute."

33  Brecht, "Humanity of Christ," 66. This is not intended to assert that any or every religious form or institution (even some substantially perverse rites) can mediate Christ's salvation, but rather to maintain that his saving work reaches people beyond the institutions that constitute the church's sacramental life.

34  See Jacques Dupuis, "Christianity and Religions: Complementarity and Convergence," in *Many Mansions? Multiple Religious Belonging and Christian Identity*, ed. Catherine Cornille (Maryknoll, N.Y.: Orbis Books, 2002), 61–75.

35  Catherine Cornille, *The Im-possibility of Interreligious Dialogue* (New York: Crossroad, 2008).

36  Cornille, *Im-possibility*, 39.

37  Cornille, *Im-possibility*, 87–89; Cornille quotes Dupuis, *Christianity and the Religions*, 229.

38  Cornille, *Im-possibility*, 198–99.

39  See note 8 above.

40  Cornille, *Im-possibility*, 140–41.

41  Dupuis, *Christianity and the Religions*, 336–52.

42  Cornille, *Im-possibility*, 110–21.

43  Gavin D'Costa, review of Jacque Dupuis' *Toward a Christian Theology of Religious Pluralism*, in *Journal of Theological Studies* 59 (1998): 910–14.

44  D'Costa, review of Jacques Dupuis, 910, 911.

45  D'Costa, review of Jacques Dupuis, 914.

46  D'Costa, review of Jacques Dupuis, 911, 912.

47  Dupuis, *Toward a Christian Theology*, 353–56.

48  Dupuis, *Toward a Christian Theology*, 344. In equivalent terms, Vatican II's Dogmatic Constitution on the Church followed Thomas Aquinas in presenting Christ as "the head" not only of the Church but also of all human beings (*Lumen gentium* 16, 17).

49  Gavin D'Costa, *Christianity and World Religions: Disputed Questions in the Theology of Religions* (Oxford: Wiley-Blackwell, 2009), 19–23.

50  D'Costa, *Christianity and World Religions*, 22.

51  For details on *Mystici corporis* and the teaching of Aquinas, see O'Collins, *Second Vatican Council*, 27–31, 48–49.

52  Francis A. Sullivan, *Salvation outside the Church? Tracing the History of the Catholic Response* (Mahwah, N.J.: Paulist, 1992), 157, 160. See also Sullivan, "Introduction and Ecclesiological Issues," in *"Sic et non": Encountering "Dominus Iesus,"* ed. Stephen J. Pope and Charles Hefling (Maryknoll, N.Y.: Orbis Books, 2002), 50–51.

53  Dupuis, *Toward a Christian Theology*, 350–51; see Dupuis, *Christianity and the Religions*, 210–11.

54  D'Costa, *Christianity and the World Religions*, 180–86.

55  Gavin D'Costa, "Pluralist Arguments," in *Catholic Engagement with World Religions: A Comprehensive Survey*, ed. Karl J. Becker and Ilaria Morali (Maryknoll, N.Y.: Orbis Books, 2010), 337.

56  Dupuis, *Toward a Christian Theology*, 367.

57  Dupuis, *Christianity and the Religions*, 178–79. On "the combined action of God's Word and of his Spirit," see Dupuis, *Toward a Christian Theology*, 321.

58  D'Costa, "Pluralist Arguments," in Becker and Morali, *Catholic Engagement*, 337. Dupuis himself states that he has "nothing in common" with "the pluralist paradigm" of Hick and Knitter, in his *Christianity and the Religions*, 263.

59  D'Costa, "Pluralist Arguments," in Becker and Morali, *Catholic Engagement*, 583n65.

60  The CDF states at the end of the preface to the *Notification*: "The present *Notification* is not meant as a judgment on the author's subjective thought, but rather as a statement of the Church's teaching on certain aspects of the above-mentioned doctrinal truths, and as a refutation of erroneous or harmful opinions, which, prescinding from the author's intentions, *could* be derived from reading the ambiguous statements and insufficient explanations found in certain sections of the book [sections which are never specified]. In this way, Catholic readers will be given solid criteria for judgment, consistent with the doctrine of the Church, in order to avoid the serious confusion and misunderstanding which *could* result from reading this book" (emphasis added). The CDF was obviously at pains *not* to pass any judgment (of innocence or guilt) on the intentions of Dupuis. There is also a patent tentativeness about the repeated "could," with no claim being made that "erroneous or harmful opinions" or "serious confusion and misunderstanding" have actually resulted from reading Dupuis' book. What the *Notification* says turns out to be notably "weaker" than what we read in 2 Peter about the letters of St. Paul and what they have provoked: "There are some things in them hard to understand, which the ignorant and unstable twist to their own destruction" (2 Pet 3:16). Note that for 2 Peter some sections of Paul's letters not only *could* be misunderstood but also were *actually* twisted to the spiritual destruction of people.

61  D'Costa, "Pluralist Arguments," in Becker and Morali, *Catholic Engagement*, 583.

62  Dupuis, *Christianity and the Religions*, 140. This book, which significantly clarifies Dupuis' views and introduces the term "inclusivise pluralism," appears neither in the text nor in the long bibliography of D'Costa, *Christianity and World Religions*. Yet D'Costa (p. 24), without providing any reference, writes of Dupuis calling his own position "inclusivist pluralism." Did D'Costa pick this up from a personal communication from Dupuis? Or had he in fact read *Christianity and the Religions*?

63  Dupuis, *Christianity and the Religions*, 144, 145.

64  St. Thomas Aquinas, *Summa theologiae*, 3a.16.10.

65  Public documentation about this is not yet available.

66  Congregation for the Doctrine of the Faith, "*Dominus Iesus*," in *AAS* 92 (2000): 745; translated in Pope and Hefling, "*Sic et non*," 5 (no. 4).

67  Dupuis, *Toward a Christian Theology*, 299; see Dupuis, *Christianity and the Religions*, 144.

68  Dupuis, *Toward a Christian Theology*, 298–99.

69  Denzinger and Hünermann, *Enchiridion symbolorum*, nos. 556–58; Neuner and Dupuis, *Christian Faith*, nos. 635–37.

70  St. Thomas Aquinas, *Summa contra Gentiles*, 4.35.8.

71  Dupuis, *Christianity and the Religions*, 144.

72  St. Thomas Aquinas, *Summa theologiae*, 3a.13.1.

73  Dupuis, *Toward a Christian Theology*, 299.

74  Ilaria Morali, "Salvation, Religions, and Dialogue with Roman Magisterium," in Becker and Morali, *Catholic Engagement*, 138.

75  Ilaria Morali, "Overview of Some Francophone and Italian Trends," in Becker and Morali, *Catholic Engagement*, 325.

76  Morali, "Overview," in Becker and Morali, *Catholic Engagement*, 326. See Jacques Dupuis, *Jesus Christ at the Encounter of World Religions*, trans. (from French) Robert R. Barr (Maryknoll, N.Y.: Orbis Books, 1997), 92, 104–10.

77  Morali, "Overview," in Becker and Morali, *Catholic Engagement*, 326.

78  Morali, "Overview," in Becker and Morali, *Catholic Engagement*, 579n97.

79  Morali, "Overview," in Becker and Morali, *Catholic Engagement*, 326. Morali is quoting Jacques Dupuis, "La teologia del pluralismo religioso rivisitata," *Rassegna di Teologia* 40 (1999): 692.

80  Morali, "Overview," in Becker and Morali, *Catholic Engagement*, 326–27.

81  Don Schweitzer, *Contemporary Christologies* (Minneapolis: Fortress, 2010); on Dupuis, principally 115–25.

82  Dupuis, *Jesus Christ at the Encounter* (1991); Dupuis, *Who Do You Say I Am?* (1994).

83  Schweitzer, *Contemporary Christologies*, 116–17, 122.

84  Schweitzer, *Contemporary Christologies*, 118.

85  Schweitzer, *Contemporary Christologies*, 118, 120.

86  Schweitzer, *Contemporary Christologies*, 122, 123.

87  Keith E. Johnson, *Rethinking the Trinity & Religious Pluralism: An Augustinian Assessment* (Downers Grove, Ill.: IVP Academic, 2011).

88  Johnson, *Rethinking the Trinity*, 100.

89  Johnson, *Rethinking the Trinity*, 42.

90  Johnson, *Rethinking the Trinity*, 126–35.

91  Johnson, *Rethinking the Trinity*, 129, 133, 134, 135 (emphasis added).

92  Johnson, *Rethinking the Trinity*, 131–33.

93  Johnson, *Rethinking the Trinity*, 130.

94  Johnson, *Rethinking the Trinity*, 187.

95  Johnson, *Rethinking the Trinity*, 99.

96  O'Collins, *Second Vatican Council*, *passim*.

97  For details, see O'Collins and Jones, *Jesus Our Priest*, *passim*.

98  See O'Collins and Jones, *Jesus Our Priest*, 92–95 (Augustine) and 224–29 (Torrance).

99  See once again what the Constitution on the Divine Liturgy taught: "Jesus Christ, the High Priest of the New and Eternal Covenant, when he assumed a human nature, introduced into this land of exile the hymn that in heaven

is sung throughout all ages. He unites the whole community of human kind with himself and associates it with him in singing the divine canticle of praise" (*Sacrosanctum concilium* 83).

## Chapter 8

1   Dupuis, *Toward a Christian Theology*; D'Costa, review of Jacques Dupuis, 910.

2   D'Costa, *Christianity and World Religions*, 19–23, at 22.

3   Gavin D'Costa, "The Trinity in Interreligious Dialogue," in *Oxford Handbook of the Trinity*, ed. Gilles Emery and Matthew Levering (Oxford: Oxford University Press, 2011), 578–79.

4   D'Costa, "Pluralist Arguments," in Becker and Morali, *Catholic Engagement*, 337.

5   See, e.g., Dupuis, *Toward a Christian Theology*, 321, 367.

6   Gavin D'Costa, "Christian Theology of Religions," in *The Routledge Companion to Modern Christian Thought*, ed. Chad Meister and James Beilby (London: Routledge, 2013), 666. As far as I can find out (with the expert help of Simon Wayte), before D'Costa in 2009 first called Dupuis a neo-Rahnerian, the term had appeared in the London *Tablet* for June 29, 1996. In an article on "Girard's Breakthrough," James Allison referred approvingly to John Milbank's 1990 book, *Theology and Social Theory: Beyond Secular Reason* (Oxford: Basil Blackwell, 1990), and spoke of "neo-Rahnerian individualism" (849). But Allison did not apply the term to Dupuis, nor had Milbank, who had simply written of Rahner's "integralism" (220).

7   For a bibliography of reviews of and reactions to *Toward a Christian Theology of Religious Pluralism*, see Kendall and O'Collins, *In Many and Diverse Ways*, 270–81; for further comments on Dupuis' work, see Gerald O'Collins, "Jacques Dupuis: The Ongoing Debate," *Theological Studies* 74 (2013): 632–54.

8   Francis X. Clooney, *Comparative Theology: Deep Learning across Religious Borders* (Oxford: Wiley-Blackwell, 2010), 16.

9   For details, see Kendall and O'Collins, *In Many and Diverse Ways*, 232, 234, 235, 237, 239, 240, 241, 243, 245, 247, 248, 249.

10  For details of reviews, see Kendall and O'Collins, *In Many and Diverse Ways*, 231–69. Given the large number of books that Dupuis regularly reviewed, the fact that over the years he reviewed seven volumes of *Theological Investigations*, *Foundations of Christian Faith*, and a few other works by Rahner did not mean paying more than ordinary attention to him.

11  *The Teaching of the Catholic Church*, trans. Geoffrey Stevens (Cork: Mercier, 1967), described as "compiled by" Heinrich Roos and Josef Neuner and "edited by" Karl Rahner.

12  Neuner and Dupuis, *Christian Faith*.

13  From vol. 5 to vol. 22 of *Theological Investigations* (1966–1991), Rahner repeatedly reflected on Vatican II, with thirteen chapters expressly dedicated

to conciliar topics, and other chapters regularly quoting or at least referring to the Council's teaching. Rahner was also an influential member of the editorial committee for H. Vorgrimler, ed., *Commentary on the Documents of Vatican II*, 5 vols. (London: Burns & Oates, 1967–1969).

14   For details, see Kendall and O'Collins, *In Many and Diverse Ways*, 233.

15   For details, see Gerald O'Collins, *Living Vatican II: The 21st Council for the 21st Century* (Mahwah, N.J.: Paulist, 2006), 45–47.

16   This article is reproduced in O'Collins, *Living Vatican II*, 173–201.

17   Jacques Dupuis, *Jesus Christ at the Encounter of World Religions*, trans. Robert R. Barr (Maryknoll, N.Y.: Orbis Books, 1991); Dupuis, *Who Do You Say I Am?*

18   Brecht, "Humanity of Christ," 54.

19   Schweitzer, *Contemporary Christologies*, 115–25.

20   Quoted by Merrigan, "Appeal to Congar," in Flynn, *Yves Congar*, 452 (emphasis in original).

21   In a lecture given in April 1961, Rahner expressed a similar conviction, but typically he spoke of what was anthropologically rather than theologically realistic. Given their social nature and radical solidarity with each other, for followers of other religions to "have a positive saving relationship with God, they are going to have it *within that religion*" which is at their disposal. Rahner, "Christianity and the Non-Christian Religions," 129 (emphasis added).

22   Dupuis, as quoted by Merrigan, "Appeal to Congar," in Flynn, *Yves Congar*, 453. Here Dupuis agreed with the view—promoted by Henri de Lubac, Rahner, and others—that human beings are created with a supernatural goal, which is intrinsic to human nature as it actually exists. Hence there is no such thing as the "purely natural" or the "merely human." For further details, see O'Collins, *Second Vatican Council*, 53–54.

23   Merrigan, "Appeal to Congar," in Flynn, *Yves Congar*, 453. Merrigan is quoting Dupuis, *Toward a Christian Theology*, 212.

24   See O'Collins, *Living Vatican II*, 233–34.

25   Jacques Dupuis, "Apostolic Exhortation *Evangelii nuntiandi* of Pope Paul VI," *Vidyajyoti* 40 (1976): 230.

26   Dupuis, *Jesus Christ at the Encounter*, 281–96. The bibliography lists twenty-two entries under the name of Rahner, but eighteen of these entries are all particular chapters in *Theological Investigations*, and only four are books. The eleven entries that follow the name of Raymond Panikkar are all books.

27   Dupuis, *Jesus Christ at the Encounter*, 109; see 136. On pp. 129–30 Dupuis detects ambiguity in the difference between Rahner's "anonymous Christianity" and "explicit Christianity," but finds this ambiguity "erased" in his *Foundations of Christian Faith*. What Dupuis does not, however, note is the way in which Rahner did more than merely clarify the difference between "anonymous" and "explicit" Christianity. He distanced himself from the

language of "anonymous Christianity"; for details, see O'Collins, *Second Vatican Council*, 56–57.

28   Dupuis, *Jesus Christ at the Encounter*, 184–88.

29   Dupuis, *Jesus Christ at the Encounter*, 109; Dupuis cites Gavin D'Costa, *Theology and Religious Pluralism: The Challenge of Other Religions* (Oxford: Basil Blackwell, 1986), 136.

30   Rahner, *Foundations of Christian Faith*, 176–321.

31   Dupuis, *Who Do You Say I Am?* 24–25.

32   Dupuis, *Who Do You Say I Am?* 91–92.

33   Dupuis, *Who Do You Say I Am?* 117, 121.

34   Dupuis, *Who Do You Say I Am?* 95, 118, 136–37. Here Dupuis quotes Karl Rahner, "On the Theology of the Incarnation," in *Theological Investigations*, vol. 4, trans. Kevin Smyth (London: Darton, Longman & Todd, 1974), 117.

35   Dupuis, *Who Do You Say I Am?* 160.

36   Dupuis, *Jesus Christ at the Encounter*, 104–10; corresponds to Dupuis, *Who Do You Say I Am?* 157–62.

37   Dupuis, *Toward a Christian Theology*, 143–49; on D'Costa, 147n15.

38   Dupuis, *Toward a Christian Theology*, 149.

39   Dupuis, *Toward a Christian Theology*, 353–56. In his review of this book for *Journal of Theological Studies*, D'Costa wrote of Dupuis "severing" Christ and his kingdom from the church and so "breaking the indissoluble bond between Christology and ecclesiology" (910, 912, 913). This extreme language of "severing" and "breaking" does not express accurately what Dupuis wrote: for instance, "The presence of the Church as sign in the world bears witness . . . that God has established in this world his Reign in Jesus Christ" (*Toward a Christian Theology*, 354).

40   Dupuis, *Toward a Christian Theology*, 314. For Dupuis, to call Hinduism, for instance, provisional and transitory would ignore much historical data: Hinduism as a way of salvation has endured and often endured vigorously for twenty centuries after the time of Christ. Below we take up this question biblically and historically.

41   Dupuis, *Toward a Christian Theology*, 282.

42   Dupuis, *Christianity and the Religions*.

43   Dupuis, *Christianity and the Religions*, 87–95, 255.

44   D'Costa, *Christianity and World Religions*, 34.

45   Dupuis, *Christianity and the Religions*, 89

46   Dupuis, *Toward a Christian Theology*, 144.

47   For instance, Dupuis, *Toward a Christian Theology*, 248, 294, 305.

48   Dupuis, *Christianity and the Religions*, e.g., 90, 158, 220–38, 256. Apropos of terminology, we should also note that, like the documents from Vatican II, Dupuis never called those of other faiths "pagans," whereas Rahner continued to use this term; for details see O'Collins, *Second Vatican Council*, 52–53.

49   Dupuis, *Toward a Christian Theology*, 326–29.

50  Dupuis, *Toward a Christian Theology*, 326–28. See O'Collins, *On the Left Bank*, 248–49.
51  Dupuis, *Christianity and the Religions*, 255–58.
52  D'Costa, review of Jacques Dupuis, 911. Others have also noted the significance of Dupuis' Trinitarian emphasis; see, e.g., Daniel L. Migliore, "The Trinity and the Theology of Religions," in *God's Life in Trinity*, ed. Miroslav Volf and Michael Welker (Minneapolis: Fortress, 2006), 101–17; Jon Paul Sydnor, "Beyond a Text: Revisiting Jacques Dupuis' Theology of Religions," *International Review of Mission* 96 (2007): 56–71.
53  Dupuis, *Christianity and the Religions*, 81, 90–95, 100–115, 156, 178–80.
54  Rahner, *Foundations of Christian Faith*, 311–21.
55  Rahner, *Foundations of Christian Faith*, 153–61; see Dupuis, *Toward a Christian Theology*, 219–20.
56  Dupuis, *Christianity and the Religions*, 102.
57  Dupuis, *Toward a Christian Theology*, 32–33.
58  Dupuis, *Christianity and the Religions*, 100–103.
59  Dupuis, *Christianity and the Religions*, 109.
60  D'Costa, *Christianity and World Religions*, 22.

# A Bibliography of ·
# Gerald O'Collins, SJ (2000–2013)

## 2000

"Between the Lines of the Easter Story." *Tablet*, April 22/29, 551–52.

"Easter Stories." *Way* suppl. 99 (*Resurrection and Beyond: The Fourth Week*): 35–43.

"The Incarnation Summit." *Furrow*, July/August, 339–42.

"The King and the Maiden." *Tablet*, December 23/30, 1738.

"Obituary: Orietta Doria Pamphilj." *Tablet*, November 25, 1615–16.

"Redemption." In *Oxford Companion to Christian Thought*, ed. Adrian Hastings, 598–61. Oxford: Oxford University Press.

"The Resurrection of Jesus: The Debate Continued." *Gregorianum* 81: 589–98.

(With Edward G. Farrugia) *A Concise Dictionary of Theology*. 2nd rev. ed. Mahwah, N.J.: Paulist.

| Book Reviews | In |
|---|---|
| Gavin D'Costa. *The Meeting of Religions*. Edinburgh: T&T Clark. | *Tablet*, November 4, 1489–90. |
| Geza Vermes. *The Changing Faces of Jesus*. London: Allen Lane. | *Tablet*, July 1, 895–96. |

## 2001

"Christmas: A Feast of Love." *America*, December 24–31, 7–8.

"The Humanity of God." *Tablet*, December 22/29, 1809.

| Book Reviews | In |
|---|---|
| Mark Elliot. *The Song of Songs and Christology in the Early Church*. Tübingen: Mohr Siebeck. | *Gregorianum* 82: 793–94. |
| Richard Holloway. *Doubts and Loves: What Is Left of Christianity*. Edinburgh: Cannongate. | *Tablet*, October 27, 1529–30. |
| Hans Hübner. *An Philemon: An die Kolosser; An die Epheser*. Tübingen: Mohr Siebeck. | *Gregorianum* 82: 595. |
| Hans Hübner. *Die Weisheit Salomonis*. Göttingen: Vandenhoeck & Ruprecht. | *Gregorianum* 82: 385–86. |

## 2002

"The Holy Trinity: The Debate Continued." *Gregorianum* 83: 363–70.

"How Much Can We Know?" *Tablet*, November 2, 15. Nom de plume Stewart Peters.

"I documenti dottrinali della chiesa cattolica." *Gregorianum* 83: 757–60.

*Incarnation*. London: Continuum. Trans. into Italian, Norwegian, and Spanish.

"The Incarnation: The Crucial Issues." In *The Incarnation*, edited by Stephen Davis, Daniel Kendall, and Gerald O'Collins, 1–27. Oxford: Oxford University Press.

"The Love That Moves the Sun." *Tablet*, April 6, 2.

"The Resurrection of Jesus: Some Contemporary Issues." In *Hear O Islands: Theology and Catechesis in the New Millennium*, edited by J. Redford, 178–204. Dublin: Veritas.

"A Theological Pilgrimage." In *Shaping a Theological Mind*, edited by D. C. Marks, 97–101. Aldershot, U.K.: Ashgate.

"This Beautiful Baby." *Tablet*, December 21/28, 14.

(With Stephen Davis and Daniel Kendall, eds.) *The Incarnation*. Oxford: Oxford University Press.

| Book Reviews | In |
|---|---|
| E. A. Dreyer, ed. *The Cross in Christian Tradition from Paul to Barnabas*. Mahwah, N.J.: Paulist. | *Gregorianum* 83: 375. |
| R. Harries. *God Outside the Box*. London: SPCK. | *Tablet*, October 12, 17. |
| Hans Hübner. *Nietzsche und das Neue Testament*. Tübingen: Mohr Siebeck. | *Gregorianum* 83: 375–76. |

## 2003

"Christ and the Religions." *Gregorianum* 84: 347–62.

*Easter Faith: Believing in the Risen Jesus.* London: Darton, Longman & Todd. Trans. into Italian.

"Jacques Dupuis's Contribution to Interreligious Dialogue." *Theological Studies* 64: 388–97.

(With Mario Farrugia) *Catholicism: The Story of Catholic Christianity.* Oxford: Oxford University Press. Trans. into Bulgarian, Italian, and Spanish.

(With Daniel Kendall) *In Many and Diverse Ways: In Honor of Jacques Dupuis.* Maryknoll, N.Y.: Orbis Books.

| Book Reviews | In |
|---|---|
| D. Brown. *The Da Vinci Code.* New York: Doubleday. | *America*, December 15, 15–17. |
| J. D. G. Dunn. *Jesus Remembered: Christianity in the Making.* Vol. 1. Grand Rapids: Eerdmans. | *Pacifica* 16, 325–27. |
| Andrew M. Greeley. *The Great Mysteries: Experiencing Catholic Faith from Inside Out.* Lanham, Md.: Sheed & Ward. | *Tablet*, December 20/27, 34. |
| B. Hoose, ed. *Authority in the Roman Catholic Church.* Burlington, Vt.: Ashgate. | *Tablet*, January 4, 18–19. |
| W. Madges and M. J. Daly, eds. *Vatican II: Forty Personal Stories.* Mystic, Conn.: Twenty-Third. | *Tablet*, June 21, 18. |
| T. Peters et al., eds. *Resurrection: Theological and Scientific Assessments.* Grand Rapids: Eerdmans. | *Theological Studies* 64, 855–57. |
| N. T. Wright. *The Resurrection of the Son of God.* London: SPCK. | *Tablet*, April 19, 28–29. |

## 2004

"Faith and History." In *Was den Glauben in Bewegung Bringt: Festschrift für Karl H. Neufeld*, edited by A. R. Batlogg, M. Delgado, and R. A. Siebenrock, 320–27. Freiburg: Herder.

"An Integral Vision." In *Sapere teologico e unità della fede: Studi in onore del Professore; Jared Wicks*, edited by C. A. Valls, C. Dotolo, and G. Pasquale, 314–23. Rome: Gregorian University Press.

"Jesus as Lord and Teacher." In *Who Do You Say That I Am? Confessing the Mystery of Christ*, edited by John C. Cavadini and Laura Holt, 51–61. Notre Dame, Ind.: University of Notre Dame Press.

"Redemption: Some Crucial Issues." In *The Redemption*, edited by Stephen Davis, Daniel Kendall, and Gerald O'Collins, 1–22. Oxford: Oxford University Press.

"The Second Adam." *America*, April 12, 10–12.

"La teologia della rivelazione dopo la 'Dei Verbum': Prospettive e problemi." *Rivista di Teologia dell'Evangelizzazione* 8: 427–35.

(With Stephen Davis and Daniel Kendall, eds.) *The Redemption*. Oxford: Oxford University Press.

| Book Reviews | In |
|---|---|
| G. Frosini. *La risurrezione: inizio del mondo nuovo*. Bologna: Dehoniane. | *Theological Studies* 65: 409–10. |
| Hans Hübner. *Goethes Faust und das Neue Testament*. Göttingen: Vandenhoeck & Ruprecht. | *Gregorianum* 85: 203. |
| R. Swinburne. *The Resurrection of God Incarnate*. Oxford: Oxford University Press. | *Theological Studies* 65: 677–78. |
| A. Torres Queiruga. *Repensar la resurrección: La differencia cristiana en la continuidad de las religiones y de la cultura*. Madrid: Trotta. | *Gregorianum* 85: 181–83. |

## 2005

"Born in the Shadow of Calvary." *Tablet*, December 31, 12–13.

"The Busy Pope with Time to Pray." *Faith Alive*, May 23.

"Come 'ringiovanire' teologia e vita Cristiana." *Vita pastorale*, March, 104–5.

"Heart of the Council." *Tablet*, December 10, 4–5.

"Jacques Dupuis, S.J. (1923–2004): In Retrospect." *Vidyajyoti* 69: 450–59.

"John Paul II." *Wanted in Rome*, April 6.

"Obituary: Jacques Dupuis." *Tablet*, January 8, 36.

"Seeking the Godhead." *Tablet*, November 12, 20.

"A Theologian Looks into *The Da Vinci Code*." *Origins*, January 27, 513–15.

"Vatican II at Age 40." *America*, December 5, 8–11.

"Why One Couple Prayed the Liturgy of the Hours." *Faith Alive*, March 7.

| Book Reviews | In |
|---|---|
| L. W. Hurtado. *Lord Jesus Christ: Devotion to Jesus in Earliest Christianity.* Grand Rapids: Eerdmans. | *Biblica* 86: 283–87. |
| *La résurrection chez les Pères.* Strasbourg: Université Marc Bloch. | *Gregorianum* 86: 221. |
| Richard Lennan. *Risking the Church: The Challenges of Catholic Faith.* Oxford: Oxford University Press. | *Gregorianum* 86: 415–16. |
| Santiago Madrigal Terras. *Memoria del Concilio: Diez evocaciones del Vaticano II.* Madrid: Universidad Pontificia Comillas. | *Gregorianum* 86: 931–32. |
| Thomas Marschler. *Auferstehung und Himmelfahrt Christi in der scholastichen Theologie bis zu Thomas von Aquin.* Münster: Aschendorff. | *Theological Studies* 66: 931–32. |

## 2006

"Being the Good News." *Tablet*, August 12, 1–15.
"Il fenomeno 'Codici da Vinci.'" *La Civiltà Cattolica*, June 3, 473–79.
"Forgive as We Forgive." *Church* 22: 5–8.
"Hell's Armies Flee." *Pastoral Review* 2: 8–10.
"Implementing *Nostra aetate*." *Gregorianum* 87: 714–26.
"John Donne on the Trinity." In *God's Life in Trinity*, edited by M. Volf and M. Welker, 200–210, 253–54. Minneapolis: Fortress.
*Living Vatican II: The 21st Council for the 21st Century.* Mahwah, N.J.: Paulist.
*The Lord's Prayer.* London: Darton, Longman & Todd.
"Proclaiming Peter's Message." *Tablet*, April 15, 12–13.
"Redenzione come liberazione vittoriosa." In *Verità e responsabilità: Studi in onore di Aniceto Molinaro*, edited by L. Messinese and C. Göbel, 657–63. Rome: Studi Anselmiana.
"Teologia della visione: Il Risorto vincitore della morte." In *Il Corpo Glorioso*, edited by C. Bernardi et al., 15–17. Pisa: Giardini Editori.

| Book Reviews | In |
|---|---|
| C. E. Curran. *Loyal Dissent: Memoir of a Catholic Theologian.* Washington, D.C.: Georgetown University Press. | *Tablet*, June 3, 27. |

| | |
|---|---|
| Hans Hübner. *Evangelische Fundamentaltheologie der Bibel*. Göttingen: Vandenhoeck & Ruprecht. | *Gregorianum* 87: 175–76. |
| O. Rush. *Still Interpreting Vatican II: Some Hermeneutical Principles*. Mahwah, N.J.: Paulist. | *Gregorianum* 87: 932–33. |

## 2007

"Being Sentimental at Christmas." *Pastoral Review* 3, no. 6: 59–61.

"A Challenge for Theologians: Three Puzzling Positions." *America*, September 17, 23–24.

"The Feast of the Sacred Heart." *Pastoral Review* 3, no. 3: 3–6.

"The God of All Comfort." *Pastoral Review* 3, no. 2: 10–15.

*Jesus Our Redeemer: A Christian Approach to Salvation*. Oxford: Oxford University Press. Trans. into Italian and Polish.

"John Paul II on Christ, the Holy Spirit, and World Religions." *Irish Theological Quarterly* 72: 323–37.

"Led by a Flickering Star." *Tablet*, January 6, 8–9.

"The Love of the Christ Child." *Reality*, December, 30–31.

"Mary, Catholicism and Priesthood." In *Behold Your Mother: Priests Speak about Mary*, edited by S. J. Rossetti, 131–41. Notre Dame, Ind.: Ave Maria.

"The Second Journey of John Henry Newman." *Way* 46, no. 2: 49–57.

"Softly, Softly." *Tablet*, December 15, 10–11.

(With Daniel Kendall and Jeffrey LaBelle, eds.) *Pope John Paul II: A Reader*. Mahwah, N.J.: Paulist.

| Book Reviews | In |
|---|---|
| Giuseppe Alberigo, ed. *History of Vatican II*. Vol. 5. Maryknoll, N.Y.: Orbis Books. | *Theological Studies* 68: 191–92. |
| Jeffrey Archer. *The Gospel according to Judas*. London: Macmillan. | *Pastoral Review* 3, no. 4: 83–85. |
| Pope Benedict XVI. *Jesus of Nazareth*. London: Bloomsbury. | *Pastoral Review* 3, no. 5: 90–91. |
| Pope Benedict XVI. *Jesus of Nazareth*. New York: Doubleday. | *America*, June 4–11, 22–23. |
| Gabriel Flynn. *Yves Congar's Vision of the Church in a World of Unbelief*. Aldershot, U.K.: Ashgate. | *Ecclesiology* 4, no. 1: 122–25. |

| Robert Gascoyne, ed. *John Paul II, Legacy and Witness*. Strathfield, N.S.W.: St. Paul's. | *Pacifica* 20: 347–48. |
|---|---|
| John Nolland. *The Gospel of Matthew*. Grand Rapids: Eerdmans. | *Pacifica* 20: 360–62. |
| Donna Orsuto. *Holiness*. London: Continuum. | *Pastoral Review* 3, no. 3: 84–85. |
| Ormond Rush. *Still Interpreting Vatican II: Some Hermeneutical Principles*. Mahwah, N.J.: Paulist. | *Gregorianum* 87: 932–33. |

## 2008

*Catholicism: A Very Short Introduction*. Oxford: Oxford University Press.
"The Contagion of Mary." *Pastoral Review* 4, no. 4: 38–40.
"Four Homilies and a Conference." *Pastoral Review* 4, no. 3: 12–17.
"The Hidden Story of Jesus." *New Blackfriars* 89: 710–14.
"Images of Prayer." *Pastoral Review* 4, no. 5: 34–39.
*Jesus: A Portrait*. London: Darton, Longman & Todd. Trans. into Arabic and Italian.
"Jesus and the Call to Love." *Pastoral Review* 4, no. 1: 17–21.
"John Paul II and the Development of Doctrine." In O'Collins and Hayes, *Legacy of John Paul II*, 1–16.
"John Paul II on Christ, the Holy Spirit, and World Religions." *Irish Theological Quarterly* 72: 323–37.
"The Message of the Annunciation." *Pastoral Review* 4, no. 2: 4–5.
Obituary: Cardinal Avery Dulles. *Tablet*, December 20/27, 61.
"The Pope's Easter Proclamation." *America*, March 24, 11–14. Reprinted by *Il Regno*; and then *Compass* 42: 3–5.
"In Praise of Christmas Cards." *Pastoral Review* 4, no. 6: 20–22.
"A Prayer and a Reflection." In *Mosaic: Favourite Prayers and Reflections from Inspiring Australians*, edited by R. Bradley, 46, 136. Sydney: ABC Books.
"A Resurrection That Works?" About episode four of the BBC's *The Passion, Thinking Faith*, March 23. www.thinkingfaith.org/.
*Salvation for All: God's Other Peoples*. Oxford: Oxford University Press. Trans. into Italian.
"Saved by Hope: Insights from Pope Benedict's New Encyclical." *America*, January 21–28, 27–30.
"The Virginal Conception and Its Meanings." *New Blackfriars* 89: 431–40.
"With Complete Acceptance and Baffling Logic." *Tablet*, March 29, 14–15.
(With Michael Hayes, eds.) *The Legacy of John Paul II*. London: Continuum.

| Book Reviews | In |
|---|---|
| Richard Bauckham. *Jesus and the Eyewitnesses: The Gospels as Eyewitness Testimony.* Grand Rapids: Eerdmans. | *Heythrop Journal* 49: 309–10. |
| David B. Burrell. *Deconstructing Theodicy: Why Job Has Nothing to Say to the Problem of Suffering.* Grand Rapids: Brazos. | *Tablet*, November 8, 27. |
| Oliver D. Crisp. *Divinity and Humanity.* Cambridge: Cambridge University Press. | *Theological Studies* 69: 232. |
| Philomena Cullen et al., eds. *Catholic Social Justice: Theological and Practical Explorations.* London: Continuum. | *Pastoral Review* 4, no. 1: 91–92. |
| Hans Hübner. *Erlösung bei Richard Wagner und im Neuen Testament.* Neukirchen: Neukirchener Verlag. | *Gregorianum* 89: 930–31. |
| Kevin J. Madigan and Jon D. Levenson. *Resurrection: The Power of God for Christians and Jews.* New Haven, Conn.: Yale University Press. | *Tablet*, August 23, 23. |
| Vitor Westhelle. *The Scandalous God: The Use and Abuse of the Cross.* Minneapolis: Fortress. | *Horizons* 35: 400–401. |
| Barrie Wilson. *How Jesus Became Christian.* London: Weidenfeld & Nicolson. | *Tablet*, May 3, 22. |

## 2009

"The Beautiful Jesus and Young People." *Le Chéile*, December, 4.

"The Case against Prayer." *Pastoral Review* 5, no. 5: 34–37.

*Christology: A Biblical, Historical, and Systematic Study of Jesus.* 2nd ed. Oxford: Oxford University Press.

Contribution to review symposium, *Horizons* 36, on O'Collins, *Salvation for All: God's Other Peoples*, 120–42.

"The Hand of God Can Be Seen in Some Events We Cannot Explain." *Herald Sun*, December 22, 34–35.

"I Have Seven Dreams. . . ." *Tablet*, September 19, 8–9.

"In Praise of Paul." *Pastoral Review* 5, no. 3: 24–29. Reprinted in *In Praise of Paul*, edited by Michael A. Hayes, 17–26. London: St Paul's.

"It Starts at Dawn and Lights the World for All Time." *Tablet*, April 11, 20–21.

"Jesus Our Priest." In *Priesthood: A Life Open to Christ*, edited by D. P. Cronin, 144–46. London: St Paul's. Reproduced by *Thinking Faith*. www.thinkingfaith.org/.

"A Presentation of *Jesus: A Portrait*." *Letters and Notices* 99: 141–42.

*Reflections for Busy People: Making Time for Ourselves, Jesus, and God*. Mahwah, N.J.: Paulist.

"Righteousness." *Preacher*, the first Sunday of Advent, 21–22.

"Starting Our Christmas Retreat." *Pastoral Review* 5, no. 6: 30–36.

"Thinking about Christ's Resurrection in the Year of St Paul." *Thinking Faith*. Easter, www.thinkingfaith.org/.

"Trashing the Truth: 'Angels and Demons.'" *Pastoral Review* 5, no. 4: 46–49.

"Two Poems on the Passion." *Pastoral Review* 5, no. 2: 53–54.

"Vatican II and Fundamental Theology." *Irish Theological Quarterly* 74: 379–88.

| Book Reviews | In |
|---|---|
| Pope Benedict XVI. *Priests of Jesus Christ*. Oxford: Family. | *Pastoral Review* 5, no. 3: 91. |
| Lawrence Cunningham. *An Introduction to Catholicism*. Cambridge: Cambridge University Press. | *Tablet*, May 30, 26. |
| John J. Hughes. *No Ordinary Fool: A Testimony to Grace*. Mustang, Okla.: Tate. | *Tablet*, February 21, 29. |
| Anthony J. Kelly. *The Resurrection Effect: Transforming Christian Life and Thought*. Maryknoll, N.Y.: Orbis Books. | *Theological Studies* 70: 478–80. |
| André Lacoque. *The Trial of Innocence: Adam, Eve and the Jahwist*. Eugene, Ore.: Cascade. | *Heythrop Journal* 50: 1007–8. |
| Alan Spence. *Christology: A Guide for the Perplexed*. London: Continuum. | *Pastoral Review* 5, no. 4: 94–96. |
| Milton Walsh. *Second Friends: C. S. Lewis and Ronald Knox in Conversation*. San Francisco: Ignatius. | *Pastoral Review* 5, no. 1: 96–97. |
| J. Webster, K. Tanner, and I. Torrance, eds. *The Oxford Handbook of Systematic Theology*. Oxford: Oxford University Press. | *Heythrop Journal* 50: 745–47. |

2010

"15th and 16th Sunday in Ordinary Time." *Kairos*, July 24, 34.

Address at Melbourne Town Hall, June 7, on the occasion of receiving a doctorate *honoris causa* from Australian Catholic University. *Jesuit Life* 93: 21–23.

"Biblical Theology"; "Redemption"; "Roman Catholic Church and Theology"; "Tradition: A Roman Catholic Perspective"; "Vatican Council II." In *The Cambridge Dictionary of Christianity*, edited by Daniel Patte. New York: Cambridge University Press.

"Dupuis, Jacques." In *New Catholic Encyclopedia Supplement 2010*, ed. Robert L. Fastiggi, 1:420–22.

"Ecumenism in Advent." *Pastoral Review* 6, no. 6: 56–58.

"Good Man Jesus, Scoundrel Pullman." *Kairos*, September 19–October 2, 27.

"Holy Saturday." *Pastoral Review* 6, no. 2: 4–5.

"Introduction"; and "The Prayer of One Couple." In *His Handmaid: Maureen McCarthy in Recollection*, edited by Teresa de Bertodano, xv–xx, 74–75. North Palm Beach, Fla.: privately printed.

" 'Light from Light' in Oxford." *Kairos*, May 2, 17.

"Living Next Door to the Pope." *Guardian*, September 18.

"Obituary: Geoffrey Chapman." *Age* (Melbourne), May 21.

"Obituary: James Peters." *Age* (Melbourne), October 4.

*Philip Pullman's Jesus*. London: Darton, Longman & Todd.

"Philip Pullman on the Miracles of Jesus." *American Theological Inquiry*, July. www.atijournal.org.

"Philosophical Theology, Philosophy of Religion, and Fundamental Theology." *Irish Theological Quarterly* 75: 217–24.

"The Presence of Jesus and Our Presence to Each Other"; and "How Is Christ Present?" *Kairos*, August 8–22, 26–27; August 22–September 4, 18–19.

"A Real Australian Saint." *Herald Sun* (Melbourne), October 8.

"Writing My Next Book." *Jesuit Life* 92: 22–25.

(With Michael Keenan Jones) *Jesus Our Priest: A Christian Approach to the Priesthood of Christ*. Oxford: Oxford University Press.

(With D. Kendall and J. LaBelle, eds.) *Seek God Everywhere: Reflections on the Spiritual Exercises of St. Ignatius*. New York: Doubleday. Trans. into Indonesian, Korean, Polish, and Spanish.

| Book Reviews | In |
|---|---|
| Robert J. Daly. *Sacrifice Unveiled: The True Meaning of Sacrifice*. London: Continuum. | *Pastoral Review* 6, no. 1: 97. |
| Keith Dyer and David Neville, eds. *Resurrection and Responsibility: Essays on Theology, Scripture, and Ethics in Honor of Thorwald Lorenzen*. Eugene Ore.: Wipf & Stock. | *Pacifica* 23: 112–13. |
| Peter Hünermann, ed. *Exkommunikation oder Kommunikation?* Freiburg: Herder. | *Theological Studies* 71: 740–42. |
| Craig Keener. *The Historical Jesus of the Gospels*. Grand Rapids: Eerdmans. | *Pacifica* 23: 358–59. |
| Geza Vermes. *The Resurrection*. New York: Doubleday. | *International Journal for the Study of the Christian Church* 10: 365–66. |

## 2011

"2nd and 3rd Sunday of Easter." *Kairos*, May 1–14, 38.

"Contemporary Apologetics." *Furrow* 62: 225–30.

"Distant Neighbours." *Tablet*, August 27, 14.

"Finding Life in Holy Week." *Kairos*, April 17–30, 4–5.

"The Gospel of Christ and Our Bodies." *Pastoral Review* 7, no. 5: 10–12.

"Growing Old: A Glory Crowned." *Pastoral Review* 7, no. 2: 30–32.

"The Holy Ghost Is in the Fields." *Preacher*, April, 24–25.

"Imagination Needed to Sell Our Faith." *Herald Sun* (Melbourne), August 6.

"Imagining Jesus." *Tablet*, December 17/24, 25–26.

"Jesus and the Homeless." *Thinking Faith*, February 3. www.thinkingfaith .org/.

"Jesus and the Ordained Ministry: A Christocentric View of Priesthood." *Irish Theological Quarterly* 76: 20–34.

"Justification: Roman Catholic View"; and three responses. In *Justification: Five Views*, edited by James Beilby and Paul Eddy, 127–30, 171–75, 215–18, 281–90. Downers Grove, Ill.: InterVarsity.

"Living the Sacrament of Matrimony." *Pastoral Review* 7, no. 1: 40–43.

*Pause for Thought: Making Time for Prayer, Jesus and God*. Mahwah, N.J.: Paulist.

"A Pope for All People." *Kairos*, February 8–19, 4–5.

"The Presence of Jesus." *Pastoral Review* 7, no. 4: 10–15.

"The Resurrection: Nine Recent Approaches." *Australian eJournal of Theology* 18: 1–18.

"The Resurrection and Bereavement Experiences." *Irish Theological Quarterly* 76: 224–37.

*Rethinking Fundamental Theology: Toward a New Fundamental Theology.* Oxford: Oxford University Press.

*A Short Guide to Writing a Thesis: What to Do and What Not to Do.* Adelaide: Australian Theological Forum.

"Una teologia narrativa della rivelazione: Gesù il rivelatore nel vangelo di Giovanni." In *Amore e Verità: Sintesi prospettiva di Teologia Fondamentale,* edited by Gianluigi Pasquale and Carmelo Dotolo, 377–90. Rome: Lateran University Press. Festschrift for Rino Fisichella's sixtieth birthday.

"What Is Real Freedom?" *Pastoral Review* 7, no. 6: 10–15.

"What Priests Are For." *Tablet,* February 19, 16.

| Book Reviews | In |
|---|---|
| Richard Bauckham. *Jesus and the God of Israel.* Milton Keynes, U.K.: Paternoster. | *Heythrop Journal* 52: 822. |
| Christopher D. Denny and Christopher McMahon, eds. *Finding Salvation in Christ: In Honor of William P. Loewe.* Eugene, Ore.: Pickwick. | *Pacifica* 24: 345–46. |
| Francis Schüssler Fiorenza and John P. Galvin, eds. *Systematic Theology: Roman Catholic Perspectives.* Minneapolis: Fortress. | *Horizons* 38: 355–56. |
| Daniel A. Smith. *Revisiting the Empty Tomb: The Early History of Easter.* Minneapolis: Fortress. | *Theological Studies* 72: 188–89. |

## 2012

"Art of the Possible: New Head of the Congregation for the Doctrine of the Faith." *Tablet,* July 14, 6–7.

*Believing in the Resurrection: The Meaning and Promise of the Risen Christ.* Mahwah, N.J.: Paulist. Trans. into Russian.

"A Brief Rule for Prayer." *Pastoral Review* 8, no. 4: 48–50.

"Cosmological Christology: Arthur Peacocke, John Polkinghorne and Pierre Teilhard de Chardin in Dialogue." *New Blackfriars* 93: 516–23.
"The Cross over Bethlehem." In *"Godhead Here in Hiding": Incarnation and the History of Human Suffering*, edited by Terrence Merrigan and Frederik Glorieux, 25–36. Leuven: Peeters.
"The Direction of Catholic Thinking." *Kairos*, March 4–17, 30.
"The Diversity of Ministries: What Would Paul Say?" *Pastoral Review* 8, no. 5: 16–19.
"Does the Second Vatican Council Represent Continuity or Discontinuity?" *Theological Studies* 73: 768–94.
"In Praise of Mark." *Pastoral Review* 8, no. 1: 4–7.
*A Midlife Journey*. Ballan, Australia: Connor Court.
"Obituary: Alex Lynch." *Age* (Melbourne), April 27.
"Obituary: Cardinal Carlo Maria Martini." *Age* (Melbourne), September 4.
"Obituary: Cardinal Martini." *Eureka Street*, September 6.
"Obituary: Peter Steele." *Age* (Melbourne), July 3.
"The Origins and Scope of Biblical Spirituality." In *The Bloomsbury Guide to Christian Spirituality*, edited by Richard Woods and Peter Tyler, 20–29. London: Bloomsbury.
"Our Risen Selves." *America*, April 9, 10–14. Italian trans. in *La Civiltà Cattolica*, May 19, 379–85.
"Peter as Witness to Easter." *Theological Studies* 73: 263–85.
"Preface." In *Vatican II: Reception and Implementation in the Australian Church*, edited by Neil Ormerod et al., xi–xviii. Melbourne: Garratt.
"Putting Justice on the Agenda." *America*, October 8, 33–34.
"*Ressourcement* and Vatican II." In *Ressourcement: A Movement for Renewal in Twentieth-Century Catholic Theology*, edited by Gabriel Flynn and Paul D. Murray, 72–91. Oxford: Oxford University Press.
"Vatican II on the Liturgical Presence of Christ." *Irish Theological Quarterly* 77: 3–17.
"Who'll Take the Son?" *Pastoral Review* 8, no. 2: 26–27.
(With Mary Ann Meyers, eds.) *Light from Light: Scientists and Theologians in Dialogue*. Grand Rapids: Eerdmans. See esp. (with Meyers) "Introduction," 1–13; "Light from Light: The Divine Light Reflected in and by the Son and the Holy Spirit," 103–21.

| Book Reviews | In |
| --- | --- |
| Henry Bettenson and Chris Maunder, eds. *Documents of the Christian Church*. 4th ed. Oxford: Oxford University Press. | *Theological Studies*: 73: 735–36. |
| Markus Bockmuehl. *The Remembered Peter: In Ancient Reception and Modern Debate.* Tübingen: Mohr Siebeck. | *Pacifica* 25: 191–92. |
| Yves Congar. *My Journal of the Council.* Trans. M. J. Ronayne and M C. Boulding. Collegeville, Minn.: Liturgical. | *Theological Studies*: 73: 977–78. |
| James D. G. Dunn. *Jesus, Paul and the Gospels.* Grand Rapids: Eerdmans. | *Theological Studies* 73: 454–55. |
| Craig A. Evans, ed. *The World of Jesus and the Early Church: Identity and Interpretation in Early Communities of Faith.* Peabody, Mass.: Hendrickson. | *Theological Studies* 73: 732–33. |
| James Heft, ed. *Catholicism and Interreligious Dialogue.* New York: Oxford University Press. | *Theological Studies* 73: 737–38. |
| John Paul Heil. *Worship in the Letter to the Hebrews.* Eugene, Ore.: Cascade Books. | *Theological Studies*: 73: 696–97. |

## 2013

"All Are Called to Real Holiness." *Pastoral Review* 9, no. 6: 16–20.

"Christology." In *Routledge Companion to Modern Christian Thought*, edited by Chad Meister and James Beilby, 412–22. London: Routledge.

"*Dei Verbum* and Revelation." *Asian Horizons* 7: 18–35.

"Developments in Christology: The Last Fifty Years." *Australasian Catholic Record* 90: 161–71.

"Easter Grace." In *Immense, Unfathomed, Unconfined: The Grace of God in Creation, Church, and Community; Essays in Honour of Norman Young*, edited by Sean Winter, 78–91. Melbourne: Uniting Academic.

"For All or for Many?" *Pastoral Review* 9, no. 1: 30–32.

"A Helping Hand to Muslims." *Kairos*, July 7, 28–29.

"In Defence of Jacques Dupuis" (letter to the editor). *Tablet*, July 6, 16.

"Jacques Dupuis: The Ongoing Debate." *Theological Studies* 74: 632–54.

"The Jesuit Pope." *Pastoral Review* 9, no. 3: 34–37.

"Legacy of Benedict XVI." *Wanted in Rome*, March 6, 3.

"Naming the Ministries." *Pastoral Review* 9, no. 5: 29–33.

*On the Left Bank of the Tiber.* Ballarat, Australia: Connor Court.
"The Papal Audit." *Tablet*, March 16, 11.
"The Priesthood of Christ and the Followers of Other Faiths." *Irish Theological Quarterly* 78: 262–78.
"Revisiting Christology." *Pacifica* 26: 88–101.
"Revisiting Soteriology." *Pacifica* 26: 311–25.
"The Second Vatican Council and Other Living Faiths." *Pacifica* 26: 155–70.
*The Second Vatican Council on Other Religions.* Oxford: Oxford University Press.
"Still Far to Go." *Tablet*, February 9, 10–11.
"There Are No Outsiders." *Preacher*, July, 21–22.
"They Made the Most of Their Limited Choices." *Tablet*, December 21–28, 26.
"A Universal Symbol: Remembering Pope Benedict XVI." *Australian Catholics*, Easter, 9.
"Unlock the Door: The Case for Women in the Diaconate." *Tablet*, May 25, 4–5.
"Vatican II's Constitution on Divine Revelation, *Dei Verbum.*" *Pastoral Review* 9, no. 2: 12–18.
"War die Lehre des Zweiten Vatikanischen Konzils vom Wort Gottes genährt und geleitet?" *Theologische Quartalschrift* 193: 116–40.
"Was Jacques Dupuis a Neo-Rahnerian?" *Asian Horizons* 7: 237–60.
(With Edward G. Farrugia) *A Concise Dictionary of Theology.* 3rd rev. ed. Mahwah, N.J.: Paulist.

| Book Reviews | In |
|---|---|
| Craig Evans. *Matthew.* New Cambridge Bible Commentary. New York: Cambridge University Press. | *Theological Studies* 74: 241–42. |
| James L. Heft with John O'Malley, eds. *After Vatican II: Trajectories and Hermeneutics.* Grand Rapids: Eerdmans. | *Theological Studies* 74: 519–20. |
| Graham Redding. *Prayer and the Priesthood of Christ in the Reformed Tradition.* London: T&T Clark. | *Participatio*, supp. vol. 2: 156–58. |

# Works Cited

Alangaram, A. *Christ of the Asian Peoples: Towards an Asian Contextual Christology.* Bangalore: Bangalore Asian Trading Corporation, 2001.

Alkier, Stefan. *The Reality of the Resurrection: The New Testament Witness.* Translated by Leroy A. Huizenga. Waco, Tex.: Baylor University Press, 2013.

Anglican Roman-Catholic International Commission [ARCIC]. *The Final Report.* London: SPCK, 1982.

Aquinas, St. Thomas. *Summa contra Gentiles.* 4 vols. Notre Dame, Ind.: University of Notre Dame Press, 1975.

———. *Summa theologiae.* 61 vols. London: Eyre & Spottiswood, 1964–1966.

Attridge, Harold. *The Epistle to the Hebrews.* Philadelphia: Fortress, 1989.

Augustine. *Letters 100–155.* Translated by Roland Teske. Hyde Park, N.Y.: New City, 2003.

Ayres, Lewis. *Augustine on the Trinity.* Cambridge: Cambridge University Press, 2010.

———. *Nicaea and Its Legacy: An Approach to Fourth-Century Trinitarian Theology.* Oxford: Oxford University Press, 2004.

Barrett, Charles Kingsley. *The Acts of the Apostles.* Vol. 1. Edinburgh: T&T Clark, 1994.

———. *The Gospel according to John.* 2nd ed. London: SPCK, 1978.

Bauckham, Richard. *Gospel Women: A Study of the Named Women in the Gospels.* Grand Rapids: Eerdmans, 2002.

———. *Jesus and the Eyewitnesses: The Gospels as Eyewitness Testimony.* Grand Rapids: Eerdmans, 2006.

Bauer, Walter. *A Greek-English Lexicon of the New Testament and Other Early Christian Literature*. 3rd ed. Revised by Frederick William Danker. Chicago: University of Chicago Press, 2000.

Becker, Karl J., and Ilaria Morali, eds. *Catholic Engagement with World Religions: A Comprehensive Survey*. Maryknoll, N.Y.: Orbis Books, 2010.

Betz, Hans-Dieter. "Jesus and the Cynics: Survey and Analysis of a Hypothesis." *Journal of Religion* 74 (1994): 453–75.

Blass, Friedrich, and Albert Debrunner. *A Greek Grammar of the New Testament and Other Early Christian Literature*. Translated and revised by Robert W. Funk. Cambridge: Cambridge University Press, 1961.

Bockmuehl, Markus. *The Remembered Peter: In Ancient Reception and Modern Debate*. Tübingen: Mohr Siebeck, 2010.

Bovon, François. *Das Evangelium nach Lukas*. Vol. 4. Neukirchen: Neukirchener Verlag, 2009.

———. *Luke 1: Commentary on the Gospel of Luke 1:1–9:50*. Translated by Christine M. Thomas. Minneapolis: Fortress, 2002.

Brecht, Mara. "The Humanity of Christ: Jacques Dupuis' Christology and Religious Pluralism." *Horizons* 35 (2008): 54–71.

Brett, Mark G. *Decolonizing God: The Bible in the Tides of Empire*. Sheffield, U.K.: Sheffield Academic, 2008.

Brown, David. "The Incarnation in Twentieth-Century Art." In Davis, Kendall, and O'Collins, *Incarnation*, 332–74.

Brown, Raymond E. *The Epistles of John*. New York: Doubleday, 1982.

———. *The Gospel according to John XIII–XXI*. New York: Doubleday, 1970.

———. "John 21 and the First Appearance of the Risen Jesus to Peter." In *Resurrexit*, edited by Eduard Dhanis, 246–65. Rome: Libreria Editrice Vaticana, 1974.

Brown, Raymond E., Karl P. Donfried, and John Reumann, eds. *Peter in the New Testament: A Collaborative Assessment by Protestant and Roman Catholic Scholars*. Minneapolis: Augsburg, 1973.

Bruce, F. F. *1 and 2 Corinthians*. London: Oliphants, 1971.

Bryan, Christopher. *The Resurrection of the Messiah*. New York: Oxford University Press, 2011.

Bulgakov, Sergius. *The Lamb of God*. Translated by Boris Jakim. Grand Rapids: Eerdmans, 2008.

Bullivant, Stephen. *The Salvation of Atheists and Catholic Dogmatic Theology*. Oxford: Oxford University Press, 2012.

Burrows, William R., ed. *Jacques Dupuis Faces the Inquisition: Two Essays by Jacques Dupuis on* Dominus Iesus *and the Roman Investigation of His Work*. Eugene, Ore.: Pickwick, 2012.

Bynum, Caroline Walker. "The Power in the Blood: Sacrifice, Satisfaction, and Substitution in Late Medieval Soteriology." In Davis, Kendall, and O'Collins, *Redemption*, 177–204.

Byrne, Brendan. "Peter as Resurrection Witness in the Lukan Narrative." In Kendall and Davis, *Convergence of Theology*, 19–33.

Carey, John, ed. *John Donne*. Oxford: Oxford University Press, 1990.

Clarke, Clifton R. *African Christology: Jesus in Post-missionary African Christianity*. Eugene, Ore.: Pickwick, 2011.

Clooney, Francis X. *Comparative Theology: Deep Learning across Religious Borders*. Oxford: Wiley-Blackwell, 2010.

Coakley, Sarah. "What Does Chalcedon Solve and What Does It Not? Some Reflections on the Status and Meaning of the Chalcedonian Definition." In Davis, Kendall, and O'Collins, *Incarnation*, 143–63.

Collins, Adela Yarbro. *Mark: A Commentary*. Minneapolis: Fortress, 2007.

Collins, Raymond F. *First Corinthians*. Collegeville, Minn.: Liturgical, 1999.

Comité de redaction. " 'Tout récapituler dans le Christ': A propos de l'ouvrage de J. Dupuis, *Vers une théologie Chrétienne du pluralisme religieux*." *Revue Thomiste* 98 (1998): 591–630.

Congregation for the Doctrine of the Faith. "*Dominus Iesus*." In *AAS* 92 (2000): 742–65. Translated in Pope and Hefling, "*Sic et non*," 3–23.

Cornille, Catherine. *The Im-possibility of Interreligious Dialogue*. New York: Crossroad, 2008.

Cross, Frank Leslie, and Elizabeth Anne Livingstone, eds. *The Oxford Dictionary of the Christian Church*. 3rd rev. ed. Oxford: Oxford University Press, 2005. See esp. "Paul, St"; "Peter, St."

Cullmann, Oscar. *Peter: Disciple, Apostle, Martyr; A Historical and Theological Study*. Translated by Floyd V. Filson. London: SCM Press, 1962.

Davis, Stephen T., Daniel Kendall, and Gerald O'Collins, eds. *The Incarnation: An Interdisciplinary Symposium on the Incarnation of the Son of God*. Oxford: Oxford University Press, 2002.

Davis, Stephen T., Daniel Kendall, and Gerald O'Collins, eds. *The Redemption: An Interdisciplinary Symposium on Christ as Redeemer*. Oxford: Oxford University Press, 2004.

D'Costa, Gavin. *Christianity and World Religions: Disputed Questions in the Theology of Religions*. Oxford: Wiley-Blackwell, 2009.

———. "Christian Theology of Religions." In *The Routledge Companion to Modern Christian Thought*, edited by Chad Meister and James Beilby, 661–72. London: Routledge, 2013.

———. "Pluralist Arguments." In Becker and Morali, *Catholic Engagement*, 329–44.

———. Review of Jacques Dupuis' *Toward a Christian Theology of Religious Pluralism*. In *Journal of Theological Studies* 59 (1998): 910–14.

———. *Theology and Religious Pluralism: The Challenge of Other Religions*. Oxford: Basil Blackwell, 1986.

———. "The Trinity in Interreligious Dialogue." In *Oxford Handbook of the Trinity*, edited by Gilles Emery and Matthew Levering, 573–85. Oxford: Oxford University Press, 2011.

Denzinger, Heinrich, and Peter Hünermann, eds. *Enchiridion symbolorum, definitionum et declarationum*. 37th ed. Freiburg im Breisgau: Herder, 1991.

Dupuis, Jacques. "Apostolic Exhortation *Evangelii nuntiandi* of Pope Paul VI." *Vidyajyoti* 40 (1976): 218–30.

———. "Christianity and Religions: Complementarity and Convergence." In *Many Mansions? Multiple Religious Belonging and Christian Identity*, edited by Catherine Cornille, 61–75. Maryknoll, N.Y.: Orbis Books, 2002.

———. *Christianity and the Religions: From Confrontation to Dialogue*. Translated by Phillip Berryman. Maryknoll, N.Y.: Orbis Books, 2002.

———. *Il Cristianesimo e le religioni: Dallo scontro all'incontro*. Brescia: Queriniana, 2001.

———. *Jesus Christ at the Encounter of World Religions*. Translated by Robert R. Barr. Maryknoll, N.Y.: Orbis Books, 1991.

———. "La teologia del pluralismo religioso rivisitata." *Rassegna di Teologia* 40 (1999): 667–93.

———. *Toward a Christian Theology of Religious Pluralism*. Maryknoll, N.Y.: Orbis Books, 1997.

———. " 'The Truth Will Make You Free': The Theology of Religious Pluralism Revisited." *Louvain Studies* 24 (1999): 211–63.

———. *Who Do You Say I Am? Introduction to Christology*. Maryknoll, N.Y.: Orbis Books, 1994.

Fiddes, Paul S. *Past Event and Present Salvation: The Christian Idea of Atonement*. London: Darton, Longman & Todd, 1989.

Fitzmyer, Joseph A. *The Acts of the Apostles*. New York: Doubleday, 1998.

———. *First Corinthians*. New Haven, Conn.: Yale University Press, 2008.

———. *The Gospel according to Luke I–IX*. New York: Doubleday, 1981.

———. *The Gospel according to Luke X–XXIV*. New York: Doubleday, 1985.

———. *Romans*. New York: Doubleday, 1993.

Flynn, Gabriel, and Paul D. Murray, eds. *Ressourcement: A Movement for Renewal in Twentieth-Century Catholic Theology.* Oxford: Oxford University Press, 2012.

Funk, Robert W. *Honest to Jesus: Jesus for a New Millennium.* San Francisco: HarperSanFrancisco, 1996.

*The Gospel of Mary.* In *The Nag Hammadi Library in English*, 3rd ed., edited by James M. Robinson, 523–27. Leiden: Brill, 1988.

Grappe, Christian. *Images de Pierre aux deux premiers siècles.* Paris: Presses Universitaires de France, 1995.

Hays, Richard B. *1 Corinthians.* Louisville, Ky.: Knox, 1997.

Heft, James L., ed. *Catholicism and Interreligious Dialogue.* New York: Oxford University Press, 2012.

Hengel, Martin. *Der unterschätzte Petrus: Zwei Studien.* Tübingen: Mohr Siebeck, 2006.

———. *Saint Peter: The Underestimated Apostle.* Translated by Thomas H. Trapp. Grand Rapids: Eerdmans, 2010.

Henn, William. "The Church as Easter Witness in the Thought of Gerald O'Collins, S.J." In Kendall and Davis, *Convergence of Theology*, 208–20.

Hug, Joseph. *La finale de l'Évangile de Marc.* Paris: Gabalda, 1978.

Hunsinger, George. *How to Read Karl Barth: The Story of His Theology.* New York: Oxford University Press, 1991.

Iammarrone, Giovanni, ed. *La Cristologia contemporanea.* Padua: Edizioni Messaggero, 1992.

Jenkins, Philip. *Hidden Gospels: How the Search for Jesus Lost Its Way.* New York: Oxford University Press, 2001.

Jeremias, Joachim. *Eucharistic Words.* Translated by Norman Perrin. London: SCM Press, 1966.

John Paul II. "*Ecclesia de Eucharistia.*" In *AAS* 95 (2003): 433–75.

Johnson, Keith E. *Rethinking the Trinity & Religious Pluralism: An Augustinian Assessment.* Downers Grove, Ill.: IVP Academic, 2011.

Johnson, Luke Timothy. *The First and Second Letters to Timothy.* New York: Doubleday, 2001.

Kasper, Walter. *Jesus the Christ.* Translated by V. Green. Mahwah, N.J.: Paulist, 1976.

Kelly, William. "Towards a Christology of Presence: Uncovering and Relating Themes from Scripture, Philosophy and Theology." Doctoral thesis, Gregorian University, Rome, 1996.

Kendall, Daniel, and Stephen T. Davis, eds. *The Convergence of Theology.* Mahwah, N.J.: Paulist, 2001.

Kendall, Daniel, and Gerald O'Collins, eds. *In Many and Diverse Ways: In Honor of Jacques Dupuis.* Maryknoll, N.Y.: Orbis Books, 2003.

————. "The Uniqueness of the Easter Appearances." *Catholic Biblical Quarterly* 54 (1991): 287–307.

Kessler, William Thomas. *Peter as the First Witness of the Risen Lord: An Historical and Theological Investigation*. Rome: Editrice Pontificia Università Gregoriana, 1998.

Koester, Craig R. *Hebrews*. New York: Doubleday, 2001.

Kremer, Jacob. "*Horaō*." In *Exegetical Dictionary of the New Testament*, vol. 2, edited by Horst Balz and Gerhard Schneider. Grand Rapids: Eerdmans, 1991.

Kurian, George Thomas, ed. "Propitiation." In *The Testament Christian Dictionary*. New York: Random House, 2001.

Lapham, Frederick. *Peter: The Myth, the Man and the Writings*. London: Sheffield Academic, 2003.

Leahy, Brendan. "John Paul II and Hans Urs von Balthasar." In *The Legacy of John Paul II*, edited by Gerald O'Collins and Michael A. Hayes, 31–50. London: Continuum, 2008.

Levering, Matthew. "Israel and the Shape of Thomas Aquinas's Soteriology." *Thomist* 63 (1999): 65–82.

————. "Juridical Language in Soteriology: Aquinas's Approach." *Angelicum* 80 (2003): 309–26.

Licona, Michael R. *The Resurrection of Jesus: A New Historiographical Approach*. Downers Grove, Ill.: IVP Academic, 2010.

Lincoln, Andrew T. *The Gospel according to St John*. London: Continuum, 2005.

Louw, Johannes P., and Eugene A. Nida, eds. *Greek-English Lexicon of the New Testament Based on Semantic Domains*. Vol. 1. New York: United Bible Societies, 1988.

Luz, Ulrich. *Matthew 8–20*. Translated by James E. Crouch. Minneapolis: Fortress, 2001.

————. *Matthew 21–28*. Translated by James E. Crouch. Minneapolis: Fortress, 2005.

Mack, Burton L. *The Lost Gospel*. San Francisco: HarperCollins, 1993.

Marcus, Joel. *Mark 8–16*. New Haven, Conn.: Yale University Press, 2009.

Marshall, I. Howard. *The Pastoral Epistles*. London: T&T Clark, 1999.

Martin, Ralph. *Will Many Be Saved? What Vatican II Actually Teaches and Its Implications for the New Evangelization*. Grand Rapids: Eerdmans, 2012.

Meier, John P. *A Marginal Jew*. Vol. 2, *Rethinking the Historical Jesus*. New York: Doubleday, 1994.

————. *A Marginal Jew*. Vol. 3, *Companions and Competitors*. New York: Doubleday, 2001.

Merrigan, Terrence. "The Appeal to Congar in Roman Catholic Theology of Religions: The Case of Jacques Dupuis." In *Yves Congar: Theologian of the Church*, edited by Gabriel Flynn, 427–57. Louvain: Peeters, 2005.

———. "Exploring the Frontiers: Toward a Christian Theology of Religious Pluralism." *Louvain Studies* 23 (1998): 338–59.

Migliore, Daniel L. "The Trinity and the Theology of Religions." In *God's Life in Trinity*, edited by Miroslav Volf and Michael Welker, 101–17. Minneapolis: Fortress, 2006.

Milbank, John. *Theology and Social Theory: Beyond Secular Reason*. Oxford: Basil Blackwell, 1990.

Miller, John Michael. *The Shepherd and the Rock: Origins, Development, and Mission of the Papacy*. Huntington, Ind.: Our Sunday Visitor, 1995.

Moloney, Francis J. *The Gospel of Mark: A Commentary*. Peabody, Mass.: Hendrickson, 2002.

———. *The Resurrection of the Messiah: A Narrative Commentary on the Resurrection Accounts in the Four Gospels*. Mahwah, N.J.: Paulist, 2013.

Moltmann, Jürgen. *The Way of Jesus Christ: Christology in Messianic Dimensions*. Translated by Margaret Kohl. London: SCM Press, 1990.

Morali, Ilaria. "Overview of Some Francophone and Italian Trends." In Becker and Morali, *Catholic Engagement*, 325–28.

———. "Salvation, Religions, and Dialogue with Roman Magisterium." In Becker and Morali, *Catholic Engagement*, 122–42.

Morris, T. V. *The Logic of God Incarnate*. Ithaca, N.Y.: Cornell University Press, 1986.

Moulton, James H., and George Milligan. *The Vocabulary of the Greek Testament*. London: Hodder & Stoughton, 1930.

Murdoch, Brian O. *Adam's Grace: Fall and Redemption in Medieval Literature*. Cambridge: D. S. Brewer, 2000.

Murphy, Francesca A., ed. *The Oxford Handbook of Christology*. Oxford: Oxford University Press, forthcoming.

Neuner, Josef, and Jacques Dupuis, eds. *The Christian Faith: In the Doctrinal Documents of the Catholic Church*. 7th ed. Bangalore: Theological Publications in India, 2001.

Newman, John Henry. "A Letter Addressed to His Grace, the Duke of Norfolk on Occasion of Mr Gladstone's Recent Expostulation." In *Certain Difficulties Felt by Anglicans in Catholic Teaching Considered*, 2:171–378. London: Longmans, Green, 1891.

———. "On the Priesthood of Christ." In *Sermon Notes of John Henry Cardinal Newman 1849–1878*, 69–70. London: Longmans, Green, 1914.

Nieuwenhove, Rik van. " 'Bearing the Marks of Christ's Passion': Aquinas' Soteriology." In *The Theology of Thomas Aquinas*, edited by R. van Nieuwenhove and Joseph P. Wawrykow, 227–302. Notre Dame, Ind.: University of Notre Dame Press, 2005.

Nolland, John. *The Gospel of Matthew*. Grand Rapids: Eerdmans, 2005.

Novello, Henry L. *Death as Transformation: A Contemporary Theology of Death*. Farnham, U.K.: Ashgate, 2011

Nutt, Roger W. "An Office in Search of Its Ontology: Mediation and Trinitarian Christology in Jacques Dupuis' Theology of Religious Pluralism." *Louvain Studies* 32 (2007): 383–407.

O'Brien, Peter T. *The Letter to the Hebrews*. Grand Rapids: Eerdmans, 2010.

O'Collins, Gerald. *Believing in the Resurrection: The Meaning and Promise of the Risen Lord*. Mahwah, N.J.: Paulist, 2012.

———. "A Challenge for Theologians: Three Puzzling Positions." *America*, September 17, 2007.

———. "Christ and the Religions." *Gregorianum* 84 (2003): 347–62.

———. *Christology: A Biblical, Historical, and Systematic Study of Jesus*. Expanded and rev. ed. Oxford: Oxford University Press, 2009.

———. *Christology: A Biblical, Historical, and Systematic Study of Jesus*. Oxford: Oxford University Press, 1995.

———. *The Easter Jesus*. New ed. London: Darton, Longman & Todd, 1980.

———. *Interpreting the Resurrection*. Mahwah, N.J.: Paulist, 1988.

———. "Jacques Dupuis." In *New Catholic Encyclopedia Supplement 2010*, 420–22. Detroit: Gale, 2010.

———. "Jacques Dupuis: The Ongoing Debate." *Theological Studies* 74 (2013): 632–54.

———. *Jesus: A Portrait*. London: Darton, Longman & Todd, 2008.

———. "Jesus Christ the Liberator: In the Context of Human Progress." *Studia Missionalia* 47 (1998): 21–35.

———. *Jesus Our Redeemer: A Christian Approach to Salvation*. Oxford: Oxford University Press, 2007.

———. *Jesus Risen: An Historical, Fundamental and Systematic Examination of Christ's Resurrection*. Mahwah, N.J.: Paulist, 1987.

———. *Living Vatican II: The 21st Council for the 21st Century*. Mahwah, N.J.: Paulist, 2006.

———. *On the Left Bank of the Tiber*. Leominster: Gracewing, 2013.

———. "Peter as Easter Witness." *Heythrop Journal* 22 (1981): 1–18.

————. *Rethinking Fundamental Theology: Toward a New Fundamental Theology.* Oxford: Oxford University Press, 2011.

————. Review of Richard Bauckham, *Jesus and the Eyewitnesses: The Gospels as Eyewitness Testimony.* Grand Rapids: Eerdmans, 2006. In *Heythrop Journal* 69 (2008): 309–10.

————. *Salvation for All: God's Other Peoples.* Oxford: Oxford University Press, 2008.

————. *The Second Vatican Council on Other Religions.* Oxford: Oxford University Press, 2013.

————. "Vatican II and the Liturgical Presences of Christ." *Irish Theological Quarterly* 77 (2012): 3–17

————. *What Are They Saying about Jesus?* 1977. Rev. ed., New York: Paulist, 1983.

————. "Wisdom in the Universe: A Biblical and Theological Reflection." In *Is God Incarnate in All That Is?* edited by Niels H. Gregersen and Mary Ann Meyers. Minneapolis: Fortress Press, forthcoming.

O'Collins, Gerald, and Daniel Kendall. *The Bible for Theology: Ten Principles for the Theological Use of Scripture.* Mahwah, N.J.: Paulist, 1997.

————. "Mary Magdalene as Major Witness to Jesus' Resurrection." *Theological Studies* 48 (1987): 631–46.

————. "On Not Neglecting Hatred." *Scottish Journal of Theology* 47 (1994): 511–18.

O'Collins, Gerald, and Michael Keenan Jones. *Jesus Our Priest: A Christian Approach to the Priesthood of Christ.* Oxford: Oxford University Press, 2010.

O'Collins, Gerald, and Mary Ann Meyers, eds. *Light from Light: Scientists and Theologians in Dialogue.* Grand Rapids: Eerdmans, 2012.

Oakes, Edward T. *Infinity Dwindled to Infancy: A Catholic and Evangelical Christology.* Grand Rapids: Eerdmans, 2011.

Origen. *Contra Celsum.* Translated by Henry Chadwick. 1953. Reprint, Cambridge: Cambridge University Press, 1980.

Perkins, Pheme. *Peter: Apostle for the Whole Church.* Columbia: University of South Carolina Press, 1994.

Pesch, Rudolf. *Die biblischen Grundlagen des Primats.* Quaestiones disputatae 187. Freiburg im Breisgau: Herder, 2001.

————. *Simon Petrus: Geschichte und geschichtliche Bedeutung des ersten Jüngers Jesu Christi.* Stuttgart: Anton Hiersemann, 1980.

Peterson, Brandon. "Paving the Way? Penalty and Atonement in Thomas Aquinas' Soteriology." *International Journal of Systematic Theology* 15, no. 3 (2013): 265–83.

Pius XII. *Christian Worship: Encyclical Letter (*Mediator Dei*) of His Holiness Pius XII. . . .* Translated by Canon G. D. Smith. London: Catholic Truth Society, 1959.

Pope, Stephen J., and Charles Hefling, eds. *"Sic et non": Encountering "Dominus Iesus."* Maryknoll, N.Y.: Orbis Books, 2002.

Puglisi, James F., ed. *How Can the Petrine Ministry Be of Service to the Unity of the Universal Church?* Grand Rapids: Eerdmans, 2010.

Quinn, Jerome D., and William C. Wacker. *The First and Second Letters to Timothy.* Grand Rapids: Eerdmans, 2000.

Rahner, Karl. *Foundations of Christian Faith: An Introduction to the Idea of Christianity.* Translated by William V. Dych. New York: Seabury, 1978.

———. *Meditations on Priestly Life.* Translated by Edward Quinn. London: Sheed & Ward, 1973.

———. *Servants of the Lord.* Translated by Richard Strachan. London: Burns & Oates, 1968.

———. *Spiritual Exercises.* Translated by Kenneth Baker. New York: Herder & Herder, 1965.

———. *Theological Investigations.* Vol. 4. Translated by Kevin Smyth. London: Darton, Longman & Todd, 1966. See esp. "On the Theology of the Incarnation."

———. *Theological Investigations.* Vol. 5. Translated by Karl-Heinz Kruger. London: Darton, Longman & Todd, 1966. See esp. "Christianity and the Non-Christian Religions."

———. *Theological Investigations.* Vol. 6. Translated by Karl-Heinz Kruger and Boniface Kruger. London: Darton, Longman & Todd, 1969. See esp. "Anonymous Christians."

———. *Theological Investigations.* Vol. 12. Translated by David Bourke. London: Darton, Longman & Todd, 1974. See esp. "The Point of Departure in Theology for Determining the Nature of the Priestly Office"; "Theological Reflections on the Priestly Image of Today and Tomorrow."

———. *Theological Investigations.* Vol. 19. Translated by Edward Quinn. Darton, Longman & Todd, 1983. See esp. "The Spirituality of the Secular Priest"; "The Spirituality of the Priest in the Light of His Office."

———. *Theological Investigations.* 23 vols. London: Darton, Longman & Todd, 1961–1992.

Roos, Heinrich, and Josef Neuner, comps. *The Teaching of the Catholic Church.* Edited by Karl Rahner. Translated by Geoffrey Stevens. Cork: Mercier, 1967.

Rouët de Journel, Marie Joseph. *Enchiridion patristicum*. Barcelona: Herder, 1965.

Schiller, Gertrud. *Iconography of Christian Art*. Vol. 2. Translated by Janet Seligman. London: Lund Humphries, 1971.

Schnackenburg, Rudolf. *God's Rule and Kingdom*. Translated by John Murray. London: Burns & Oates, 1968.

Scholer, John M. *Proleptic Priests: Priesthood in the Epistle to the Hebrews*. Sheffield, U.K.: Sheffield Academic, 1991.

Schrage, Wolfgang. *Der erste Brief an die Korinther*. Vol. 4. Düsseldorf: Benziger Verlag, 2001.

Schweitzer, Don. *Contemporary Christologies*. Minneapolis: Fortress, 2010.

Scott, Mark S. M. "Guarding the Mysteries of Salvation: The Pastoral Pedagogy of Origen's Universalism." *Journal of Early Christian Studies* 18 (2010): 347–68.

———. *Journey Back to God: Origen on the Problem of Evil*. New York: Oxford University Press, 2012.

Sherman, Robert J. "Christ the Priest: The Son's Sacrificial Offering." In *King, Priest, and Prophet: A Trinitarian Theology of Atonement*, 169–218. New York: T&T Clark, 2004.

Smith, Daniel A. *Revisiting the Empty Tomb*. Minneapolis: Fortress, 2010.

Sobrino, Jon. *Christ the Liberator: A View from the Victims*. Translated by Paul Burns. Maryknoll, N.Y.: Orbis Books, 2001.

———. *Jesus the Liberator: A Historical-Theological Reading of Jesus of Nazareth*. Translated by Paul Burns and Francis McDonough. Maryknoll, N.Y.: Orbis Books, 1993.

Solano, Jésus. *Sacrae theologiae summa*. Vol. 3. Madrid: Biblioteca de Autores Cristianos, 1956.

Stinton, Diane B. *Jesus of Africa: Voices of Contemporary African Christology*. Maryknoll, N.Y.: Orbis Books, 2004.

Stump, Eleonore. "Aquinas' Metaphysics of the Incarnation." In Davis, Kendall, and O'Collins, *Incarnation*, 197–218.

Sturch, Richard. *The Word and the Christ*. Oxford: Clarendon, 1991.

Sullivan, Francis A. "Introduction and Ecclesiological Issues." In Pope and Hefling, *"Sic et non,"* 47–56.

———. *Salvation outside the Church? Tracing the History of the Catholic Response*. Mahwah, N.J.: Paulist, 1992.

Sydnor, Jon Paul. "Beyond a Text: Revisiting Jacques Dupuis' Theology of Religions." *International Review of Mission* 96 (2007): 56–71.

Tannehill, Robert C. *The Narrative Unity of Luke–Acts: A Literary Interpretation*. Vol. 1. Philadelphia: Fortress, 1986.

Teilhard de Chardin, Pierre. "The Mass on the World." In *Hymn of the Universe*, translated by Gerald Vann, 19–37. London: Collins, 1965.

Thayer, Joseph H. *Greek-English Lexicon of the New Testament*. Peabody, Mass.: Hendrickson, 1999. Reprint of the 4th ed. of 1896.

Thiselton, Anthony. *The First Epistle to the Corinthians*. Grand Rapids: Eerdmans, 2000.

Tillard, Jean-Marie-Roger. *The Bishop of Rome*. Translated by John de Satgé. London: SPCK, 1983.

Torrance, Tom F. *Theology in Reconciliation: Essays Toward Evangelical and Catholic Unity in East and West*. Eugene, Ore.: Wipf & Stock, 1996.

Towner, Philip H. *The Letters to Timothy and Titus*. Grand Rapids: Eerdmans, 2006.

Vanhoye, Albert. *Old Testament Priests and the New Priest*. Translated by Bernard Orchard. Petersham, Mass.: St. Bede's, 1986.

Vermes, Geza. *Resurrection*. New York: Doubelday, 2008.

Vorgrimler, H., ed. *Commentary on the Documents of Vatican II*. 5 vols. London: Burns & Oates, 1967–1969.

Wallace, Daniel B. *Greek Grammar beyond the Basics: An Exegetical Syntax of the New Testament*. Grand Rapids: Zondervan, 1996.

Wills, Garry. *Why Priests? A Failed Tradition*. New York: Viking, 2013.

Harold Winstone, ed. *The Sunday Missal*. London: Collins, 1975.

Woolf, Rosemary. *The English Mystery Plays*. Berkeley: University of California Press, 1980.

Wright, N. T. *The Resurrection of the Son of God*. Minneapolis: Fortress, 2003.

# Credits

"Developments in Christology: The Last Fifty Years" (ch. 1) appeared in *Australasian Catholic Record* 90 (2013): 161–71; "Revisiting Christology" (ch. 2), in *Pacifica* 26 (2013): 88–101; "Revisiting Soteriology" (ch. 3), in *Pacifica* 26 (2013): 311–25; "The Appearances of the Risen Christ: A Lexical-Exegetical Examination of St. Paul and Other Witnesses" (ch. 4), in *Irish Theological Quarterly* 79 (2014): 128–43; "Peter as Witness to Easter" (ch. 5), in *Theological Studies* 73 (2012): 263–85; "The Priesthood of Christ and Followers of Other Faiths" (ch. 6), in *Irish Theological Quarterly* 78 (2013): 262–78; "Jacques Dupuis: The Ongoing Debate" (ch. 7), in *Theological Studies* 74 (2013): 632–54; "Was Jacques Dupuis a Neo-Rahnerian?" (ch. 8), in *Asian Horizons* 7 (2013): 568–88. Chapter 1 is reprinted with the permission of *Australasian Catholic Record*; chapter 8, with the permission of *Asian Horizons*; and all other chapters, with the permission of *Sage Publications*.

# Index of Names

Abelard, Peter, 11
Achebe, Chinua, 23
Adams, Marilyn McCord, 13
Alangaram, Arockiam, 11, 145, 189
Alberigo, Giuseppe, 178
Aletti, Jean-Noël, 32
Alison, James, 169
Alkier, Stefan, 144, 189
Allison, Dale C., 9
Amalorpavadass, Duraisamy S., 136
Amato, Angelo, 165
Angela of Foligno, 11
Anselm of Canterbury, 11
Aparicio Valls, María Carmen, 175
Aquinas, Thomas, 19, 37–38, 59, 117,
    120–23, 127–28, 148–49, 155, 166–
    68, 189, 194, 196–97, 199
Archer, Jeffrey, 178
Attridge, Harold W., 162, 189
Augustine of Hippo, 7, 14, 19–20, 45,
    99, 126, 128, 144, 146, 168, 189
Ayres, Lewis, 12, 18–21, 27–28, 126,
    146–47, 189

Bacon, Francis, 23
Baker, Kenneth, 161, 198
Balthasar, Hans Urs von, 6–7, 24, 143,
    150, 194
Balz, Horst, 153–55, 194
Barnes, Michel R., 126
Barr, Robert R., 168, 170, 192
Barrett, Charles Kingsley, 160, 189

Barth, Karl, 3–4, 7, 24, 39, 143, 193
Batlogg, Andreas R., 175
Bauckham, Richard, 25–26, 67, 147,
    157, 180, 184, 189, 197
Bauer, Walter, 52, 55, 62–63, 153–54,
    156, 190
Becker, Karl J., 166–69, 190, 192, 195
Beilby, James K., 169, 183, 186, 191
Benedict XVI, Pope, 41, 178–79, 181,
    186–87
Bernardi, Claudio, 177
Bernardi, Peter J., 23, 14–17
Berryman, Phillip E., 145, 192
Bettenson, Henry, 186
Betz, Hans-Dieter, 144, 190
Blass, Friedrich, 51–52, 153, 190
Bloch, Ernst, 5
Bockmuehl, Markus, 156, 186, 190
Boersma, Hans, 32–34, 148
Boulding, Mary Cecily, 186
Bourke, David, 161, 198
Bovon, François, 159, 190
Bradley, Ian, 12
Bradley, Ros, 179
Bradshaw, Timothy, 38–39, 150
Brecht, Mara, 113–14, 125, 127–28,
    134–35, 165–66, 170, 190
Brett, Mark G., 151, 190
Brontë, Charlotte, 118
Brown, Dan, 175
Brown, David, 23, 32, 146, 149, 190

Brown, Raymond E., 8–9, 63, 75–76, 81, 83, 144, 156–57, 159–61, 190
Bruce, F. F., 152–53, 190
Bryan, Christopher, 158–60, 190
Bulgakov, Sergius, 12, 145, 190
Bullivant, Stephen, 38, 150–51, 190
Bultmann, Rudolf, 4–5
Burns, Paul, 146–47, 199
Burrell, David B., 38, 150, 180
Burrows, William R., 14, 145, 190
Bynum, Caroline W., 11, 13, 32, 144, 149, 191
Byrne, Brendan, 159, 191

Calvin, John, 99, 128
Canobbio, Giacomo, 165
Capizzi, Nunzio, 165
Carey, John, 163, 191
Carroll, Denis, 21–23, 27, 147
Catherine of Genoa, 11
Cavadini, John C., 175
Chadwick, Henry, 155, 197
Chagall, Marc, 23
Chancey, Mark A., 18
Chapman, Geoffrey, 182
Clarke, Clifton E., 144, 191
Clement of Alexandria, 69
Clement of Rome, 78
Clooney, Francis X., 38–42, 44, 132, 150, 169
Coakley, Sarah, 11–12, 144, 147, 191
Collins, Adela Yarbro, 158, 160, 191
Collins, Raymond, 51–52, 54, 57, 152–55, 191
Congar, Yves, 5, 89, 111–12, 118, 135–36, 165, 170, 178, 186, 195
Colzani, Gianni, 165
Cornille, Catherine, 39, 41–44, 115–16, 127, 150–51, 166, 191–92
Cornwell, Peter, 34, 37, 149
Cozzi, Alberto, 164–65
Crisp, Oliver D., 12, 180
Crociata, Mariano, 165
Cronin, Daniel P., 181
Crosbie, Paul, 34, 149
Cross, Frank L., 160, 191
Cross, Richard, 13
Crossan, John Dominic, 9

Crouch, James E., 159–60, 194
Cullen, Philomena, 180
Cullmann, Oscar, 65, 156, 191
Cunningham, Lawrence, 181
Curran, Charles E., 177

Daley, Brian E., 12, 32
Daley, Michael J., 175
Dalferth, Ingolf, 13
Daly, Michael J., 175
Daly, Robert J., 12, 183
Daniélou, Jean, 5
Danker, Frederick W., 52, 55, 62–63, 153, 156, 190
Dante Alighieri, 118
Davis, Stephen T., 13, 32, 143–44, 159, 161, 174, 176, 190–91, 193, 199
D'Costa, Gavin, 38, 39–40, 42–43, 111, 114, 116–24, 127–29, 131–41, 150, 166–67, 169, 171–73, 191–92
Deane-Drummond, Celia, 11
De Bertodano, Teresa, 182
Debrunner, Albert, 51–52, 153, 190
Delgado, Mariano, 175
Denny, Christopher D., 184
Denzinger, Heinrich, 133, 158, 168, 192
Dhanis, Eduard, 159, 190
Donfried, Karl P., 156–57, 159–61, 190
Donne, John, 102, 163, 177, 191
Doria Pamphilj, Orietta, 173
Dostoevsky, Fyodor, 7, 118
Dotolo, Carmelo, 184
Dreyer, Elizabeth A., 174
Dulles, Avery, 179
Dunn, James D. G., 8–10, 18, 28, 147, 175, 186
Dupuis, Jacques, 13–14, 89, 91–92, 103–4, 109–41, 145, 158, 162–72, 175–76, 182, 186–87, 190, 192–93, 195–96, 199, 201
Dych, William V., 161, 198
Dyer, Keith, 183

Eddy, Paul R., 183
Edwards, Denis, 11
Egan, Anthony, 24, 146–47
Ela, Jean-Marc, 11

Elliot, Mark, 174
Ellis, E. Earle, 147
Emery, Gilles, 169, 192
Endo, Shusaku, 23
Evans, C. Stephen, 13, 32
Evans, Craig A., 186–87
Evdokimov, Paul, 12, 139
Ezigbo, Victor I., 34, 149

Farrugia, Edward G., 173, 186
Farrugia, Mario, 175
Fasiggi, Robert L., 164, 182
Fee, Gordon D., 31
Fernandes, Angelo, 136
Fichte, Johann G., 7
Fiddes, Paul S., 12, 145, 192
Filson, Floyd V., 156, 191
Fiorenza, Elizabeth Schüssler, 11
Fiorenza, Francis Schüssler, 184
Fisichella, Rino, 184
Fitzmyer, Joseph A., 50–53, 152–53,
    158–60, 192
Flanagan, Donal, 147
Florovsky, George, 139
Flynn, Gabriel, 143, 165, 170, 178, 185,
    193, 195
Francis, Pope, 41
Freyne, Sean, 18
Friedrich, Gerhard, 52
Fritschel, Ann, 39
Frosini, Giordano, 176
Funk, Robert W., 9, 22, 146, 153, 190,
    193

Galvin, John P., 184
García Márquez, Gabriel, 23
Gascoyne, Robert, 179
Geldhof, Joris, 32, 148
Gesteira, Manuel, 147
Girard, René, 14, 169
Gladstone, William E., 104, 163, 195
Glorieux, Frederik, 185
Göbel, Christian, 177
Grappe, Christian, 65, 69–70, 83,
    156–58, 193
Greeley, Andrew M., 175
Gregerson, Niels H., 144, 197
Gregory the Great, Pope, 79, 160

Grelot, Pierre, 68
Griffiths, Paul, 39, 40–42, 45, 150
Gunton, Colin, 12
Gutiérrez, Gustavo, 8, 25

Hadley, John, 147
Haight, Roger, 119, 131
Harries, Richard, 174
Hastings, Adrian, 173
Hayes, Michael A., 144, 179–80, 194
Hays, Richard B., 153, 193
He Qui, 23
Heaney, Seamus, 23
Hefling, Charles C., 166–67, 198–99
Heft, James L., 26–28, 147, 186–87,
    193
Hegel, Georg W. F., 4, 7
Heidegger, Martin, 6, 133
Heil, John Paul, 186
Hengel, Martin, 8–9, 65–69, 144, 156–
    58, 161, 193
Henn, William, 161, 193
Hick, John, 124, 167
Hippolytus of Rome, 79, 160
Holloway, Richard, 69, 174
Holt, Laura, 176
Hoose, Bernard, 175
Houlden, Leslie, 28, 147
Hübner, Hans, 174, 176, 178, 180
Hug, Joseph, 154, 193
Hughes, John J., 181
Huizenga, Leroy A., 144, 189
Hultgren, Arland J., 12
Hünermann, Peter, 158, 168, 183, 192
Hunsinger, George, 143, 193
Hurtado, Larry W., 10, 177

Iammarrone, Giovanni, 15, 145, 193
Ignatius Loyola, 90, 182
Ignatius of Antioch, 69, 78
Imbelli, Robert P., 23, 26, 34, 37, 147,
    149
Ipgrave, Michael, 40, 150
Irenaeus of Lyons, 7, 69, 78–79, 104,
    119, 140, 163

Jenkins, Philip, 79, 144, 193
Jenson, Robert W., 12

Jeremias, Joachim, 50–51, 152, 193
Johnson, Elizabeth, 11
Johnson, Keith E., 110, 126–27, 168, 193
Johnson, Luke Timothy, 154, 162, 193
John Chrysostom, 90, 128
John Paul II, Pope, 36, 41, 70–71, 101, 107, 110, 115, 143, 163–64, 176, 178–79, 194
Jones, Michael K., 146, 148, 161–63, 165, 168, 182, 197
Joyce, James, 23
Julian of Norwich, 11
Justin Martyr, 69, 78

Käsemann, Ernst, 4, 7, 9
Kasper, Walter, 7–8, 144, 193
Kazantzakis, Nikos, 146
Keener, Craig S., 183
Kelley, Dean M., 147
Kelly, Anthony J., 181
Kelly, William, 147, 193
Kendall, Daniel, 14, 25–26, 143–44, 146–48, 154–55, 157, 159–62, 164–65, 169–70, 174–76, 178, 182, 190–91, 193, 197, 199
Kenny, J. Peter, 147
Kessler, W. Thomas, 156, 194
Khodr, Georges, 119, 131
Kiely, Robert, 32, 34
Knitter, Paul, 116, 119, 124, 126, 131, 167
Knox, Ronald, 181
Koester, Craig R., 162, 194
Kohl, Margaret, 145, 195
Kremer, Jacob, 57–58, 153–55, 194
Krieg, Robert A., 150
Kruger, Boniface, 164, 198
Kruger, Karl-Heinz, 161, 164, 198
Kurian, George T., 149, 194

LaBelle, Jeffrey, 178, 182
LaCoque, André, 181
Lapham, Frederick, 73–74, 159, 194
Leahy, Brendan, 143–44, 194
Leftow, Brian, 13
Lennan, Richard, 177
Leo the Great, Pope, 79, 160

Levenson, Jon D., 180
Levering, Matthew, 148, 150, 169, 192, 194
Lewis, C. S., 181
Licona, Michael R., 153, 155, 194
Lincoln, Andrew T., 75–76, 159–60, 162, 194
Livingstone, Elizabeth Anne, 160, 191
Loewe, William P., 184
Lonergan, Bernard, 24
Lorenzen, Thorwald, 183
Lossky, Vladimir, 139
Loughlin, Gerard, 32, 34, 148
Louth, Andrew, 12–13
Louw, Johannes P., 152, 194
Lubac, Henri de, 5, 143, 170
Luther, Martin, 14, 99, 104, 106
Luz, Ulrich, 159–60, 194
Lynch, Alex, 185

Mack, Burton L., 21, 146, 194
Macut, Ivan, 165
Madangi, Jean de Dieu, 147
Madigan, Kevin J., 180
Madges, William, 175
Madrigal Terras, Santiago, 177
Maréchal, Joseph, 6, 133
Marcus, Joel, 73–74, 158–60, 194
Marks, Darren C., 174
Marschler, Thomas, 177
Marshall, I. Howard, 154, 194
Martin, Ralph, 35–36, 149–50, 194
Martini, Carlo Maria, 185
Marxsen, Willi, 59, 158
Massa, James, 147
Maunder, Chris, 186
Maurice, Frederick Denison, 39
Maximus the Confessor, 7
Mbiti, John, 11
McCarthy, Maureen, 182
McDonough, Francis, 146, 199
McGowan, Andrew T. B., 36–37, 149
McGrath, James F., 24–26, 29, 147
McIntyre, John, 12, 30, 147
McMahon, Christopher, 184
Meier, John P., 9–10, 18, 22, 144–46, 194
Meister, Chad, 169, 186, 191

Melito of Sardis, 14
Merrigan, Terrence, 109–12, 124, 127–28, 135, 164–65, 170, 185, 195
Messinese, Leonardo, 177
Meyendorff, John, 12, 139
Meyers, Mary Ann, 144, 149, 185, 197
Michaelis, Wilhelm, 164
Migliore, Daniel L., 172, 195
Milbank, John, 169, 195
Miller, John Michael, 71, 158, 195
Milligan, George, 62, 155, 195
Molinaro, Aniceto, 177
Moloney, Francis J., 144, 158, 195
Moloney, Robert, 24, 32, 147–48
Moltmann, Jürgen, 4–5, 7, 17, 24, 145, 195
Montague, George T., 18, 28, 148
Morali, Ilaria, 123–27, 166–69, 190, 192, 195
Morris, Thomas V., 143, 195
Mostert, Christiaan, 34, 37, 149
Moule, Charles D. F., 9
Moulton, James Hope, 62, 155, 195
Murdoch, Brian O., 163, 195
Murdoch, Iris, 23
Murphy, Ann, 32, 34, 148
Murphy, Francesca A., 15, 145, 195
Murray, John, 146, 199
Murray, Paul D., 143, 185, 193

Neufeld, Karl Heinz, 175
Neuner, Josef, 133, 158, 168–69, 195, 198
Neville, David, 183
Newlands, George, 21–22, 148
Newman, Carey C., 18, 148
Newman, John Henry, 99, 104–5, 128, 163, 178, 195–96
Nickson, Anne, 26, 148
Nida, Eugene A., 152, 194
Nieuwenhove, Rik van, 37, 149, 196
Nolland, John, 159–60, 179, 196
Novello, Henry L., 149
Nutt, Roger W., 165, 196

Oakes, Edward T., 15, 145, 197
O'Brien, Peter T., 162, 196
Ochs, Peter, 32

O'Connell, Patrick, 148
O'Malley, John, 187
O'Neill, Eugene, 23
Ong, Walter J., 27
Orchard, Bernard, 162
Origen, 40, 59, 106, 132, 151, 155, 197, 199
Ormerod, Neil, 185
Orsuto, Donna, 179

Palamas, Gregory, 138–39
Panikkar, Raymond, 136, 170
Pannenberg, Wolfhart, 4, 7, 24, 29
Parr, John, 18–20, 24, 28, 148
Pasquale, Gianluigi, 175, 184
Patte, Daniel, 182
Paul VI, Pope, 84, 112, 136, 170
Peacocke, Arthur, 185
Perkins, Pheme, 18, 26, 148, 157, 197
Perrin, Norman, 152, 193
Pesch, Rudolf, 65, 67–69, 156–57, 197
Peters James S., 182
Peters, Stewart, 174
Peters, Ted, 175
Peterson, Brandon, 37–38, 150, 197
Pfammatter, Josef, 52
Phan, Peter C., 12, 39, 41–42, 44–45, 150
Phillips, John B., 50, 152
Picachy, Lawrence, 136
Pieris, Aloysius, 115, 140
Pius XI, Pope, 99
Pius XII, Pope, 100, 117, 163, 198
Plantinga, Alvin, 13
Platts, Timothy C., 148
Polkinghorne, John, 185
Pope, Stephen J., 166–67, 198–99
Portier, William L., 26, 148
Price, Richard, 13
Puglisi, James F., 161, 198
Pullman, Philip, 182

Quinn, Edward, 161–62, 198
Quinn, Jerome D., 154–55, 162, 198
Quirini, Fiorella, 165

Rad, Gerhard von, 4–5

Rahner, Karl, 5–6, 44, 89–92, 100, 105, 114, 116–17, 131–41, 143, 150–51, 161, 164–65, 169–72, 198
Ratzinger, Joseph: see Benedict XVI, Pope
Redding, Graham, 187
Redford, John, 174
Rengstorf, Heinrich, 52
Reumann, John 156–57, 159–61, 190
Richard, Lucien J., 148
Robinson, James M., 160, 163
Roloff, Jürgen, 68
Ronayne, Mary John, 186
Roos, Heinrich, 133, 169, 198
Rossetti, Stephen J., 178
Rouët de Journel, Marie J., 7, 144, 199
Ruether, Rosemary R., 11
Rush, Ormond, 178–79
Rushdie, Salman, 23
Russo, Adolfo, 141, 165

Saldarini, Anthony, 22–24, 148
Salvadagi, Paolo, 165
Satgé, John de, 158, 200
Schelling, Friedrich W. J. von, 7
Schillebeeckx, Edward, 8, 26
Schiller, Gertrud, 163, 199
Schnackenburg, Rudolf, 7, 22, 146, 199
Schneider, Gerhard, 153–55, 194
Scholer, John M., 162, 199
Schrage, Wolfgang, 51–53, 61, 152–53, 155, 199
Schweitzer, Don, 113, 125–27, 135, 168, 170, 199
Scott, Mark S. M., 40, 151, 199
Segundo, Juan Luis, 8
Seitz, Christopher R., 31
Seligman, Janet, 163, 199
Sesboüé, Bernard, 12
Sherman, Robert J., 92, 162, 199
Shults, E. LeRoy, 34–37, 149
Shuster, Marguerite, 32
Siebenrock, Roman A., 175
Siniscalchi, Glenn B., 39, 149–50
Smith, Daniel A., 159, 163, 184, 199
Smith, G. D., 163, 198
Smyth, Kevin, 171, 198
Snodgrass, Klyne R., 27, 148

Sobrino, Jon, 8, 24–25, 146–47, 199
Solano, Jésus, 143, 199
Spence, Alan, 181
Staniloae, Dumutru, 12
Steele, Peter, 185
Stevens, Geoffrey, 169, 198
Stinton, Diane B., 144, 199
Strachan, Richard, 161, 198
Stump, Eleonore, 11, 13, 32, 144, 199
Sturch, Richard, 143, 199
Sullivan, Francis A., 118, 166, 199
Swinburne, Richard, 1213, 176
Sydnor, Jon Paul, 172, 199

Tannehill, Robert C., 74–75, 159, 199
Tanner, Kathryn, 181
Teilhard de Chardin, Pierre, 21, 101, 118, 143, 163, 185, 200
Tertullian, 7
Teske, Roland J., 146, 189
Thayer, Joseph, 51, 152, 200
Thiel, John E., 148
Thiselton, Anthony C., 51–52, 59, 152–53, 155, 200
Thomas, Christine M., 159, 190
Thomas, Dylan, 23
Ticciati, Susannah, 32–33, 148
Tillard, Jean-Marie-Roger, 71, 158, 161, 200
Tillich, Paul, 3
Tilley, Terrence W., 129
Torrance, Iain, 181
Torrance, Thomas F., 113, 128, 165, 168, 200
Torres Queiruga, Andrés, 176
Towner, Philip H., 154, 200
Trapp, Thomas H., 156, 193
Treiyer, Humberto, 148
Tyler, Peter, 185

Valls, Carmen Aparicio, 175
Vanhoye, Albert, 162, 200
Van Inwagen, Peter, 13
Vann, Gerald, 163, 200
Vargas Llosa, Mario, 23
Venantius Fortunatus, 101
Verheyden, Joseph, 148
Vermes, Geza, 8–9, 144, 173, 183, 200

Volf, Miroslav, 172, 177, 195
Vorgrimler, Herbert, 170, 200

Wacker, William C. 154–55, 162, 198
Wales, Sean, 32, 149
Wallace, Daniel, B., 51–52, 152, 154, 200
Walsh, Milton, 181
Ware, Kallistos, 12, 139
Warhol, Andy, 23
Wawrykow, Joseph P., 149, 196
Wayte, Simon, 151, 169
Webster, John, 181
Weger, Karl-Heinz, 133
Welker, Michael, 172, 177, 195
Westhelle, Vitor, 180

Wicks, Jared, 175
Wills, Garry, 42, 148, 151, 200
Wilson, Barrie, 180
Wilson, Charles A., 22, 146, 148
Winstone, Harold, 162, 200
Winter, Sean, 186
Woolf, Rosemary, 163, 200
Woolf, Virginia, 23
Woods, Richard, 185
Wright, N. T., 9–10, 29, 31, 153, 155, 175, 200

Young, Frances, 12
Young, Norman, 186

Zizioulas, John D., 12